Y0-BTB-621

789

10

'0

RE

TARGET NATION

Canada and the Western Intelligence Network

James Littleton

A Lester & Orpen Dennys/CBC Enterprises Co-publication

FIRST EDITION

Canadian Cataloguing in Publication Data

Littleton, James.
  Target nation

Co-published by CBC Enterprises.
Bibliography: p.
Includes index.
ISBN 0-88619-118-1 (bound) — ISBN 0-88619-120-3 (pbk.)

1. Intelligence service — Canada — History — 20th century.
2. Canada — Military relations — United States.   3. United States — Military relations — Canada. 4. Canadian Security Intelligence Service.   5. Intelligence service — International cooperation.
I. CBC Enterprises.   II. Title.

UB251.C3L57 1986   327.1'2'0971   C86-093230-3

Cover design by Bob Young/Bookends West
Design by David Shaw/Bookends East
Typeset in 11 pt Plantin by Q Composition Inc.

Printed and bound in Canada by
T.H. Best Printing Company Limited for

Lester & Orpen Dennys Limited
78 Sullivan Street
Toronto, Canada   M5T 1C1

To my parents, Charles Littleton
and Dorothy Littleton,
who first encouraged me
to ask "why?"

ACKNOWLEDGEMENTS

Canada and its place in the adversarial relations between East and West is a fascinating subject about which to write. In the 1980s the international context outlines the nature of this country more sharply than ever. Realities and myths arising outside our geographical boundaries often define the limits of discourse in Canadian political life. The line separating those realities and myths is frequently difficult to determine.

I was eleven when the Korean War ended. Like that of most Canadians of my generation, my experience of the cold war in the 1950s was quite unambivalent. The world was divided by a great conflict between East and West, and we were on the good side, the American side. It was not until the intensity of the cold war diminished in the 1960s that I began to question the reassuring assumptions on which my earlier certainty had been based.

The 1960s was a time of turbulence and optimism for my generation; we were certain that we could change society for the better. The process of reform included a dedication to try to understand the nature of our country and its place in the community of nations. The comfortable 1950s myths of childhood evaporated, along with a bit of our optimism.

My awareness that secret intelligence agencies were bound up with the mythology of the cold war developed as part of the quest to understand Canada while participating in the movement to change it. This awareness gradually evolved into an intellectual interest; however, it did not take on a professional dimension until I worked on the CBC television series "On Guard for Thee" with Donald Brittain in 1980 and 1981. I am grateful to Brittain not so much for causing me to become immersed in the world of secret agencies as for showing me something quite different: his way of going about his work demonstrated to me the importance of irreverence and irony in the creative process. This approach is particularly necessary when one attempts to peel away the layers of mythology that surround the kind of subject dealt with both in "On Guard for Thee" and in this book.

In the course of researching and co-producing "On Guard for Thee" I met and interviewed many of the people who have played key roles in the Canadian security and intelligence establishment. I also met some of their American counterparts, as well as a few of their enemies. Interviewing and having informal discussions with such people continued during my work as a producer for the CBC Radio Current Affairs Department. In the summer of 1983, when a controversy was raging in Canada about the new security-service legislation that was being proposed by the Trudeau government, I wrote a series of radio documentaries entitled "Dissent and Subversion" for the "Ideas" programme of CBC Radio. This work deepened my interest in and led me to expand my research on the role of the security services in Canadian life. "Dissent and Subversion" generated an unexpectedly enthusiastic response from

v

listeners in every part of the country. I was subsequently asked by CBC Enterprises to write a book based on the radio series. Radio programmes do not translate readily into books; however, this book evolved directly out of that request, and the central assumptions and ideas remain.

The impressions that I acquired from the many interviews and countless discussions that I had in preparing "On Guard for Thee" and "Dissent and Subversion" comprise a significant part of the basis for this book. When specific information in the text has been derived from a particular interview, the source is cited in the notes. However, further discussion with many of the same people has contributed still more to my general understanding of the central issues explored in this work. Also, many discussions of these matters with persons whom I cannot name have been extremely helpful. I am grateful to all of them.

It is impossible to list all the people who have contributed to the completion of this book. Of those who can be mentioned, I must first of all thank Don Wall, former assistant secretary to the Cabinet for security and intelligence. Without his encouragement, introductions, and assurance that it was time for a number of previously unpublished things to be said, I would not have had the determination or courage to complete this book. His review of several drafts of the manuscript has prevented me from making many egregious errors.

At the beginning of my work on "On Guard for Thee," Elmer MacKay generously provided encouragement and introductions that have proved to be most helpful. Neither he nor I foresaw that one of the results would be this book. I am grateful to Elmer MacKay for his acts of friendship over a good many years.

Other friends have been helpful in other ways. The long-lasting support, discussions, and criticisms of both Leo Panitch and Reg Whitaker have been invaluable. Their respective suggestions for changes in the manuscript have resulted in a less confused and greatly improved text. David Stafford's suggestions have also been of great help. I am grateful to Geoffrey Pearson for his comments on the draft of the chapter entitled "The Mythology of Treason". Mark McClung's insatiable interest in the philosophy of national security is infectious. I thank him for his enthusiasm, insight, hospitality, and many other kindnesses.

I also wish to thank other individuals who have been helpful in numerous ways. Included in this list are Jack Granatstein, John Sawatsky, Roger Bowen, and Brenda Sweeny.

Researchers in other countries who are interested in similar subjects have generously provided advice and materials; in particular I wish to thank James Bamford in Boston, Jeffrey Richelson in Washington, Desmond Ball in Canberra, Brian Toohey in Sydney, and Duncan Campbell in London.

I am grateful to the Canada Council for providing an Explorations Grant that covered the costs of research and manuscript preparation. I also wish to thank Bryce Weber for his efficient archival research in Toronto. The staff at the CBC reference library have at all times been speedy and accurate in meeting requests for material. They are unfailingly generous with their time and energy, and I am accordingly grateful to them. I also wish to thank the staff at the Canadian Armed Forces Staff College library for their courteous assistance.

My editors at the CBC, Robert Daley and Charis Wahl, are to be commended for their encouragement, advice, patience, and good humour.

Kate Hamilton not only processed these words more times than I can count, but her understanding of the agony of producing a book prevented many a catastrophe.

My gratitude to Louise Dennys for her editorial insight and guidance cannot be adequately expressed.

I wish to thank my many friends and colleagues at the CBC whose constant encouragement and tolerance, and granting of time off when it was most sorely needed, were crucial to the completion of this work. The intellectual stimulation of their company has also been of enormous benefit to me. Space precludes my mentioning each of the colleagues to whom I am indebted. But, in particular, I must state my gratitude to Andrew Simon, Anne Wright Howard, and Gloria Bishop. Peter Gzowski's wry advice about the respective plights of writers and editors has been appreciated if not always heeded. Michael Hughes' review of the manuscript was helpful on legal points; he also has a sharp editorial eye. Over many years I have benefited enormously from the insight of my friend Nicole Belanger into the arcane inner workings of an Ottawa that is not always as staid as it often appears to be on the surface.

Above all, I am deeply grateful to my wife, Cheryl, for her consistently sound editorial opinions and for her always healthy skepticism. My debt to her and to my daughters, Susan and Claire, for tolerating my mental absence while writing this book, as well as for their unfailing encouragement and inspiration, can never be fully stated or repaid.

It is customary at the conclusion of acknowledgements for writers to absolve all others of responsibility for errors and opinions contained in the work. In this case I must do so in more than a ritual way. It is important for me to state that the views expressed here are my own and to emphasize that they are not those of the CBC. As a producer I work professionally with the presentation of the opinions of other people on the CBC. One must have opinions of one's own to be able to understand the opinions of others. The discipline of stating my own opinions in this book has taught me to appreciate still more the many very different views of those whose opinions are broadcast daily on the CBC, regardless of whether I personally agree with them.

I am both proud and heartened that as a member of our public broadcasting service I have been able to explore and to write freely about the sensitive and consequential matters contained in this book.

Notes on Terminology

A few of the terms that appear frequently in this book are subject to a number of interpretations. The most important of these terms, "cold war," is usually understood to refer to the period of history spanning the years from approximately 1945 to 1957, when tensions between the United States and the Soviet Union were particularly high. In this work, "cold war" is also used as an adjective to describe political attitudes that were prominent in that period. Further, it is my view that many of the characteristic features of the cold war have continued to exist in a variety of forms up to the present. Hence, the term is not used solely to refer to the 1945-57 period, and the words are not capitalized.

A number of ambiguous terms occur frequently in most discussions of security and intelligence matters. It is hoped that their meanings will be evident from the context in which they appear in this work. However, to increase clarity, it should be observed that, in general, "intelligence" refers to information, sometimes collected by secret means, that is processed and interpreted for the use of a government. "Security" refers to institutions or practices that are directed at maintaining both the strength and the secrets of the state. There is, not surprisingly, a close relationship between acquiring secret information and protecting secrets; therefore, the concepts of "intelligence" and "security" go hand in hand. The many government agencies that are concerned with these matters are collectively known as the "security and intelligence community" or sometimes simply as the "intelligence community."

"Counter-intelligence," in the words of the CIA, refers to: "Intelligence activity intended to detect, counteract, and/or prevent espionage and other foreign clandestine intelligence activities, sabotage, international terrorist activities or assassinations for or on behalf of foreign powers. Counter-intelligence also refers to the information derived from such activity." That is the sense in which the term "counter-intelligence" is used here.

"Security intelligence," as it appears in the name of this country's Canadian Security Intelligence Service (CSIS), has a similar meaning. Specifically, it is intelligence about threats to the security of the state.

These particular usages are by no means definitive. Nuances of meaning attached to these and related terms should become apparent from the ways in which they are used in this book.

James Littleton
Toronto, April 1986

"The time has come," the Walrus said,
"To talk of many things:
Of shoes — and ships — and sealing-wax —
Of cabbages — and kings —
And why the sea is boiling hot —
And whether pigs have wings."

Lewis Carroll

Wovon man nicht sprechen kann, darüber
muss man schweigen.
(What we cannot speak about we must pass
over in silence.)

Ludwig Wittgenstein

Contents

Introduction

J ames Jesus Angleton is both a man and a symbol. He belonged to the CIA from the very beginning. He studied at
Yale and at Harvard. He was in the wartime Office of Strategic Services in London and Rome. He battled the Communists
in Italy at the start of the cold war, knew well and came within a
hair's-breadth of unmasking the greatest spy of the century, Kim
Philby, and probed the deepest secrets of the Kremlin. He had a
copy of Khrushchev's secret speech denouncing Stalin almost before it had been delivered to a closed session of the Soviet Communist Party in 1956. As Chief of the Counterintelligence Division
of the Central Intelligence Agency, Angleton scrutinized his own
organization as well as the top levels of allied governments and
their intelligence agencies for traces of Soviet spies. He cultivated
defectors from the Communist intelligence services for clues to
the identity of traitors secretly operating in the West. If he didn't
believe them, they were punished. If he did believe them, they
were taken very seriously, and treated very well. He liked and
believed one defector who told him there was a high-level spy in
Western intelligence. For years, Angleton ransacked the CIA to
find the traitor. In 1974 he was removed from his post; his search
had tied the Agency in knots.

But Angleton was revered as a great intelligence chief, a man
of cultivation and sensitivity, a reader of poetry, friend of Ezra
Pound, a brilliant and totally uncompromising enemy of Communism. To the insiders of the New Right who came to power
with the Reagan administration in 1981, Angleton represented the
conservative who was not a cowboy, the man who truly knew the
full dimensions of the Communist threat, the defender of freedom
who had fallen victim to the American malaise of the early 1970s.

I met Angleton at the Café de la Paix in Arlington, Virginia,
a few weeks after Ronald Reagan's first inauguration. I wanted to
persuade him to appear in a film that the Canadian Broadcasting
Corporation was producing. When I entered the restaurant, he
looked exactly as I expected — tall, stooped over, mid-sixties,

1

alert. Angleton wanted to know about Canada. Was the McDonald Royal Commission likely to destroy the RCMP? Might the senior officers be punished? Was Pierre Trudeau's support from the media still strong? He also asked pointed questions about the part of Canada where I grew up. What months do the salmon run in the Annapolis River? How deep is the river?

I guess I passed the preliminary test. The conversation turned to the Communist threat and the vulnerability of the West. After a very leisurely dinner we drove around in Angleton's black Mercedes. He was an amazingly fast driver for a man his age. On the dash of the Mercedes was a fluorescent blue digital display. It gave an instant read-out of the outside air temperature. If he headed into a hollow where there might be a film of ice on the road, he'd have advance warning and could slow down, he explained.

We went to the bar on top of a suburban hotel. You could see the Potomac River and the Washington Monument in the distance. Angleton described how Lenin had never meant to confine the revolution to Russia. It was to have been the beginning of a worldwide process. It had been stopped in Western Europe and America. But that didn't mean that Lenin's heirs had abandoned his plans. They had simply continued to invent other ways to implement them. Nuclear war. Infiltration of Western governments. The West, because of its naiveté, and the treachery of some of its own people, had been steadily losing. Those who understood the real nature of the battle could never stop fighting.

After the bar closed at four a.m. we drove around for another hour or so. A few weeks later Angleton told me that he had decided it would be best if he didn't appear on Canadian television. I thought of the night as fascinating but just faintly disappointing. I had been told by other journalists of the "Angleton briefing." Now I had had it. The interpretation of twentieth-century world history was articulate, well framed, riveting. But it really wasn't different in its essentials from the conspiratorial version of the Communist menace that is familiar to anyone who remembers the 1950s.

Don Wall also spent most of his working life in the world of security and intelligence. During the Second World War, he was an air gunner in the Royal Canadian Air Force. He took an M.A. in English at the University of Saskatchewan. Then he joined Canada's super-secret signals intelligence (SIGINT) agency because someone told him his facility with languages would be useful. He served as a civilian expert with the RCMP Security and Intelligence Branch in the 1950s. Eventually he became Assistant Secretary to the Cabinet for Security and Intelligence.

Don Wall is not very angular. One person said that he could be anybody's favourite uncle. He laughs easily. He does wonderful imitations of characters, ranging from stuffy mandarins and generals in Ottawa to old Scandinavian pig farmers on the prairies. He tends to admire the latter.

Wall doesn't think much of stuffiness, but he really dislikes people who are "hard eyed." He says that most people tend to become hard eyed if they stay in security and intelligence for too long. It's a nasty business, he says, and they begin to take themselves too seriously. Instead of being skeptical, they take to believing their own mythologies. That can be dangerous.

My disappointment with Angleton ("Jimmy Jesus," Wall calls him) did not surprise Don Wall. Perhaps he suspected Angleton of being a bit hard eyed. But there have been many people in the security and intelligence agencies in Canada who have taken Angleton extremely seriously. Their outlook is closer to his than to Don Wall's. They believe that a man of Angleton's brilliance and accomplishments, with access to the information he has had, must have profound understanding and insight into what is really going on. To them, he represents unflinching dedication to the ceaseless battle against the hidden designs of Lenin's heirs. He symbolizes the cold war.

For people who regard the cold war as the primary reality of our time, successive Canadian governments have been less than completely satisfactory. Lester Pearson at times seemed more interested in peace than in defending the nation against the Communists; John Diefenbaker allowed his stubborn pride and his nationalism to jeopardize the sanctity of our alliance with the Americans; Trudeau's past, and his conduct in office, suggested grounds for all sorts of misgivings. This has created an uncomfortable kind of ambiguity. Many operatives in the security and intelligence establishment have found themselves in a dilemma — having to reconcile the insight, convictions, and authority of the James Angletons with what seemed to them the indifference of their own government towards the gravity of the threat. Canadian political leaders, on the other hand, have had to devise ways of maintaining their own perspectives while at the same time accommodating or containing the ideological obsessions that tend increasingly to thrive within the culture of the international intelligence community.

This problem occurs to some extent in many countries, but especially in those that are considered to be of great strategic importance within the alliance systems to which they belong. Because it lies geographically directly between the United States and the Soviet Union, no country is of greater military strategic importance in the cold war than Canada. Therefore the "reliability" of any Canadian government is of great consequence to cold war planners, and their own adherence to cold war orthodoxy has inevitably led many people in the Canadian security and intelligence establishment to be uneasy about Canadian political leaders. The reluctance of Pierre Trudeau to go along with the Reagan administration's resurgent confrontational stance towards the Soviet bloc, and towards many parts of the Third World, inevitably increased the suspicion of the Western intelligence community, including at least some of its Canadian members.

I acquired a sense of the unease that this situation has created at the highest levels of the Canadian government during discussions in Ottawa over the last five years. Michael Pitfield has been a close friend of Pierre Trudeau since the early 1960s. He has been interested in the problems of the management of the security services since that time. In 1965, when he was serving as an aide to the Governor-General, with no formal responsibilities in the area of national security, Pitfield wrote a critique of the RCMP and its Security and Intelligence Branch. He presented the report to Don Wall, who still regards it as a very astute analysis of the management of the internal security apparatus. Pitfield and Trudeau discussed these issues frequently between 1965 and 1968, when Trudeau was Minister of Justice. As Prime Minister, Trudeau appointed Pitfield Clerk of the Privy Council and Secretary to the Cabinet in 1975. In that position he was not only the head of the civil service but was directly responsible for the overall planning of every aspect of national security. He therefore knew all the secrets. In 1982 Pitfield stepped down and was appointed to the Senate. That summer, he chaired a special committee that reviewed the proposed legislation for Canada's new security intelligence service. In July of that year I had several conversations with him in his Ottawa office. I was impressed by the depth of concern, which I'm sure was shared by the Prime Minister, about the inadequacy of their means of knowing with certainty the full extent of security and intelligence activities in Canada. Activities they did not know about they certainly could not control. And this worried them.

Shortly after Pierre Trudeau had left office, in the early summer of 1984, I went over the same ground with Michael Pitfield again. I wanted to be sure that in my own thinking I had not exaggerated or dramatized his (and inferentially Trudeau's) unease about the problem of what the Western intelligence community might be doing in Canada. In the intervening year, Pitfield's committee had completed its work. The Canadian Security Intelligence Service legislation had just been passed. Trudeau had embarked on a whirlwind, four-month international peace mission and then announced his retirement from politics.

Pitfield confirmed my understanding of his earlier concerns. This time he was, if anything, more direct in his opinion that the ability of the Canadian government to act autonomously is restricted in virtually any area perceived by the U.S. government to affect its own national security. This limitation applies to a wide range of matters, not the least of which is the operation of this country's security and intelligence services.

In three long conversations on successive days in that summer of political uncertainty, I could not help thinking of the words of a former Deputy Director of the CIA, General Vernon Walters, when discussing the more subtle means that are employed by the CIA to influence the policies of other countries. He had explained that the practice

> is to seek to alter in the long term the thinking in the target nation in such a way as to make them perceive that their interest does not lie in hostility to the first nation. If this can be done, then those responsible for the formation of public opinion and the key decisions may be made to see things quite differently from their original views and this can be done at considerably less cost and less loss of life than one day of open warfare. The most successful action of this type takes place without anyone in the target nation being aware of it.[1]

Operations fitting this description have certainly occurred elsewhere. From a Canadian perspective, it is impossible to know if this sort of manipulation exists largely in the realm of fantasy. In the summer of 1984, it did not seem far-fetched. As the cold war deepens, almost anything seems possible. Canada's strategic importance to the United States increases, and so does its importance as a potential target nation.

The world lurches from crisis to crisis. A rigged election in one impoverished country is followed by widespread public disorder. An airliner is blown out of the sky, and 300 innocent lives are lost. The dark presence of nuclear winter is always in the background. The state of perpetual confrontation is a global phenomenon. The nuclear arms race, and regular bouts of what Pierre Trudeau has called "megaphone diplomacy," are only the more obvious expressions of it. Defence budgets that distort national economies, propped-up dictators, and spy exchanges on the Berlin bridge are all manifestations of this phenomenon.

Canadians are now accustomed to being told by their leaders that the world has become so small that their country is no longer isolated from such unpleasant events. In fact, it is a good many decades since Canada was isolated from the realities of the rest of the world. At least since the state of perpetual confrontation known as the cold war began forty years ago, Canada has been in the front lines. The fortuitous reason for this disturbing situation is our position midway on the cold war map between the two superpowers. Our involvement in the cold war, however, cannot be attributed simply to a misfortune of geography; it has more to do with the very human matter of politics.

The cold war is insidious because it has warped the way that we think about the world. Unstated assumptions about the primacy of the perpetual conflict between East and West, Communism and capitalism, the good guys and the bad guys, underlie much of our political discourse. Many arguments used to justify or to criticize policies can ultimately be reduced to the same essence: the policy either is or isn't necessary to strengthen our side in this polarized world. The state of perpetual conflict has created a set of organizations that might be called cold war institutions. Military forces and their associated bureaucracies are the most obvious of these. Various industries, research institutes, and think tanks are also part of the structure of interests whose existence in turn depends on the continuation of the conflict. The cold war and its institutions have become self-perpetuating.

The security and intelligence organizations stand very close to the centre of the system of cold war institutions. Supplying vital information about the "enemy" to the government is the main purpose of intelligence agencies. Much of the information is collected by clandestine means. The secrecy of this process is protected by counter-intelligence or security services; the latter are also supposed to detect and assess domestic threats to their governments.

These functions give the security and intelligence agencies enormous power to influence the decisions that governments make. Surrounded by secrecy and enjoying a monopoly on the business of informing the government about foreign and domestic threats, these agencies are in an ideal position to ensure their own institutional prosperity. They are more effectively protected from the vicissitudes of political change than virtually any other kind of bureaucracy. Their secrecy is often more important as a protection against normal democratic scrutiny than it is for the supposed reasons of "national security."

The cold war conflict is fundamentally between the two superpowers; other nations participate as subsidiary players, and they too have their own cold war institutions. But there is an irresistible tendency for the cold war institutions of the superpowers, because of their primacy, to exert enormous influence on their counterparts in the allied countries. The security and intelligence agencies of each superpower and its allies form a fraternal community. Among the agencies of the major English-speaking allies this communal relationship is particularly close. So it is not surprising that tradition, organizational structures, and secrecy have all led to American influence being particularly strong in the closed inner world of the Western intelligence organizations. Most of the organizations maintain liaison officers permanently with their counterparts in the other countries. Personnel exchanges also take place frequently. In addition to shared ideological indoctrination, strong ties of both professional collegiality and personal friendship inevitably develop. The result is that the culture of security and intelligence transcends both national boundaries and political debate.

I became aware of a pattern of subdued disquiet about the issue during a series of conversations with a number of people who had been senior public servants, intelligence officers, or politicians in successive Canadian governments. By both training and inclination, such people do not readily discuss security and intelligence matters with outsiders. But the first half of the 1980s was a peculiar period in Ottawa. First, the McDonald Royal Commission's inquiry — of unprecedented thoroughness — into the RCMP was concluded in 1981. Between the autumn of that year and the summer of 1984 the Liberal government went through a tortuous procedure of implementing McDonald's principal recommendation, by separating the Security Service from the structure of the RCMP. Then there was a change in the Liberal leadership and John Turner's brief tenure as Prime Minister, followed by the Progressive Conservative victory at the polls in September 1984. The uncertainty caused by these changes was accompanied by widespread unease about the resurgence of militant cold war attitudes in the United States under the Reagan administration. These were some of the obvious factors — and I'm sure there were other factors of which I'm not fully aware — that enabled me to take part in many frank yet discreet conversations on security and intelligence.

Canada is a sovereign nation whose government has its own security and intelligence agencies. But those agencies are also an integral part of the Western intelligence community. I am convinced that persons at the highest levels of the government of Canada, who have been responsible for administering the security and intelligence machinery, have for years been deeply concerned about the ambiguous relationship between Canada and the Western intelligence community, questioning whether the ties within that community are stronger than those between the agencies and the Canadian government.

The question cannot be answered with a simple yes or no.

That ambiguous and dangerous relationship is the subject of this book. To shed some light upon it, it is necessary to take a hard look at how Canada interacts with the Western intelligence network, and most particularly the degree to which America's cold war stance has influenced Canada over the years. Because U.S. influence is so much greater in Canada than that of the Soviet Union, the book is particularly concerned with the relationship between the Western security and intelligence community and the democratic political process in Canada. It does not attempt to equate the roles or the strategic manoeuvrings of the two superpowers.

I am disturbed by the implications of some of the matters about which I have written. But the fact that questions on such sensitive matters can be raised is evidence that we Canadians enjoy far more freedom than do the people of most other countries.

1

Areas of Influence

The sun was shining on the sea
Shining with all his might:
He did his very best to make
The billows smooth and bright —
And this was odd, because it was
The middle of the night.

During the last four decades relations among nations have been dominated by one overwhelming fact — the relentless struggle between the two superpowers, the United States and the Soviet Union. Each antagonist is aided, with varying degrees of enthusiasm, by its allies. The struggle between the two power blocs takes many forms: they compete in terms of the development of their respective economies, for superiority in military strength, for strategic advantage, and in terms of politics and ideology.

The period in which tension between the superpowers reached its zenith, roughly from 1945 to 1957, came to be known as the cold war. But since these tensions escalated further in the late 1970s, there has been increasing recognition that the cold war never really ended; it has continued as the fundamental fact of international relations for the last four decades. The cold war has been with us for so many years that it is widely taken for granted; it is simply a fact of life. But a look at its origins suggests that this state of protracted international tension is founded on some very questionable assumptions.

The intensity of the cold war has varied since it began at the close of World War Two, although mutual suspicion and hostility have characterized relations between the Soviet Union and the West almost continually since the Russian Revolution of 1917.

The wartime alliance between the Western countries and the Soviet Union against the Fascist powers had been a temporary arrangement. It was doomed to break up even before the defeat of Hitler. The wartime conferences at Teheran and Yalta succeeded in co-ordinating wartime strategy among the Americans, the British, and the Soviets; but they were not as successful in laying plans for the post-war configuration of Europe. The Yalta Conference in February 1945 provided for what amounted to a Soviet sphere of influence in Eastern Europe and British and American predominance in Western Europe. This agreement can be broadly interpreted as being a matter of Churchill, Roosevelt, and Stalin formalizing what would in any case have been inevitable. The *de facto* division of areas of influence was roughly co-extensive with the parts of the continent that were about to be occupied by their respective armies.

One of the fundamental causes of the cold war was the political instability that prevailed throughout Europe in the aftermath of the defeat of the Nazi empire. The devastation and impoverishment after years of occupation and the unprecedented violence of modern warfare had created a dreadful situation in both Eastern and Western Europe. Hunger, the widespread dislocation of whole populations, and an absence of that fundamental social organization essential to any civilized society were common conditions in many European countries.

There is little evidence that the Americans, the British, or the Canadians genuinely thought that the Red Army was going to sweep over Europe as far as the Atlantic Ocean in the early post-war period. There was, however, concern that left-wing parties that had gained influence during the war, and legitimacy in the resistance against the Nazis, would increase their power in certain European countries, especially in Greece, Italy, and France.[1] The resistance to Nazi occupation in Western Europe, as in Greece and Yugoslavia, had included people with revolutionary expectations, and some Communists played leading roles in the resistance movements. The arbitrary means by which Communist governments were installed under the aegis of the Red Army between 1946 and 1948 in Poland, Hungary, Romania, and Bulgaria encouraged fears in the West that similar situations might develop in countries not occupied by the Red Army. These fears peaked after the Communist seizure of power in Soviet-occupied Czechoslovakia in 1948.

The leaders of the Western nations were most concerned about the strength of the left in the Western European countries. The strong showing of the Communist parties in elections in Italy and France in 1946 alarmed both the Americans and the British. Efforts, particularly by the Americans, to undermine the Communists in these countries were begun within a year of the end of the war. One of the first major tasks of the CIA after its formation in 1947 was to develop a covert action programme in Western Europe that would finance and strengthen various anti-Communist organizations.[2] It also worked to weaken the influence of the Communists in the trade-union movements of France and Italy. By the end of 1948, Communist influence throughout Western Europe had diminished significantly.

It is noteworthy that for all Stalin's aggressiveness in the post-war period, the Soviet Union did very little to expand its power beyond the sphere of influence that it had achieved by international agreement in 1945. The Red Army did not advance beyond the cease-fire lines established on VE Day. The Soviets did little to encourage the Communist parties in Western European countries, where they had achieved some degree of legitimacy, to attempt to seize power in any unconstitutional way. In Greece, the left-wing resistance forces controlled most of the country when the Nazis were driven out in 1944. But they were soon engaged in a civil war against the British-backed right, which they stood a good chance of winning. Nevertheless, the Soviets did not support the left in recognition of the fact that Stalin and Churchill had agreed in Moscow in 1944 that Greece would be in the Western sphere of influence.[3] The result was that the Greek left was defeated in 1948 and suffered repression for years after.

In post-war Europe, Communist parties for the most part acted in a constitutional manner. Their strategy, in keeping with the position taken by Stalin during the war, did not include insurrectionary activity. Stalin's main interest was to consolidate his territorial gains in Eastern Europe after the defeat of Hitler's armies and to begin the enormous task of rebuilding Soviet industry. As always, Stalin suffered from a paranoid vision of Western intentions to undo his regime. Consequently, his policy was to employ belligerent rhetoric, to insulate the Soviet people from outside influences and, at the same time, to avoid open conflict with the Western powers. Communist parties in Western countries that had sought alliances with social democratic and liberal parties until 1947 subsequently became increasingly isolated from the mainstream of political life.[4]

In spite of the caution of the Communists and their tendency to act legally, they were regarded by Western leaders as dangerous and subversive of liberal democracy. The result was that the principal Western powers in the late 1940s co-operated closely in forming the Atlantic Alliance. Its ostensible purpose was to deter Soviet military aggression. It is arguable, however, that this aggression was perceived to be taking place more through the activities of Communist parties in Western European countries than through military action by the Red Army. The Brussels Pact of 1948 and the formation of the North Atlantic Treaty Organization, NATO, a year later were intended implicitly to counter the danger of Communist subversion. NATO was formed as a military alliance, but its political importance should not be underestimated.[5]

The early phase of the cold war was marked by events such as the Berlin Blockade, the Korean War, and the development of the nuclear arms race. Domestically, both the United States and the Soviet Union went through a prolonged period in the late 1940s and the 1950s in which efforts were made to suppress internal dissent. In the Soviet Union, and in Soviet-controlled Eastern Europe, Joseph Stalin's obsession with foreign agents and foreign-inspired plots took on grotesque proportions. The years preceding Stalin's death in 1953 were characterized by savage attacks by the state on anyone suspected of a lack of commitment to Stalin's policies. The horrors of the *gulag* and the ubiquity of the Soviet Secret Police are all too familiar. Simultaneously, in the United States, the phenomenon known as McCarthyism dominated the political scene. A vision of the world threatened by an implacable enemy gripped the imagination of the American people. Those suspected of harbouring "Communist sympathies," or of being associated with Communists in the past, or of being "subversive" in some other way, were liable to be exposed to public ridicule, hounded from their jobs, or prevented from pursuing their professions. The accusations alone were, in many cases, enough to ruin a career. Anti-Communism in effect became an official creed — a quasi-

12

religious belief — and ordinary citizens and political leaders alike were expected to reaffirm their belief whenever asked. Both East and West were haunted by what the British writer David Caute has aptly called "The Great Fear."

Anti-Commmunism as a quasi-religious belief must, of course, be distinguished from the stance of being critical of Communism. The tumultuous history of the Soviet Union in the aftermath of the 1917 Revolution, the cruel excesses of Stalinism, the subordination of almost all national Communist parties to the Communist Party of the Soviet Union — these and many other tragic aspects of the history of the twentieth century provided grounds for serious, wide-ranging criticism of the Communist movement. But anti-Communism as a creed is a different matter; as it became a quasi-religion, it was institutionalized. In this form, anti-Communism has on occasion served as a pretext for the suppression of civil liberties in the United States and in other countries; many atrocities have been committed in its name in Third World countries; it has also provided the ideological underpinning for the arms race.

During World War Two, FBI Director J. Edgar Hoover argued that Communists and "pseudo liberals" were as great a threat to the American way of life as were the very Nazis against whom the war was being waged.[6] The onset of the cold war provided a new legitimacy for these views. Hoover welcomed the cold war and helped to generate additional support for its assumptions. He engaged enthusiastically in the propaganda of the period, warning that

> Something new has taken root in America during the past generation, a Communist mentality, representing a systematic, purposive, and conscious attempt to destroy Western Civilization and roll history back to the age of barbaric cruelty and despotism, all in the name of "progress." Evil is depicted as good, terror as justice, hate as love, and obedience to a foreign master as patriotism.[7]

In the United States, the cold war provided an occasion for an alliance between right-wing politicians and the internal security organizations of the Executive Branch of government. The political careers of dozens of members of Congress were built on the increasingly frenzied hunts for Communists and "subversives" in government. The internal security organizations of the state, in

13

particular the FBI, had a symbiotic relationship with the congressional witch-hunters. Each tended to legitimize the activities of the other. The congressional investigations between 1946 and 1957 also legitimized for a time the formula that equated espionage, Communist beliefs, subversion, and dissent.

Americans were encouraged to become informers against their fellow citizens. Although the informer, as Victor Navasky has pointed out, has traditionally been a figure of opprobrium in almost every culture, including the American culture, during the cold war a new archetype of the informer as public hero was developed.[8]

Ordinary Americans were urged by their government to keep a sharp eye out for subversive activities by friends and neighbours, and to report anything suspicious to the FBI. A plea for popular informing was broadcast on CBS Radio by Irving Saypol, a man lauded by *Time* magazine as "the nation's number one hunter of top Communists,"[9] on behalf of the United States Department of Justice. Saypol's pitch was dramatic:

> Many times a small bit of information might furnish the data we are seeking. If you have any information on sabotage, espionage, or subversive activities, contact the FBI. A citizen may overhear a conversation in a public place — at a ball game, in a theatre, at a dance — conversation dealing with movement of ships, supplies, military movements, the suggestion of delay in an industry devoted to production of essential materials.[10]

Saypol's radio interlocutor pointed out that of course the FBI was simply looking for facts, and Saypol answered,

> Exactly so. And regardless of how inconsequential they may appear to the citizen, if they deal with that subject or are related, no harm is done in conveying them.[11]

The phrase "witch-hunting" has been widely used to describe the rooting-out process. There is indeed a resonance between the anti-Communist hysteria of the 1950s and the witch-hunts of the Middle Ages. In each case the process revealed more about the hunter than the hunted.

Once witch-hunting starts it is extremely difficult for it to be stopped. If the enemy might be anywhere, then it is necessary to hunt for him everywhere. As the search for subversives became more widespread, with almost no results, it had to be broadened further. The cold war had begun under the Democratic administration of President Harry S. Truman. But eventually the Democratic Party itself, including its conservative members, became a victim of the process. During the 1952 election campaign, Senator Joseph McCarthy and other Republicans did not hesitate to accuse the Democratic Party of treason. In one speech, McCarthy said that "the hard fact is that those who wear the label 'Democrat' worked with the stain of a historic betrayal. The Democrat Party has time after time and irrevocably labelled itself as the party which stands for the government of, by and for Communists, crooks and cronies. You can't get away from that. Not a single one of those now in the leadership of the Party have raised their voices against this type of treason ... which means that with their return to power, you'll get another twenty years of the same."[12]

By 1952 the cold war consensus was sufficiently strong that such attacks did serious political harm to the Democratic Party. Twenty years of Democratic rule came to an end with the election of the Eisenhower administration.

In Canada, the Liberal Party had also been in power since the 1930s. Although there are very substantial differences resulting from diverging political traditions, the Liberal Party of Canada tended to occupy a place on the political spectrum roughly equivalent to that held by the Democrats in the United States. Both parties maintained essentially liberal policies on social issues; both had used Keynesian techniques to mitigate the effects of the Depression. Each, when in government, had executed the war against the Nazis enthusiastically; both had been relatively tolerant of the left up until 1945. But despite the sensation caused by the defection of Igor Gouzenko from the Soviet Embassy in Ottawa shortly after the end of the war, the leadership of the Liberal Party was largely inclined to prevent Communism from becoming a public spectacle.

The fear of Communist subversion in Canada did not start with the cold war. The Russian Revolution in 1917 had been sufficiently unnerving to Canadian political leaders that a contingent of regular army troops, as well as members of the RCMP, was sent to Siberia in 1918 to fight the Bolsheviks. This mission met with no more success than did the interventions in the Russian Civil War by British, American, Czech, and other foreign armies; but it did initiate a tradition of Canadian hostility to Communism that often

15

featured the RCMP in the vanguard. The Winnipeg General Strike in 1919 was seen by many business and political leaders as a manifestation of the Soviet-directed, international Communist conspiracy. In 1931 eight leaders of the Communist Party were prosecuted for membership in an illegal association. The part of the Criminal Code under which this was done, Section 98, was later repealed under pressure from civil libertarians; but the Communist Party continued to be an object of intense interest to the RCMP throughout the 1930s.

After the beginning of World War Two, the Communist Party was declared an illegal organization and several dozens of its leaders were interned for as much as two years. Following the German attack on the Soviet Union in June 1941, most of the Communist leaders were released and a number of them subsequently served in the Canadian Armed Forces. The Communist Party of Canada adopted a new identity as the Labour Progressive Party and functioned unhindered throughout the war. It acquired unprecedented respectability from the fact that Canada and the Soviet Union were allies. The Communists discouraged militancy among trade unionists on the ground that unrestrained effort should be devoted to winning the war. The popularity of the Communist Party reached an all-time high in 1945 when it had about 30,000 members, received more than 100,000 votes in the federal election, and re-elected a Member of Parliament, Fred Rose, from a downtown Montreal riding.

Cold war hysteria never became as acute in Canada as it did in the United States. A benign view would be that the Canadian government tried to limit the spillover effect of the hysteria that swept the United States. Such a view would be simplistic though not without some truth.

The Liberal Party, through its control of Parliament and the public service, did what it could to avoid the witch-hunt that might work to its own detriment. Social Credit and some Conservative Members of Parliament made a number of rather weak attempts to initiate purges in the public service. These efforts received little public support and the government was able to resist them. Instead of a public inquisition, the government devised much less conspicuous means of safeguarding the nation's secrets.

In the summer of 1946 it established a Security Panel, chaired by the Secretary to the Cabinet, Arnold Heeny. It included permanent representatives of the Department of External Affairs and the RCMP; other departments were represented as required. The purpose of the security panel was to co-ordinate the security measures taken by various departments and to advise the Cabinet on security matters. The actual gathering of information in the field was done by the RCMP. The security panel did not assess the security reports it received from the RCMP, but passed them on to the security officers of individual government departments where decisions on individual cases were made. But the process of turning raw information into processed intelligence inevitably involves a good deal of discretion and judgement, and this function was carried out by the RCMP. The result was that in some cases a good deal of power over the careers of civil servants rested with the police.[13]

The Commissioner of the RCMP, S.T. Wood, went on public record in early 1947, claiming that a purge of the civil service similar to that taking place in the United States was under way. He called on civil servants to maintain "constant vigilance of their office associates."[14] The government, however, was not inclined to move in this direction. Eventually Prime Minister King went some distance to assure the public that there would be no "loyalty board" of the kind then being established by the Truman administration.

From the beginning of the cold war, tension between the RCMP and the government existed concerning questions of internal security policy. The Gouzenko affair had served as a catalyst for the development of cold war attitudes. It also provided a vehicle for certain RCMP officers to build reputations as experts on espionage and subversion.

The defection of Igor Gouzenko, the well-known cipher clerk, from the Soviet Embassy in Ottawa on September 5, 1945, helped to precipitate Canada's plunge into the cold war. The papers Gouzenko pilfered from the Embassy showed that the Soviet military intelligence service, the GRU, had been operating an espionage ring in Canada for about two years. It is likely that the GRU operation was not particularly sophisticated. The value of most of the information that it acquired is doubtful. But the revelation of its existence set off a reaction that would have reverberations for years to come.

For five months after Gouzenko's defection, the Canadian government did not take action publicly. Prime Minister Mackenzie King's initial response was a desire not to harm relations between

Canada and the Soviet Union. King and his principal lieutenants travelled to Washington to confer with President Truman, and to London to see Prime Minister Clement Attlee, before deciding on a course of action. Meanwhile, the RCMP quietly investigated persons who seemed to be implicated in the espionage ring to which Gouzenko's documents were pointing. No arrests were made and the government placed Gouzenko and his family out of the way at a wartime training camp for secret agents, Camp X, on the outskirts of Oshawa, Ontario.

By the beginning of 1946, increasing numbers of people in Washington were becoming aware of the case; Mackenzie King came under pressure to make it public. On February 13, the outline of the Gouzenko affair was leaked by a United States government source to Drew Pearson, a *New York Herald Tribune* columnist. The story claimed that the Canadian government was concealing a Soviet defector who had evidence of massive Soviet espionage operations against both Canada and the United States. The news caused a sensation on both sides of the border. On February 15, the King government was forced to acknowledge Gouzenko's defection. Thirteen people were immediately arrested and detained without charges being laid. This was done under the provisions of the *War Measures Act*, which was still in force. The detainees were held incommunicado and interrogated night and day, without legal counsel, at the RCMP barracks at Rockcliffe. The Prime Minister immediately appointed a Royal Commission to formally investigate Gouzenko's allegations.

The Royal Commission was headed by two Supreme Court Justices, R.L. Kellock and Robert Taschereau. Their mandate was to investigate Gouzenko's allegations of Soviet espionage in Canada and to recommend measures to prevent the continuation of such activities. The Royal Commission began its secret hearings in February and continued until June 1946. The people who had been arrested under the *War Measures Act* were questioned exhaustively. They represented a cross-section of Canadians, including MP Fred Rose, several military officers, an eminent scientist, two secretaries, and two academics. Most had no legal counsel when testifying before the Royal Commission. Igor Gouzenko testified at length, arguing that a vast conspiracy involving the Soviet Embassy and the Communist Party was spying on Canada in preparation for war.[15]

The Royal Commission issued interim reports in March and

May and a final report in June 1946. Before the Commission's work had been completed, charges had been laid against twenty-one of the people named by the Royal Commission as spies. Their trials went on throughout 1946, with Gouzenko acting as the main witness for the prosecution in most cases. Of the twenty-one people charged, eleven were convicted and ten acquitted. In many of the successful prosecutions, the evidence was based to a considerable extent on the words of the accused, spoken under interrogation by the RCMP or before the Royal Commission, without legal counsel. The detainees who had exercised their legal right to remain silent were all acquitted.[16]

The Soviets were indeed running a spy ring in Canada. What is in doubt is whether its importance was kept in perspective. Civil libertarians were outraged at the way in which the Kellock-Taschereau Commission conducted its inquiry and at the courts making use of evidence obtained under questionable circumstances. However, most Canadians did not exhibit much concern about civil liberties; the widely held public perception, based largely on press coverage, was that a very dangerous threat to the safety of Canada had been exposed just in time. Igor Gouzenko became a folk hero. With shrewdness, cynicism, and megalomania, he built a thirty-seven-year career as a professional defector. He had two books authored under his name and sold his story to a number of major magazines for large sums of money. He possessed an astute sense of theatre. He dramatized and sustained interest in himself by appearing in public with a bag over his head, to protect himself, he said, against revenge from the Russians. In fact, for most of his career Gouzenko's whereabouts were a very poorly kept secret. Any journalist with a few hundred dollars to spend could get in touch with him in minutes. His message over the years remained the same: the conspiracies of the Kremlin posed a deadly threat to the West, and anyone who didn't believe this might well be a Soviet agent.[17]

This perspective, expressed in its most vulgar form by Igor Gouzenko, is at the heart of cold war ideology. If the premise is established that the Soviet Union is bent on world conquest, and will employ every means to accomplish this goal, then all political activity, including the normal working of the liberal-democratic process, tends to be seen through this prism. Cold war ideology in its extreme form demands that any view that does not assent to the primacy of the cold war itself, as a basic fact of contemporary history, is subversive; to suggest that events occur for their own reasons, instead of being made to happen by the enemy, simply helps the enemy. This bizarre reasoning became very pervasive in the 1950s.

The Gouzenko revelations of a GRU espionage ring did provide a fragment of truth on which the exaggerated cold war edifice could be built; the importance of the GRU operation lay in its political consequences, rather than in its espionage success. In terms of the quality of the information it obtained and the professionalism of its members, it was a rather pathetic operation. As a number of the alleged conspirators have pointed out, in the context of World War Two it was possible for well-meaning, politically naive citizens to pass information to the Soviet Union, Canada's ally in the battle against the Nazis, without considering themselves to be traitors.[18] Raymond Boyer, for example, was a brilliant Montreal chemist who was convicted of giving the Soviets information on the technique for producing the high-explosive substance RDX, a process he had developed. In his early seventies, Boyer has retained the poise and self-confidence he inherited as a member of the old French-Canadian elite of Montreal. In the 1930s he had been trained as a research chemist in Montreal and Paris. At about that time he became dissatisfied with conventional social and political values — the failures of which became evident during the Great Depression — and like many other intellectuals of his generation, Boyer took up the politics of the left. He regarded Russia twenty years after the Bolshevik revolution as the ally of those people seeking progressive change in the West. The Hitler-Stalin pact of 1939 was seen as a necessary tactical move by the Soviets, and after it ended with the Nazi invasion in June 1941, the Soviets were open allies of the West. So Boyer could see nothing wrong in sharing with them his technique for producing RDX.

For this, Boyer spent four years in prison. He then gave up his career as a chemist to devote himself to penal reform. He still sees nothing wrong with what he did during the war. His modest flat is not far from the McGill campus. Speaking calmly, he points out that approximately a year before he passed on the information to the Russians, an official delegation from the Soviet Embassy visited his laboratory in Montreal, accompanied by representatives of the Canadian government. The Soviet visitors had been given access to the entire facility by the federal government.[19]

A similar sense of having done nothing that seemed traitorous in the context of the period has been expressed by a number of the other alleged conspirators.[20] Freda Linton was also named by the Kellock-Taschereau Commission as a member of the Soviet spy ring. Before the suspects were arrested in February 1946, Freda Linton disappeared. More than three years later, she was discovered by the FBI in the United States and deported to Canada. Charges against her were dropped, but she has often been mentioned as having been a key part of the operation.

Freda Linton has lived under another name for more than thirty years. She is an energetic, quick woman. She has had the strength to raise her daughter free of the burden of her own political past. Freda Linton has rarely been able to share the past with anyone.

A number of bright young men and women in the 1930s — many of them children of a generation of immigrants to Canada — became convinced of the need to organize for revolutionary change. They became dedicated Communists. They did what they thought necessary to achieve their political objectives. In their world at that time, there was virtually no distinction to be made between the interests of revolutionary Russia and the revolutionary prospects of the working class in other countries. Each needed the support of the other.

Although she did not go to prison, it is obvious that Freda Linton has paid a price for the political convictions of her youth. Three decades of silence, living with a false identity, always fearful of being discovered and humiliated, exact an emotional toll of pain and isolation. Perhaps worst of all is the realization that a grievous political mistake was made in the 1940s. The mistake in her view was not her adherence to the values of equality and the struggle against social injustice; rather it was in failing to make the crucial distinction between the interests of the Stalinist state and the interests of the Canadian workers. Freda Linton did not choose the path of the apostate, ready to renounce her past sins. Her regret is at her own political naiveté. It is also at what she regards as the cynical way in which that naiveté was exploited by the Royal Commission.

The Gouzenko case promoted the growth of the idea that Canadian society was in danger from a fifth column, an internal enemy bent on worming its way into positions of power and influence in order to further the Soviet aim of world domination. As cold war ideology developed, the internal enemy was believed to work by subverting the Canadian way of life and Canadian institutions, and by destroying the moral fibre of the nation. The fear of this subversion was enhanced by the concurrent fear that Western Europe and perhaps the whole Western world was about to fall victim to the Red Army.

The internal enemy was defined not in terms of any actions that actually occurred, but in terms of the political beliefs to which people subscribed. Those people who held left-wing views were automatically suspected of being agents of the Soviet enemy and of being subversive of Canadian society. In the cold war vision, Communists were invested with greatly exaggerated powers; they were seen as being enormously skilful and resourceful in their ability to influence and manipulate events. Those thought to be "tainted" by Communism had to be rooted out because of the enormous damage they were thought to be capable of causing. In the light of this menace, the Canadian government turned its attention to developing its own internal security measures.

In the immediate post-war period, the dominant external influence on the RCMP, and the Canadian intelligence community, still tended to be British. Sir William Stephenson, a Canadian whose exploits during the war as head of British Security Coordination in New York have been both celebrated and exaggerated, was in contact with senior figures in Ottawa in relation to the Gouzenko case. Subsequently, the Canadian government acquired the services of an experienced British intelligence officer. Peter Dwyer had worked for a number of years with MI6, the British Secret Intelligence Service. From 1945 until 1948 he had represented that organization in Washington. (He was succeeded in that post in 1949 by Kim Philby, who later wrote admiringly of Dwyer's professionalism and competence.)[21] Canada's signals intelligence agency (SIGINT), the super-secret Communications Branch of the National Research Council, employed Peter Dwyer from 1949 until 1952. He then moved to the Privy Council Office, where he served as Secretary to the Security Panel. Dwyer devoted his efforts to reforming the internal security procedures of the federal government. He understood the limitations of the RCMP Security and Intelligence Branch and strove to develop higher standards of professionalism, as well as a more humane approach to the handling of civil servants who were considered to be security risks. The long process of reform of the Canadian security services undoubtedly began with Peter Dwyer.[22]

The British, as an imperial power, had been involved in foreign espionage and the closely related field of internal security operations for a longer time than had the United States. The British were therefore thought to be more expert in these areas. They had considerable influence on the Americans in the early stages of the formation of the wartime Office of Strategic Services (OSS), the predecessor of the CIA. However, in the late 1940s, as the British empire declined, the American organizations became increasingly dominant in influencing and controlling various Western security and intelligence services.

Security services tend to be inherently conservative organizations. Their fundamental reason for existence is the protection of the state against change, whether the impetus for change is external or internal. The rise of the American empire was concurrent with the development of the cold war, with its characteristic obsession with Communism, and its tendency to equate dissent with subversion. This had the effect of causing United States security and intelligence organizations to become in many cases *de facto* agents for the propagation of the cold war view of the world.[23] Security and intelligence organizations of countries that have been closely allied with the United States have tended to embrace a similar perspective. This is caused partly by their own inherent characteristics and partly by the dominance of the American organizations.

The interrelationship between secret intelligence organizations and liberal democratic governments is necessarily uneasy. It involves a continuous tension between two often contradictory sets of values. A number of liberal democratic governments have experienced additional tensions with their security establishments because of the intimate ties that usually exist between their own secret services and the American-dominated Western intelligence fraternity.

In the cold war period, Canada adopted some internal security practices that were similar to those of the United States. Thousands of civil servants were investigated by the RCMP. Regulations concerning access to sensitive information were tightened. Plans for the detention of "subversives" in time of crisis were made. However, in contrast to the practice in the United States during the same period, the Canadian government did not enact restrictive labour legislation such as the *Taft-Hartley Act* of 1947, or anti-Communist legislation comparable to the U.S. *Internal Security Act* of 1950. As Mackenzie King had promised, Canada did not establish a loyalty oath programme. The Federal Cabinet stated in 1947 that it was "not considered possible or desirable to establish any rigid criteria for testing loyalty."[24] Justice Minister J. Lorimer Ilsley observed in 1947 that while certain other countries had attempted to determine a citizen's political beliefs, these policies proved to be counter-productive. "Loyalty," he said, "is not susceptible to any precise series of tests."

Although the government of Canada made an effort to pursue policies consistent with this view, it did not always succeed. The impact of the U.S. congressional investigations of the 1950s has continued to be felt in both the United States and Canada right up to the present. Political investigations by the FBI were closely linked to the activities of the congressional inquisitors in Washington. Unfortunately, in certain instances the RCMP also played a part, through its intimate connections with the United States security and intelligence community.

2

The Mythology of Treason

The moon was shining sulkily
Because she thought the sun
Had got no business to be there
After the day was done —
"It's very rude of him," she said,
"To come and spoil the fun!"

A ttitudes and suspicions formed in the 1950s tended to be
made permanent in the institutional memories of the security agencies, where these dark visions were nurtured
long after they ceased to have any currency in political discourse.
They have formed an undercurrent in Canadian political life that
from time to time swirls to the surface; then the public is tantalized
with the spectre of betrayal in high places.

Thus, for example, directly over a picture of the scantily clad
"Sunshine Girl" of April 12, 1981, the *Toronto Sun* ran an article
headed "Were Commies in Control Here?" with a subtitle, "Spy
Probe Identified 245 Agents of Influence."[1] The writer, Robert
Reguly, summarized the argument that Canada has been betrayed
by Soviet agents masquerading as civil servants, diplomats, and
politicians since the Russian Revolution. Reguly's sources in the
RCMP and the CIA had filled him in on the much-rumoured but
top-secret Operation Featherbed. The operation had been started
in 1958, Reguly claimed, because the RCMP had received word
from the FBI of Communism in high places in Ottawa. Featherbed
was claimed to have uncovered twelve senior civil servants who

were spies and "245 prominent 'agents of influence', including 138 in politics and the civil service."[2]

The treason dated from 1923, because it was then, Reguly alleged, that O.D. Skelton, the "father of the civil service," was recruited as a Comintern agent. He "hand-picked" men who were to be the leaders in the Canadian civil service for the following half-century. The article, typical of the genre, implied that both Robert Bryce, Secretary to the Cabinet from 1954 to 1963, and Lester B. Pearson, Liberal Prime Minister from 1963 to 1968, were suspected of treachery.

The origins of much of this mythology lie in the tragic case of Herbert Norman, a brilliant Canadian scholar and diplomat whose suicide in Cairo in 1957 shocked the world. The extent to which it also involved an effort by Washington witch-hunters to intimidate a Canadian Prime Minister, Lester B. Pearson, has until now never been made public. The Norman case draws together and is a powerful symbol of the paranoia, the exaggerations, and the vicious consequences of cold war witch-hunting. It also reveals the close relations among the agencies of the international intelligence community.

Herbert Norman was the son of Canadian Christian missionaries. Born in Karuizawa, Japan in 1909, he spoke Japanese fluently and enjoyed a subtle and far-reaching appreciation of the history and culture of Japan. He studied Classics at the University of Toronto, and continued his studies at Trinity College, Cambridge, from which he received a second B.A. in 1935. Norman returned to Canada, married Irene Clark in Hamilton on August 31, 1935, and taught at Upper Canada College. He did graduate work in Far Eastern Studies at Harvard University, and in 1938 he wrote his doctoral dissertation, which later became a widely acclaimed book, *Japan's Emergence as a Modern State*. At the same time, he served as a research associate with the Institute of Pacific Relations in New York. A year later he joined the Canadian Department of External Affairs, and was soon after assigned as a language officer to the Canadian Embassy in Tokyo.[3]

When the Japanese attacked Pearl Harbor, their government interned the Canadian diplomats. Two years later they were returned to Canada, and Norman found himself back in Ottawa. There he made an important contribution to the Canadian war effort against Japan until VJ Day in 1945. He was head of the Special Intelligence Section in the Department of External Affairs, analysing Japanese communications being monitored by the National Research Council Examination Unit. As soon as the war was over, he was sent by the Department of External Affairs first to the Philippines and then back to Tokyo, where he served as head of the Research and Analysis Branch of the Counter-Intelligence Section of the General Headquarters of the United States Army occupying Japan. He returned briefly to Ottawa, and in 1946 was appointed head of the Canadian liaison mission to the Allied Occupation Government of Japan. During the following four years, Norman was frequently consulted by the head of the Occupation Government, General Douglas MacArthur, because of his knowledge and understanding of the people and culture of Japan.

Herbert Norman was a serious student of Japanese politics. His published writing clearly shows he approached Japanese history using concepts available to a scholar familiar with Marxist thought. He made no effort to conceal this influence on his way of thinking, and his interpretation of the dynamics of history is evident to anyone who reads his work carefully. Norman had been interested in a radical critique of society since his undergraduate days. When he went to Cambridge in 1933, large numbers of students in several British universities were responding to the crisis of the Depression and the increasing power of European Fascism by participating in left-wing political activities. According to one description, written in the 1930s,

> By 1933 the crisis had broken into a political storm, and the conditions for a great anti-war and anti-Fascist movement gradually came into existence. Hitler's success in Germany made brutally clear the importance of Anti-Fascist propaganda among the students and the middle class, and brought many students up against political questions for the first time in their lives.[4]

Herbert Norman was one of the students who did respond to these questions. Not surprisingly, he became active in left-wing politics. The arena in which he acted was not politically sectarian, for

> In Cambridge no specific Marxist or Communist society had been set up in rivalry to the old Socialist Society. The left-wing students had simply won leading positions and majority support, and in 1933-34 had succeeded in giving the Socialist Society a very radical programme of action and speakers.[5]

A Labour Party group split off in the summer of 1934, but

27

the two groups merged again the following year. Norman may have joined the Communist Party in that period. If not, he almost certainly did later. His friend and fellow Canadian at Cambridge, Robert Bryce, recalled that he was "never sure whether Norman belonged to the party there or not. I didn't ask him. But subsequent evidence indicates that he did join the Party at some stage in his career."[6]

Norman's subsequent conduct contrasts sharply with that of some other left-wing Cambridge students of the early 1930s. Kim Philby, as well as Anthony Blunt, Guy Burgess, and Donald Maclean, went on to become Soviet agents. In so doing, they laundered themselves. They ceased to take part in left-wing politics. They did not write, or enter into political debate, nor were they seen with other known Communists. But Herbert Norman, like many others on the left acting out of honest conviction, was quite open about his views: his published articles and books express his Marxist interpretation of history and society.

The early period of General MacArthur's occupation of Japan was marked by a determination to bring about democratic reforms. These included breaking up the monopolistic corporations that had dominated much of the Japanese economy, redistributing land in favour of poor peasants, and encouraging democratic political activity. Norman assisted in this programme with great enthusiasm. But after 1946 and the onset of the cold war, General MacArthur's policies became more conservative, and many of the reforms that had been started were abandoned. Instead, priority was given to reinforcing the more traditionally powerful elements in Japanese society in order to enhance their ability to resist the perceived threat of Communism.

Norman did not agree with the general thrust of these changes, but he continued to function in apparent harmony with Douglas MacArthur for four more years. Then, in 1951, Herbert Norman and Lester Pearson were caught up in the whirlwind that ripped through the United States at the height of the cold war.

The 1949 victory of the Communists in the Chinese Civil War led to great anger and widespread recriminations in Washington. The crisis atmosphere was further exacerbated by the outbreak of the Korean War on June 25, 1950. For a decade, U.S. foreign policy had been infuriating certain figures on the extreme right of the American political spectrum. In their view, the wartime alliance with the Soviet Union — if not the war against Germany itself — the Yalta Agreement, the formation of the United Nations, and the defeat of the Chinese nationalists added up to an unforgivable series of betrayals by the Executive Branch in general and the State Department in particular. Joe McCarthy and Pat McCarran were two among a large number of senators and members of the House of Representatives who were deeply disturbed at the setbacks. These disasters, they argued, were the result of the ascendancy in the bureaucracy of "New Dealers," liberals and Communist sympathizers.[7] President Roosevelt's New Deal, with its policies of massive government intervention in the economy, was resented by both the Republican Party and the right wing of the Democratic Party. Roosevelt had been able to maintain a workable political consensus throughout the war. But without his personal leadership, along with the external pressures imposed by fighting the war, the consensus could not survive. One of the most effective weapons against the coalition was used by right-wing politicians, exemplified by Senator Martin Dies and Senator Pat McCarran, who by early 1946 were attacking veterans of the New Deal still in office in the Truman administration as Communists, Communist sympathizers, or subversives.

This was the very issue on which Senator Joe McCarthy launched his rise to prominence. In his speech in Wheeling, West Virginia, on February 7, 1950, McCarthy held aloft a list of the names of 205 people who, he claimed, were Communists working for the State Department. Within months a number of congressional committees were looking into the allegations. One of the hallmarks of this search for scapegoats was that there was no need to prove actual espionage or treason. To become a victim, a person need only have expressed views that, after the fact, could be construed as having been sympathetic to Communism. The passage of time did not matter; it was enough if the imprudent statement or association had occurred fifteen or twenty years earlier.

A search for those believed guilty of having "lost" China was undertaken by the Senate Internal Security Subcommittee headed by Senator Pat McCarran. From July 1951 until June 1952 much of its attention was directed to the Institute of Pacific Relations. The Institute had been a respected organization, founded in 1925 to foster research and study of Asian affairs. It was funded by such respectable institutions as the Rockefeller Foundation, and a number of major oil companies.

Herbert Norman had served as a research associate with the

Institute of Pacific Relations in New York in 1938.[8] The Institute published *Japan's Emergence as a Modern State* in 1940, and another work by Norman, *Soldier and Peasant in Japan*, in 1943.

On August 7, 1951, Dr. Karl Wittfogel, who had been a member of the Communist Party in pre-Hitler Germany, was testifying before the McCarran subcommittee. Under questioning by Robert Morris, the committee counsel, Wittfogel claimed that Herbert Norman had been a member of an allegedly Communist discussion group in the summer of 1938.[9] Morris then read into the record letters showing that Norman had been associated with the Institute of Pacific Relations in 1940. In the political atmosphere of 1951, to say that Norman had, thirteen years before, been a member of "a discussion group of friends,"[10] some of whom might have been Communists, was tantamount to accusing him of the gravest kind of treachery. It also amounted to an accusation that the government of Canada was complicit in treachery because it employed Norman as a senior diplomat.

Lester Pearson was Minister of External Affairs at the time. On August 10, he made a formal statement in Ottawa, affirming the confidence of the Canadian government in Herbert Norman. The Department of External Affairs lodged a protest with the United States State Department. The Canadian Embassy in Washington was instructed to express "regret and annoyance" that Norman's name was "being dragged into the hearings."

But within a matter of days, Pearson's own name was being dragged into the hearings, and he was being accused, in an executive session of the McCarran subcommittee, of having been involved with Soviet spies in wartime Washington. The accusation was without foundation; but the circumstances in which it was made illustrate the worst aspects of cold war politics.

Pearson had been posted at the Canadian Embassy in Washington from 1942 until 1946. He began as Minister-Counsellor and completed his tour as Ambassador. One of the persons attached to the Embassy during 1943 and 1944 was Hazen Sise, a distribution representative for the National Film Board of Canada.

Elizabeth T. Bentley was one of the better-known informers in cold war Washington. In August 1945 she contacted the FBI to report that she had been an underground operative of the American Communist Party. She claimed to have worked with and been the lover of Jacob Golos, said to have been an important Soviet intelligence agent until his death in 1943. Bentley was later dubbed

"The Blonde Spy Queen" by the press for her many appearances before the congressional committees. During her career as an informer she "named" a total of forty-three U.S. government employees as having belonged to the Communist underground.[11] She had alleged privately to the FBI in 1945 that Hazen Sise had supplied information for her to pass on to Jacob Golos. In June 1949, she made the same claim publicly to the United States Senate Judiciary Committee. Hazen Sise promptly denied the allegation and asserted that he had never met Elizabeth Bentley.[12]

On August 14, 1951, one week after Wittfogel's accusation against Herbert Norman, the McCarran subcommittee met to take testimony from Elizabeth Bentley. The Senators ostensibly wanted to hear about Hazen Sise; in fact, they were after Lester Pearson. In due course, Bentley agreed with the subcommittee counsel, Robert Morris, that Hazen Sise had been "a direct agent and conscious agent" and had worked directly with her. Morris then asked, "What were some of the sources of his information?" After mentioning the Film Board, Bentley came out with the stunning reply, "But his most valuable material came from Mike Pearson." The verbatim transcript, including the misspelling of Hazen Sise's name, reads as follows:

MR. MORRIS: Who is Mike Pearson?

MISS BENTLEY: That is really his nickname, it's really Lester Pearson, and he was second in charge of the Canadian Legation during that period, which would be from 1942 to 1943 when I lost Hazen Size.

MR. MORRIS: Was he a counsellor to the Canadian Legation?

MISS BENTLEY: I don't know the precise title, but Hazen said he was the top man in the legation; I understand from Hazen that Pearson knew Hazen was a Communist and was willing to help. Pearson by virtue of his position used to sit in on American functions, particularly British ones re British policies, all of which was super hush-hush.

MR. MORRIS: Then he used to give the information he obtained to Hazen Size?

MISS BENTLEY: That is correct, and he passed it on to me.

MR. MORRIS: Do you have any question now that Hazen Size was a Communist?

MISS BENTLEY: Hazen Size said knew [sic] that he was a Communist? Hazen Size said he knew.

31

MR. MORRIS: Nevertheless he was giving this information to Hazen Size?

MISS BENTLEY: That is correct.

MR. MORRIS: Hazen Size turned it over to you?

MISS BENTLEY: That is correct.

MR. MORRIS: What did you do with it?

MISS BENTLEY: That was turned over to Golos during his lifetime, and later on to his succeeding agent.

MR. MORRIS: And it went on to the Soviets?

MISS BENTLEY: That is right.[13]

The FBI followed up this revelation with another lengthy interrogation of Elizabeth Bentley. The top-secret report of that session reveals that in surroundings less dramatic than those of the McCarran subcommittee, Bentley's accusations against Pearson were much more restrained. She alleged that Sise supplied her with information from the Film Board but, according to the FBI, she allowed that

> none of this info was of any great importance to the Russians, but she accepted it anyway to make SISE feel he was accomplishing something. In addition, he supplied her with info which he obtained from LESTER PEARSON having to do with diplomatic conferences and affairs which PEARSON was party to. MISS BENTLEY states that she cannot recall details of this info.[14]

The FBI queried Bentley about Pearson's "political ideology," and was informed that she had the impression that Pearson (whom she never claimed to have met) was a "left-winger." He moved in the same circles as Sise, she alleged, and was said to have been sympathetic to the Loyalist cause in the Spanish Civil War.[15]

The FBI report concludes with this observation:

> It would appear that BENTLEY's answers to the above questions are an interpretation and an enlargement of the statements furnished by her with regard to SISE in 1945. She has stated that the info with regard to PEARSON was overlooked by her at that time.[16]

The FBI investigation of Hazen Sise that had begun in 1945 had, in fact, been closed on August 5, 1949. In the report that had concluded the case, the FBI observed that

MISS BENTLEY characterized the information obtained from SISE as gossip he overheard in the Canadian and British Embassy, Washington, D.C. He also mentioned the names of prominent British individuals who were coming to the United States as well as comments by SISE on Canada's policy as far as the war and other matters were concerned.[17]

Why was the Hazen Sise case opened again two years later, in 1951? It is difficult to escape the conclusion that Elizabeth Bentley was brought before the McCarran subcommittee in order to defame Lester Pearson. Pearson, as Secretary of State for External Affairs, had denounced the subcommittee and the cold war assumptions that underlay everything it did. He had asserted that in this area Canada would make its own decisions. This the McCarran subcommittee could not tolerate and with bravado it set out to put the Canadian Secretary of State for External Affairs in his place. In doing so, it added another branch to the tree of reckless suspicion that was becoming deeply rooted within the security and intelligence community.

The dark atmosphere where unscrupulous politicians, professional subversive-hunters, and informers gather encourages the growth of suspicion. What began as an act of cynical expediency on the part of Pat McCarran and Robert Morris was taken up by the security agencies, minutely examined by them once again, and made a part of their institutional culture. For many people in these agencies, it probably never became a matter of serious concern; but the nature of secret organizations is such that there is sometimes a tendency on the part of certain elements within them to be seized by notions of conspiracies in high places. The suspicion of treachery in the highest levels of the government of Canada became an ongoing obsession within the right wing of both the American and Canadian security organizations. Its history is almost entirely subterranean, but at certain moments its effects are felt.

The initial interest of the McCarran subcommittee in Herbert Norman was the result of an earlier move against him that had also been frustrated by the Canadian government. On October 17, 1950, the RCMP issued a secret report that raised questions about Norman's past political associations. Two days later Norman was summoned to Ottawa from Tokyo. He was subjected to six weeks of intensive interrogation by the RCMP. The Mounties did not confine their attention to Norman's background and political views, which in general were already known to the government. The RCMP wanted to turn Norman into an informer.[18]

During the long weeks when the interrogation was taking place, Norman spent a good deal of time with his old friend Robert Bryce, who was then a high-ranking public servant. Norman and Bryce had attended Cambridge together. Bryce had been a serious student of economic theory, and a socialist. His commitment to socialism did not last; his interest in economics did. He became one of the leading exponents of the theories of John Maynard Keynes. As a senior official in the Department of Finance, he was one of the architects of the Keynesian policies that were fundamental to much of the economic planning of successive post-war Canadian governments.

Bryce was a brilliantly successful civil servant. When Herbert Norman was interrogated in 1950, Bryce was Assistant Deputy Minister of Finance. Three years later he reached the pinnacle of the federal bureaucracy when he became Secretary to the Cabinet and Clerk of the Privy Council. He was implicitly trusted — and not only by the Liberal government of Louis St. Laurent. When John Diefenbaker became Prime Minister in 1957, he insisted Bryce stay on as the head of the civil service, and Bryce retained the confidence of the Chief throughout the six years of Tory government. His years as Secretary to the Cabinet coincided with the later stages of the cold war. Deeply concerned about McCarthyism, Bryce was a central figure in the effort to prevent its worst excesses from being repeated in Canada. He understood the complex considerations that could lead a person to be a socialist in the 1930s and a liberal in the 1950s.

In the 1980s Bryce is a quiet and evidently thoughtful man. He is well aware of the incomplete sovereignty that Canada's ties to the United States have created. At times one catches a glimpse of his sense of the ironies that abound in the exercise of this limited power. There is also an intuition of his pain at a recurring theme — the clash of sensibilities that has resulted from the attempt to apply mechanistic notions of the cold war retroactively to the richness of the intellectual life of the 1930s. Reflecting on Norman's ordeal under interrogation in 1950, he recalled that

> the thing that was troubling him most in these interrogations was the pressure to give information about his friends that

might indicate whether or not they were Communists or associated with Communists. Whether they had views that should be investigated. And Herbert felt that he shouldn't do this. He was loyal to his friends and he didn't want, as a means of resolving his own problems, to get them into trouble.[19]

To men like Bryce and Pearson, this principled refusal to become an informer was understandable. Indeed, they considered it an honourable course of action for Norman.

The procedure for security screening of government employees was set out in Cabinet Directive 4A, which had been passed in April 1948. The RCMP was to conduct the investigation of Norman and report its findings to the government department concerned, in this case the Department of External Affairs. It was not within the power of the RCMP to grant the security clearance; that was the responsibility of the Department of External Affairs. The findings of the protracted RCMP investigation of Herbert Norman were duly submitted to the Department. After they had been reviewed, it was decided on December 1, 1950, that there was no reason to doubt Herbert Norman's loyalty to Canada.[20]

As Minister of External Affairs, this was Lester Pearson's decision to make in consultation with senior officials and fellow cabinet ministers. The criteria used in reaching the conclusion that Norman was loyal to Canada were evidently not what the RCMP might have wished. Pearson and his colleagues affirmed that Norman was a trusted and valued public servant. In their view this was not negated by his having been a Communist in the past, or by his refusal to be an informer. But this view was heretical to the RCMP. As Bryce remarked, "if you are running a Security Service it satisfies you a lot more if a man demonstrates that he is willing to give you information about others as a way of demonstrating ... proof of his dedication to your cause."[21]

A sophisticated view of the complexities of political belief, and hence of the subtle nature of trust and honour, had come into direct conflict with the simplistic values of the police mentality and the cold war. In a sense, the Norman case, and indeed the Pearson case, were decided at this time. There is something almost dreadfully inevitable about the Norman case after December 1, 1950: the disgruntled RCMP, convinced it had been overruled by a sinister combination of treachery and favouritism; the sharing of the information from the RCMP investigation with colleagues in the FBI; the leak to the McCarran subcommittee, which precipitated the hearings; the attempt to intimidate Lester Pearson by dredging up the tired gossip of the Hazen Sise case.

So finally, after a hiatus of almost six years, the McCarran subcommittee revived its allegations against Norman. William Rusher, an assistant to committee counsel Robert Morris at the time, proudly revealed that

> the Sub-Committee had come into possession of the substance of the RCMP memorandum of October, 1950, which had been suppressed at the insistence of Lester Pearson.... What matters is that the ISSC [Internal Security Subcommittee — the McCarran Committee] knew what the RCMP had reported, and that Morris [without identifying the RCMP as the author of the memorandum] summarized it for the record in the 1957 investigation....[22]

Rusher's smug account underscores the fact that a confidential report about a senior Canadian official from the RCMP to the government of Canada had been improperly passed to the McCarran subcommittee. It is virtually certain that the intermediary in this transaction was one of the agencies in the American intelligence community.

Rusher's charge that Lester Pearson had "suppressed" the RCMP memorandum compounds the viciousness of this episode. No security report on an individual is *ever* a public document. A confidential document of this kind is in its essence "suppressed" from publication or scrutiny by a foreign agency or political committee; otherwise it would not be a confidential document. This confidentiality was violated when the report was passed to the Americans; that act illustrates all too well that ties within the Western intelligence community are sometimes stronger than the loyalty of security agencies to their own governments.

Moreover, William Rusher and the McCarran subcommittee totally misconstrued the nature of the security screening process as it existed in Canada in 1950. Its fundamental principle was that responsible officials and ministers should make considered judgements about the loyalty of Canadians, taking all factors into account. This procedure contrasted sharply with the implicit assumption that the police, or some other security agency, should somehow have the wisdom and the power to "clear" or to reject any citizen who might come to their attention. This assumption about the role of the police is necessarily subversive of democratic government.

Herbert Norman was appalled that the attack on him had been renewed in the Senate Committee after more than six years. The prospect of again having to tolerate the ignorant speculation of this smug band of fanatics was profoundly depressing to him.[23] He took his own life within a few weeks of learning that Robert Morris and the McCarran subcommittee were once again beating the drums of cold war hysteria with him as their intended victim.

To the crusaders of the cold war, Norman's death provided further evidence that he had something to hide. In that obsessively totalitarian view of the world even death itself can be explained away as the result of a conspiracy.

The story of Herbert Norman and Lester Pearson is important because it provided the foundation for the mythology of treason in high places in Canada — a mythology on which the right, both inside and outside the Western intelligence community, has fed ever since. But it is even more important for what it reveals about the motivation, and the modes of thought, of those people for whom there will always be a cold war.

3

The Self-Perpetuating System

The Walrus and the Carpenter
Were walking close at hand:
They wept like anything to see
Such quantities of sand:
"If this were only cleared away,"
They said, "it would *be grand!"*

The first round of the protracted cold war ended in the mid-1960s. It was succeeded by a period of *détente* between the two superpowers that lasted roughly from the late 1960s to the late 1970s. During that time extensive negotiations took place between the superpowers: more than a dozen formal agreements to limit various aspects of the nuclear arms race were signed; exchanges and travel between the Soviet Union and the United States increased dramatically. The general tone of East-West diplomacy and dialogue became much less shrill and accusatory than it had been during the initial cold war period.

During *détente*, tolerance of dissident opinion was increased to some extent. Nikita Khrushchev's denunciation of Stalinism in 1956 was followed by a period of attempted economic and political reform. This included a limited improvement in the human rights of Soviet citizens. Although the pace of de-Stalinization was not maintained in the post-Khrushchev period, some degree of reform continued through the 1970s.

In the United States, the attempt to repress dissent that had characterized the original cold war began to ease by the late 1950s.

Joe McCarthy and McCarthyism came to symbolize a kind of demagogy that was viewed by the majority of Americans as being incompatible with the basic principles of their constitutional democracy. The fearful conformism of the 1950s changed dramatically as millions of Americans mobilized in powerful movements of protest and social reform in the 1960s.

But *détente* did not suspend the cold war: it shifted the terms on which it was fought, and reduced the overt tensions. Cold war interests and institutions continued to exist throughout the period of *détente*. Each side remained a heavily armed camp; although international agreements imposed some restraints, the arms race continued, largely unabated. Complexes of arms-related research, development, and manufacturing organizations prospered. The respective systems of alliances, centring in the West on NATO and in the East on the Warsaw Pact, remained intact. Alliances in peripheral areas did, of course, shift. China, for example, was far too massive a power to maintain its military alliance with the Soviet Union when this arrangement ceased to be useful to it for its own political purposes. Third World countries at a distance from the two centres of global power had some scope for shifting allegiances in the flux of anti-colonial and post-colonial struggles.

The new atmosphere of *détente* between the superpowers was attenuated by the fact that both superpowers engaged in armed interventions in other countries during the period. In 1968 the military and security forces of the Soviet Union forcibly suppressed the move towards a more democratic and liberal kind of socialism in Czechoslovakia. Until its withdrawal in the early 1970s, the United States waged a brutal war in Vietnam. American involvement in the war had begun during the Kennedy administration, in the late stages of the first round of the cold war. The widespread protest this war unleashed in the United States, together with the implications of the defeat in Vietnam for the viability of the United States' global role, paradoxically contained the seeds of the new cold war. Through the years, right-wing forces in the United States began to regroup and develop a campaign to re-establish American global pre-eminence and prestige.

Détente ended when the superpowers sensed that it no longer suited their respective purposes. By the beginning of the 1980s the interests of the cold war institutions and the dominant political forces in the United States had once again converged. The cold war had begun again incrementally under the Carter presidency;

it was raised to the level of official ideology by the Reagan administration.

There are several striking features of the continuing cold war. The first is that it involves global competition between two superpowers, each of which is at the centre of what is in effect an empire. Yet these empires do not make imperial claims. They do not demand the formal political control, much less the colonization, of the less powerful nations that are dependent on them. Instead, they derive their legitimacy from their claims to support freedom, democracy, a better way of life, and the equality of individuals. Each purports to achieve these universal human goals in a different way, using very different definitions of "freedom," "democracy," and "equality." Each implicitly claims to act in the interests of its friends. Each is also prepared to suppress dissent in pursuit of its apparently benign interests.

The second feature is that from the beginning the cold war has been inextricably linked with the nuclear arms race. The two competing superpowers have long had the means to destroy one another, as well as the earth itself, many times over. The cold war has provided the necessary pretext for the continuation of this "dance of death."

The principal aims of the United States and the Soviet Union long ago ceased to be about the possibility of one side acquiring territory from the other or from its allies, if that ever was a genuine issue. It is difficult to contemplate one side successfully subduing the other in political, ideological, or military terms. In the age of nuclear overkill, the famous dictum of Clausewitz that war is the continuation of politics by other means cannot hold literally true. There can be "proxy" wars, and there have been many, and they have been fearsomely destructive. There can also be cold war. But only the most wild-eyed nuclear strategist would claim the cold war can be turned into a hot war that can actually be fought and won using nuclear weapons. Other means are preferable.

The cold war is, in a sense, about itself. It can perhaps be best understood as a system of relationships among the nations that make up the alliances. Each superpower enjoys relative dominance among its allies in the vital areas of military and security policy. This, of course, does not necessarily extend to matters of trade, diplomacy, economic policy, and other areas of public interest. But where national security is perceived to be at stake, both the Soviet Union and the United States are able to intervene with virtual impunity within their respective spheres of influence. Each is able to exert effective control over the military and security elements within its own network of alliances, and to do so in the name of values that are formally held by the other members of the alliance.[1]

The cold war provides the rationale for the development and maintenance not only of massive military organizations, but also of a vast network of supporting institutions. Arms manufacturers, energy suppliers, and communications systems are needed to sustain each superpower's cold war effort. Scientific and technological research is required on a permanent basis. Vast bureaucracies are necessary to regulate and administer these activities. A prominent characteristic of the Soviet system for decades has been the existence of a dominant and highly bloated state apparatus. In the West as well, the state sectors concerned with cold war activity have grown steadily. Under conservative administrations — which are traditionally dedicated to reducing the size of the government — military, police, and security organizations are exempted. Their budgets and establishments have continued to expand.

The organizations needed for waging the cold war on each side are in turn dependent upon it for their ongoing existence and expansion. The cold war has thus become a self-perpetuating system. The complex of related institutions that support it have a vital interest in ensuring its continuation. They must also be certain of ensuring that the pretexts for the cold war seize the hearts and minds of the people who set the political direction of the superpowers and their allies.

This is not to suggest that there is a cold war conspiracy. There is no cabal or clandestine group that deviously decides on the best strategy to prolong the cold war and the nuclear arms race. On the contrary, the majority of adherents to cold war ideology are undoubtedly sincerely convinced of the danger of the Soviet (or American) threat, of the relentless efforts by the other side to destroy or undermine free (or socialist) institutions, and of the rightness of the cause they happen to serve. In both the United States and the Soviet Union, being publicly *seen* to accept and support the assumptions of the cold war has come to represent a significant component of political respectability. Ironically, in maintaining this situation, the antagonistic cold war elites are ultimately more dependent upon one another than they are on their own allies. And this applies strongly to the intelligence organizations. What would the KGB do without the machinations of the CIA? What would the CIA do without the plots of the KGB?

The security and intelligence organizations on both sides play a particularly important part in the functioning of the cold war system. The nature of the long-running conflict between the superpowers has been essentially political; but throughout its history, it has taken on the form, if not the content, of a war. The metaphor of the cold war is that of a protracted military struggle. East-West relations, and by extension international relations in general, have been militarized. There is no precedent in modern history for the extent and duration of the military alliance systems that have dominated international relations for almost four decades. Intelligence agencies in most countries operate on an essentially military basis. Their mission is to collect "offensive" or "defensive" intelligence about "targets"; their primary purpose is to provide their governments with information on the intentions as well as the capabilities of other nations — friendly nations as well as those conventionally regarded as "the enemy." The agencies provide the information about adversary nations upon which plans and strategies for waging the cold war are based. In some respects, the work of intelligence operatives is similar to that of anyone whose profession it is to deal in information — journalists, academics, diplomats. Information is collected, evaluated, analysed, and disseminated. But intelligence agencies must perforce also sustain the system of which they are an indispensable part. Unlike journalism or scholarship or diplomacy, secret intelligence is founded upon the assumption of conflict. And of course intelligence agencies can and do use methods and technologies unavailable to other collectors of information — secret agents, electronic intercepts, surveillance satellites. Consequently, the information they generate carries a uniquely exotic quality.

Intelligence organizations of necessity operate in secret; but the secrecy of their operations also makes it impossible for the accuracy of their information or the quality of their analysis to be measured against other accepted standards. For example, only the person who knows the identity of a confidential source can accurately gauge the reliability of information coming from that source. When the official view of a situation appears to be at odds with the reality apparent to most observers, it is often argued that they would see that situation differently if they had access to the special information and insight that the state and its secret intelligence services have.

A similar set of considerations applies in the field of "security intelligence" — intelligence concerning the security of the state against foreign espionage agents, terrorists, and domestic "subversion." Here, too, there is an ideological function. In their concern with threats to the security of the state, security services (also known as domestic intelligence agencies, and internal security agencies) are necessarily interested in political thought. Not just the thinking of spies and terrorists, but also revolutionary ideas, insurgent ideas, subversive ideas. Their ostensible purpose is to detect plots, conspiracies, an incipient coup or violent upheaval, and to warn the responsible leaders of the state so they can take preventive action. In the United States and the Soviet Union, they must also ensure that those who influence or control the process of formulating public policy do not stray too far from cold war orthodoxy. Thus the ubiquity of the background check and the security clearance for public servants.

In countries that are not themselves superpowers but, like Canada, are participants in the cold war as allies of a superpower, the situation is somewhat different. There is a constant tension between the national interest and the always-present alliance interest. These differences are usually submerged in the prevailing view that what is best for the dominant partner is best for the others, although it is commonplace to deny that one country does dominate another. Harold Innis observed that the mechanism of denial "has been particularly effective in Canada with its difficulty in dealing precisely and directly with foreign problems because of divisions between French and English."[2]

The degree of tension within an alliance varies according to circumstances. Perceptions of the divergence between the national interest and the allied-superpower interest change, depending upon which group is dominant in the government of a smaller nation. To take a rather extreme example: for the Dubcek regime in Czechoslovakia in the spring of 1968, Czech interests and Soviet interests did not converge, particularly in terms of the way the political process was to operate within Czechoslovakia. But for the government of Gustav Husak, which succeeded the Dubcek

43

government in August 1968 after the Soviet tanks had rolled into Prague, there was not much of a problem about Czech interests not converging with Soviet interests.

In another obvious example, the brutal regime of the Greek colonels that began with a coup d'état on April 21, 1967, did not cause alarm among the nation's NATO allies. Indeed, it enjoyed their tacit approval until it was replaced by the Papandreou government in 1974. In fact, it can be argued that Henry Kissinger and the CIA had a hand in the coup. In contrast, the Socialist government of Andreas Papandreou that was democratically re-elected in October 1981 has experienced continuing friction within the NATO alliance.

A very different kind of example is that of the refusal of the Labour government of New Zealand to continue to allow visits to its ports by naval vessels that might be carrying nuclear weapons. The government was acting in what it took to be the national interest of New Zealand, as well as in its own political interest; this brought it into direct conflict with its superpower ally, the United States. Only hours after the New Zealand Labour Party, led by David Lange, won a general election by a landslide, an American official started warning that a Labour government would break long-standing defence ties if Lange kept his election promise to ban the nuclear ships.[3] Prime Minister Lange nonetheless went ahead with the policy after his government was sworn in some nine days later.

The United States' reaction was explained succinctly by a senior figure in the Reagan administration several months later, when he was reputed to have said, "Unless we hold our allies' feet to the fire over ship visits and nuclear deployments, one will run away and then the next."[4]

The interests of the institutions in the cold war alliances remain relatively constant, but the political life of nations is always evolving, changing, and developing. When the political life of allied nations is such that the assumptions of the cold war dominate political discourse, there tends to be harmony within the alliance. But when the political life of nations develops in such a way that serious public questions or doubts are raised about the wisdom of cold war policies, then a different situation emerges. Superpowers apply various kinds of pressures to reluctant allies. And the domestic institutions of the cold war system move, in one way or another, to counter and inhibit the public and political pressures that threaten the alliance, and to re-assert its dominance. Their institutional and bureaucratic futures depend on doing so.

Ironically, there have been occasional instances in which politicians have pressured security and intelligence agencies to develop information to support cold war positions. CIA Director William J. Casey has come under attack by conservatives in the United States Senate for harbouring an alleged "pro-Soviet bias." Senator Jesse Helms, the right-wing Republican from North Carolina, among others, charged that the CIA had deliberately or mistakenly underestimated Soviet military capabilities.[5] An earlier case involved George Bush, shortly after he was appointed Director of Central Intelligence by President Gerald Ford in 1975. Bush, in collaboration with White House officials, appointed a "B-team" made up of dedicated cold warriors who were critical of what they regarded as the CIA's "arms-control bias." Their mandate was to review the government's estimates of Soviet military strength and intentions. The B-team duly came up with ringing criticisms of the U.S. intelligence community for allegedly underestimating Soviet nuclear capabilities. This episode ultimately proved to be an important factor in the transition from *détente* to the renewed cold war.[6]

Canada has been deeply enmeshed in the Western alliance system since the beginning of the cold war. The importance of the location of the country — directly between the United States and the Soviet Union — was not lost on American planners. The strategic advantage of a permanent military presence in the Arctic was coveted by the Americans even before World War Two had ended. The American presence, justified by the exigencies of the war against Germany and Japan, was regarded as a temporary necessity by the Canadian government, and Prime Minister Mackenzie King was profoundly uneasy about its continuation after 1945.

But the theme of Canadian governments making the best of accommodating the American military presence in Canada has a long history. Invariably, the rationale in the end is that it is better for the Americans to be present with our permission than without our permission.

This awkward compromise of acquiescence and sovereignty, expedience and dignity, has generated a kind of schizophrenia in Canadian political life. From Mackenzie King on, Canadian leaders have walked the narrow path between the stone wall of Americans' perceived strategic self-interest and the wasteland of unfulfilled aspirations to national independence. Each Prime Minister has devised his own method of living with the problem. Despite his reputation for dithering, King held out on certain key issues, not the least of which was the American military presence in the Arctic. Louis St. Laurent presided over the coldest years of the cold war, in which Canada became irrevocably entangled in the Western alliance system. Lester Pearson harboured misgivings about the cold war as a diplomat in the 1940s, as Minister of External Affairs in the 1950s, and as Prime Minister in the 1960s. For this he earned the distrust, if not the outright enmity, of the more enthusiastic ideologues in the United States national security complex. This is not to suggest that Pearson actually obstructed the development of cold war institutions or ideology in Canada. On the contrary, one need only remember his role in arming the Canadian military with nuclear weapons in 1963 to recognize that Pearson was quite capable of making a significant, if somewhat reluctant, contribution to the cold war syndrome. But his lack of enthusiasm caught the imagination of the McCarthyite watchdogs.

Being formally allied with another nation offers no insurance against being spied on by that nation. One of the tasks of the superpower intelligence agencies is to keep watch on the allies and ensure that they remain reliable, a task that is enormously facilitated by gaining influence over the security and intelligence agencies of the smaller allied nations.

The other side of the alliance coin is that smaller nations must pay a good deal of attention to the intentions and the expectations of the superpower to which they are allied. This is essentially a political and diplomatic function, rather than a secret intelligence task. But the expectations of the superpowers invariably also require the security and intelligence agencies of the smaller allies to maintain a flow of information to the superpower.

Counter-intelligence is an integral part of the intelligence mission. It involves, at the very least, the protection of the state against various threats: foreign espionage in particular, but also terrorism and "subversion." In identifying and neutralizing these threats, the counter-intelligence organization uses many of the same techniques as the offensive intelligence organization. These include electronic surveillance, running secret agents, infiltration of political groups and parties, etc.

Since the 1940s, Canada has been heavily engaged in the secret collection of foreign intelligence as well as in counter-intelligence. Canadian activities in the field of foreign intelligence have been cloaked in great secrecy. Beginning during World War Two and continuing through the cold war to the present day, the Canadian government has maintained a large-scale signals intelligence (SIG-INT) operation, conducted by the little-known Communications Security Establishment (CSE), which operates a number of installations around the country at which highly sophisticated equipment monitors communications and other electronic signals from various parts of the globe. These signals yield a vast amount of information about activities within other countries. It is reliably estimated that over ninety per cent of the foreign intelligence acquired by the United States comes from this kind of operation carried out by its own agencies in a number of countries, as well as by those of Canada and other allies.[7] The activity of the CSE is carried out under a series of secret international arrangements that have existed since 1947. Known generically as the UKUSA agreements, they ensure that Canadian SIGINT activity is intimately bound up with similar activity on the part of the United Kingdom, the United States, Australia, and New Zealand. Much of the SIG-INT material collected by Canada is transmitted directly to the U.S. National Security Agency, where it is interpreted, stored, and retained. Much of it is not first processed and analysed in Canada.[8]

Canadian counter-intelligence activities are better known to the public. The RCMP had a security and intelligence capability as early as the 1920s. But it was during the cold war period that security and intelligence activity, as well as the organizational infrastructure that it required, expanded rapidly. The security and intelligence function of the RCMP was established formally in a special branch of the force in 1948. Inevitably, the Security and Intelligence Branch, predecessor of the Security Service, developed a culture of its own that explicitly embodied a cold war perspective on the world. A succinct statement of this view was contained in the introduction to a series of lectures published by the RCMP in 1952:

Freedom is our most precious possession. For the sake of freedom, since 1914, the people of Canada, with other peoples of the Commonwealth, the United States and allies have fought two terrible wars. With some allies, in 1950, Canada entered the struggle for Korea. For the sake of freedom, to guard against the ever-growing danger of a tyranny such as the world has never known, Canada signed the North Atlantic Treaty.

Not only from without is freedom threatened, it is threatened from within. We are no longer complacent towards threats from without but we must avoid complacency in the face of threats from within. The most serious of all comes from those who use their liberty to enjoy licence, whose anti-social works endanger the foundations of democracy.[9]

The connection was thus firmly established between the international and domestic cold wars. The specific nature of the internal threat against which the RCMP was defending Canada was spelled out in the first lecture of the book, where it was pointed out that

Undermining and subversive influences in Canada today thrive on ignorance and lack of appreciation of the full meaning of true democracy. A well-informed public can throw off and smash the hold of subversive ideologies. And it is the absolute duty of every Canadian citizen to become well informed, and thus to bring to light and destroy the ugly cancer which at this very moment is gnawing at the vitals of democracy.[10]

In part because of its own paramilitary organization, it was not difficult for the RCMP to adopt the cold war model of military conflict as the basis of its own ideology. Elements of this view can be traced back to the era of the Bolshevik Revolution and the Winnipeg General Strike; they became the dominant view in the RCMP, as in other security and intelligence services, in the early years of the cold war.

In commenting on the underlying meaning and causes for the treason of Kim Philby, the MI6 officer who was in fact a Soviet spy, the novelist John le Carré claims that the British Secret Intelligence Service (SIS) also found its most comfortable ideological clothing during that same period. He recalls that in the immediate post-war era:

If the prevailing political sentiment of the nation was vaguely leftist, the posture and tradition of SIS — as well as its present role — were frankly anti-Bolshevist. It was in the world of capital that SIS had its traditional heart, in the preservation of trade routes, in the defence of foreign investment and colonial wealth, in the protection of "ordered society." In re-discovering this tradition, and bringing to it the new techniques and brutalities it had learned in the war, SIS was hardly likely to win the hearts of the intellectuals whose wit had once saved it from disbandment.[11]

Labour Prime Minister Clement Attlee was enough of a cold warrior to refrain from entertaining any political misgivings about this situation. "There is no sign," le Carré writes, "that Attlee tried to put a socialist spin on our Intelligence effort. Let SIS expand, he seems to have said; in the fight against Communism, Left and Right are united."[12]

None of this is meant to suggest that the security and intelligence services, either in Canada or in other countries, are monolithic. Competition and rivalry between agencies within a country can be fierce, as has often been the case between the FBI and the CIA in the United States, or MI5 and MI6 in the United Kingdom. Internationally, there is always some distrust among intelligence organizations. It can be caused by specific problems, such as the Philby betrayal, or by differing domestic political conditions from one country to another. Examples of the latter case occur when politicians probe too deeply into the workings of their own intelligence community, thus arousing fear that secrets will be revealed.

Within the agencies of the Western intelligence community, there are several factions with differing political points of view. Opinions vary as to the exact nature of the threats to national security, and as to their relative importance. There is a recognized need to examine information as objectively as possible in order to produce the most accurate and timely intelligence. Yet there is a tendency on the part of some intelligence professionals to see the world in conspiratorial terms. In their view, no phenomenon can be assumed to be what it appears to be; it may hide a sinister meaning. No one is above suspicion. This ultra-conservative attitude has many similarities to that of Joseph McCarthy and the other witch-hunters of the 1950s. Indeed, the continuing efforts of the ultra-conservative faction to prevail not only in the United States but also in allied agencies has had enormous impact on the ways in which those organizations have developed. It has also affected the political process itself in Canada and in other allied nations.

Within the Western intelligence community, the right has become dominant. It has been eclipsed at times, as was the case during the post-Watergate reforms. But a fundamental consensus about certain assumptions that comprise the cold war orthodoxy has remained: East and West are locked in battle, and there can be no compromise, because the battle is between good and evil; the other side will stop at nothing; they will disguise themselves as do-gooders and reformers and peaceniks, but we must not be deceived; we must be resolute, but we must also learn to be as cunning as they are.

In such a world, as John le Carré pointed out, there is little room for serious political debate. Disagreement and discussion, as well as institutional rivalry, are possible, but only within the limits prescribed. When political leaders in the wider community accept similar parameters, then a relatively stable situation exists. This was more or less the case in Canada, the United States, and Britain, from the late 1940s until the early 1960s. The cold war consensus was not achieved entirely through the medium of free political thought. The history of the early cold war period is replete with evidence of both tacit and overt political coercion. The security services in each country, particularly the more zealous elements within them, played a key part in this exercise.

4

American Confidence

"It seems a shame," the Walrus said,
"To play them such a trick,
After we've brought them out so far,
And made them trot so quick!"
The Carpenter said nothing but
"The butter's spread too thick!"

During the 1970s, an ideology based specifically on the necessity of open confrontation with the Soviet Union was crystallizing among groups of Americans who were, for the most part, on the far right of the political spectrum. During the years of the Carter administration they were seen by many of their countrymen as extremists. After the 1980 election they became both respectable and influential. Organizations such as the Heritage Foundation and the Committee on the Present Danger began to advocate a massive increase in U.S. military spending, in preparation for a nuclear war. A number of articles were published making the case for a new approach to American defence policy. Their central theme was that the only way to achieve world peace would be for the United States to fight and win a protracted nuclear war against the Soviet Union.[1] The Soviets, they said, had always been committed to world conquest; they were behind most of the major problems in the world. The United States had become so weak, spiritually and militarily, that the Soviets might succeed in their sinister goal.

Although an undercurrent of such thinking had existed in the United States since the first cold war period, during *détente* those who advocated it tended to be relegated to the margins of political life. The machinery of the cold war was intact and functioning throughout, but the political discourse of civil society in the advanced countries reflected the richness and complexity of the real world. By the late 1970s, however, a number of factors combined to create conditions favourable for a reversion to the dominance of cold war values and attitudes in the United States.

One of the features of this change was a move towards more conservative social attitudes and away from the openness to social innovation that had been characteristic of the 1960s and early 1970s. Increasing emphasis tended to be placed on the importance of the traditional family structure, religion and prayer in the schools, and on a nostalgic and idealized notion of the small-town American way of life. Opposition to busing to achieve racial balance in the schools, the movement against the right to legal abortions, opposition to the movement for the equality of women, and hostility to the gay movement are manifestations of the same conservative trend. Similar changes in some social attitudes occurred in Canada. But Canada was relatively free of the polarization and moral uncertainty that had been caused in the United States by events such as the Vietnam war and the Iran hostage crisis. The election of Brian Mulroney's Progressive Conservative government in 1984 was based on a promise of maintaining the fundamental policies that had sustained the Canadian consensus for decades. The combination of frustration in the international arena and domestic social dislocation that had contributed to the surge to the right in American politics was not present in Canada. A profound shift to the right has not taken place in this country.

The assertion of conservative social values in America has been accompanied by a renewed emphasis on patriotism and military strength. Ronald Reagan's intuition that these values were again coming to have meaning and importance for many Americans was central to his electoral success in 1980. The results of the 1984 election again suggested that a substantial number of Americans supported an administration that imposed heavy cuts in social spending while authorizing unprecedented increases in peacetime military expenditures. In spite of the prevalence of this attitude, however, significant reservations about the use of military force persist. One of the legacies of the Vietnam war has been a reluctance by United States military officers to become involved in large-scale hostilities in Third World countries.

The defeat of United States military power in Vietnam in 1972 and the victory of the revolutionary forces there in 1975 were particularly traumatic for many Americans. Following the U.S. withdrawal from Vietnam an increasing number of struggles took place in various parts of the Third World against American and European domination. Between 1970 and 1984, Mozambique, Angola, and Guinea Bissau achieved independence from Portugal through revolutionary struggle. The Sandinista revolution was victorious in Nicaragua. Large-scale insurgency against United States-backed dictatorships has taken place in El Salvador and Guatemala. The victory of the Vietnamese revolution was accompanied by a loss of U.S. influence throughout Indochina, with the exception of Thailand. Many Americans have had difficulty coming to grips with the fact that the United States no longer exercises the unchallenged dominance in the world that it enjoyed in the first three decades after World War Two.

The mythology of the cold war of the 1940s and 1950s was revived by the right wing in the United States as a means of interpreting these events. Neo-conservatives have attempted to popularize the idea that the main cause of Third World revolutions and of the loss of American influence is to be found in the machinations of the Kremlin. This view takes little heed of the realities of regional or internal factors in Third World politics. There is, of course, some truth in the explanations of the New Right. The Soviet army did intervene massively in Afghanistan at the end of 1979. The Soviets have supported the presence of Cuban troops in Angola since 1975. Economic, diplomatic, and indirect military aid from the Soviet Union was in some cases crucial to the success of revolutionary movements in Third World nations in the late 1970s and early 1980s. But the scale and effectiveness of Soviet intervention has been limited by a number of factors, the most important of which is whether it is deemed by the Soviets to be in their own national interest. Thus substantial assistance was given to revolutionary movements in Indochina and parts of Africa. The Soviets have also supported non-revolutionary governments for strategic reasons — Syria is a case in point. Third World revolutionary movements regarded by the Soviets as being strategically difficult to support, however, are largely on their own — Grenada clearly fell into this category. The Soviets assisted the Communist guerrillas in Vietnam until their victory in May 1975. Since then they have continued to give economic assistance to the

Vietnamese. But the notion that anyone but the Vietnamese people themselves won the war in 1975 is not in keeping with the historical facts. The Vietnamese had been struggling against foreign domination since the 1930s, long before the Americans or the Russians became involved in their country. The Vietnamese, through their years of battle against the French, the Japanese, and the Americans, developed a strong sense of national identity and an equally strong commitment to national independence. Nevertheless, many Americans believe that they "lost" Vietnam — as if it had ever belonged to them — and that it was "taken" by the Russians. Many U.S. policy-makers see Vietnam as proof that the decline in American influence in the Third World has been directly caused by the Soviet Union.

During the period of *détente* there had been a major assertion of democratic rights against the abuses of security and intelligence agencies in the United States. The Watergate scandals in the early 1970s revealed the extent to which the Nixon administration had used the CIA, the FBI, and the National Security Agency (NSA) for its own political purposes. Social tensions caused by the Vietnam war and the protest against it led to exaggerated fears on the part of Nixon and his advisors that massive civil strife and insurrection would be fomented by anti-war protesters and other social activists. The Watergate scandals centred on Nixon's use of the clandestine techniques of the security and intelligence agencies for partisan political purposes during the 1972 presidential election campaign. In the impeachment proceedings against President Nixon in 1974, the Congress cited improper use of the intelligence-gathering powers of both the FBI and the CIA.

The Watergate investigations revealed problems with the security and intelligence agencies that went far beyond the abuses instigated by the Nixon administration. The FBI had tapped journalists' phones during the Kennedy administration; it had committed political burglaries at least that far back; Lyndon Johnson had used the FBI against political opponents during the 1968 election campaign; the FBI had been conducting its COINTELPRO dirty-tricks programme against civil rights workers, the anti-war movement, and many other dissident Americans since the 1950s. For years, the CIA, contrary to its charter, had spied upon Americans engaged in legitimate political activity. The National Security Agency routinely used its massive facilities to conduct electronic surveillance of large numbers of Americans. The military intelligence agencies were also involved in large-scale spying on civilians.[2]

National security was the standard excuse given by those responsible for these nefarious activities once they were found out. Officials of the FBI and the CIA argued that they were justified in breaking into homes and offices, intercepting mail and telephone calls, committing forgery, defaming law-abiding citizens, and using other illegal and immoral tactics, because of the importance of their mission. The protection of national security meant, in their view, that they were above the law. Exposés of the uncontrolled activities of the intelligence organizations led to popular pressure for reform. Large-scale investigations were conducted by congressional bodies. The press continued its scrutiny for a time. The result of the continuing revelations was that a number of reforms were carried out by both the Ford and the Carter administrations. Moreover, the agencies themselves were put on the defensive by the popular outrage over their conduct. Following the mid-1970s revelations, they tended to cut back on their covert activities in order to avoid the possibility of discovery and further public condemnation.

In 1972 the United States Supreme Court asserted that the rule of law and the protection of individual rights afforded by the Constitution apply to intelligence-gathering operations as they apply in every other situation. In a landmark case, the Supreme Court had warned that

> the danger to political dissent is acute where the Government attempts to act under so vague a concept as the power to protect "domestic security." Given the difficulty of defining the domestic security interest, the danger of abuse in acting to protect that interest becomes apparent.... The price of lawful public dissent must not be a dread of subjection to an unchecked surveillance power.[3]

An Executive Order issued by President Ford established that the FBI must operate within guidelines set by the Attorney-General. President Carter subsequently issued an Executive Order that deleted "subversion" from the list of activities the FBI was mandated to investigate. In 1978 Congress passed the *Foreign Intelligence Surveillance Act*, which formalized a number of checks on the activities of the security and intelligence agencies.

After prolonged bargaining involving Congress, the Carter administration, and the intelligence community, an *Intelligence Oversight Act* was passed in 1980. Among other provisions, it stipulated that the Executive Branch must keep the House and Senate intelligence committees "fully and currently informed of all intelligence activities" including any "significant anticipated" operations.[4]

The cumulative effect of the post-Watergate reforms was to quell public criticism of the security and intelligence agencies; but the changes were, in fact, modest in their impact upon the massive capabilities of the American intelligence community. The new restraints dealt almost entirely with the surveillance of American citizens. They had very little to do with the collecting of foreign intelligence. They placed few restrictions on the extent to which the American intelligence community could attempt to covertly influence other governments. Even at the height of the criticism of the United States' agencies, the reformers were silent on the issue of the manipulation of allied security and intelligence agencies. The basic assumption of the need for United States dominance, not only of the Soviets but also of U.S. allies, was never questioned.

Nevertheless, many members of the United States' intelligence community were dismayed at the reforms. A number of veterans resigned from the CIA or were eased out during the later 1970s. Some thought the Agency, and the country itself, had been betrayed in an act of profound treachery. The theme of the absolute identity of interests between the CIA and the United States itself was repeated many times. For example, in our marathon discussion that lasted from dinner in a Virginia restaurant until five a.m. in his parked Mercedes-Benz, the legendary CIA Counter-Intelligence Chief James Angleton asserted that the United States might never recover from the assault its own government had committed on the CIA. The Russians, already far more skilled in waging the secret war, would exploit the situation further against a now defenceless United States.[5]

Those who believed in the need for a powerful American security and intelligence community did not take the post-Watergate reforms lying down. Their counter-attack began in earnest during the two years preceding the 1980 presidential election. A series of papers on proposed reorganization of the intelligence community was prepared by Reagan supporters in 1979. Of particular note was a Republican National Committee paper drafted in August 1979 under the direction of Richard Allen, who subsequently became President Reagan's first National Security Advisor. Among other things, this paper proposed that the CIA should return to its pre-Watergate role of carrying out internal security operations within the United States.[6]

Between 1979 and 1981 a number of right-wing organizations prepared detailed proposals for Reagan administration policy. The Consortium for the Study of Intelligence was started as a project of the National Strategy Information Center, which had itself been founded in 1962 by William Casey, who was ultimately appointed Director of Central Intelligence by President Reagan. The Consortium was headed by Roy Godson and included a number of hard-line veterans of the CIA. Several of the key figures from this group took part in preparing the intelligence section of a report by the right-wing Heritage Foundation on a "blueprint for a conservative American government."[7]

The Heritage Foundation report was written for the Reagan transition team in 1980. It warned that "the threat to the internal security of the republic is greater today than at any time since World War Two, and the number of public men who are even aware of the threat is so small as to be negligible."[8] The report urged that the new president proclaim "the reality of subversion and ... the un-American nature of much so-called 'dissidence.' "[9] It called for investigations of groups critical of conservative policies, including "anti-defense and anti-nuclear lobbies," as well as "clergymen, students, businessmen, entertainers, labor officials, journalists and government workers who may engage in subversive activities without being fully aware of the extent, purposes or control of their activities."[10] In other words, in its conspiratorial interpretation of political life, the Heritage Foundation was advocating massive surveillance of persons engaged in innocent political activity.

The report also claimed that the CIA and allied intelligence agencies "have not been so weak since Pearl Harbor."[11] It recommended that the CIA be freed from the restrictions it had suffered since the post-Watergate reforms. There must be a green light and increased funding for both foreign intelligence collection and covert action. In advocating an increase in covert action, the Heritage Foundation was in effect calling for a stepped-up cold war: covert action is the method by which intelligence agencies actively fight against both declared and undeclared enemies. It also on occasion provides a means of manipulating or disciplining friends.

In the CIA's own definition,

> Covert action is a special activity conducted abroad in support of United States foreign policy objectives and executed so that the role of the United States Government is not apparent or acknowledged publicly. Covert action is distinct from the intelligence-gathering function. Covert action often gives the United States a foreign policy option between diplomatic and military action.[12]

The verdict of the Senate Select Committee, chaired by Senator Frank Church of Idaho, was more skeptical. The Church committee had conducted extensive investigations of the CIA during the post-Watergate upheaval. The committee had concluded that American covert action in the international arena had been a failure, because it attempted to do in secret what had already failed in public. During the prelude to the 1980 elections, the Church committee was blamed for weakening the CIA and undermining America's standing in the world.[13]

Once elected, the Reagan administration moved quickly to counteract the reforming influence of the Church committee reports and to put things right. "Unleashing" the CIA was central to the cold war vision of the new administration. A new Director of Central Intelligence, William J. Casey, was appointed. A New York millionaire described in the *Wall Street Journal* as "arrogant" and "impulsive," Casey had been Ronald Reagan's campaign manager in the 1980 election campaign.[14] Members of Congress have repeatedly expressed doubts about Casey's suitability for the job. His own financial affairs were called into question, and his resignation was demanded by the chairman of the Senate Select Committee on Intelligence, Senator Barry Goldwater. He was also questioned by the FBI about suspicions that he had a part in the theft of election material from the Carter White House during the 1980 campaign.[15] William Casey has not only survived these controversies, but has had greater influence in the top levels of the Executive Branch of the United States government than any of his recent predecessors. He acts as both Director of Central Intelligence and Senior Policy Advisor to President Reagan, taking part in cabinet meetings.

Under the Reagan administration the CIA has more than regained whatever it lost during the scandals and disillusionment of the 1970s. Its budget has grown faster than that of any other part of the United States government, including the armed forces. It is estimated to have increased at a rate of nearly twenty-five per cent each year since Reagan first took office,[16] for an annual total budget in the billions of dollars. It has approximately 20,000 employees in the Washington area alone.

True to the recommendations of the Heritage Foundation, President Reagan issued an Executive Order (12333) during his first year in office that permits the CIA to collect secret intelligence on American soil. The Agency is also given authority to conduct "special activities," a euphemism for covert action, within the United States.[17]

Covert actions against unofficial "enemies" have been pursued enthusiastically under Reagan and Casey. By mid-1984 the number of such actions was estimated to have increased fivefold over levels in the last year of the Carter administration.[18] They included paramilitary operations in Central America, and supplying arms and money to rebel groups in several African and Asian countries. Among the more grotesque beneficiaries has been Pol Pot, the notorious renegade Communist leader in Kampuchea, whose forces have been supplied through a joint effort of the CIA and the government of the People's Republic of China.[19]

Covert actions are planned in an increasingly informal manner by President Reagan, William Casey, and a handful of other senior members of the administration. Experts who might advise a more prudent course of action do not attend the sessions; the President is reported not to want to "have people around always saying why things could not be done."[20] A senior official has been quoted as complaining of the problem that "the people at the top of this Administration are fascinated with covert operations and find it easier to approve them than to discuss complicated diplomatic matters."[21]

The renewed cold war is the result of the interaction of complex factors — political, economic, technological, and strategic. It is imposed by its own institutions upon the whole world. Those institutions, and the specific actions they undertake, are controlled by a small group of men who do not want others who might know better to obstruct action.

This second round of the cold war, like the first one, has

enormous implications for Canada. In the 1980s many Canadian leaders are finding themselves as troubled about being swept along by the new cold war as their predecessors were three decades earlier. Despite his acquiescence in the testing of the cruise missile in Canadian air-space, the direction of the new cold war alarmed Prime Minister Trudeau sufficiently that he moved in opposition to the fundamental policies of the Reagan administration with his international peace mission.

The mission was launched with a powerful speech at the University of Guelph on the evening of October 7, 1983. The Prime Minister was blunt in his description of the renewed cold war:

> I will tell you right away that I am deeply troubled: by an intellectual climate of acrimony and uncertainty; by the parlous state of East-West relations; by a superpower relationship which is dangerously confrontational; and by a widening gap between military strategy and political purpose. All these reveal most profoundly the urgent need to assert the preeminence of the mind of man over machines of war.[22]

In the following three months, Trudeau embarked on an almost frantic effort to persuade world leaders that they must join him in discussions that would reduce the risk of war. He travelled to Paris, The Hague, Brussels, Rome, the Vatican, Bonn, London, Zurich, Tokyo, Peking, Washington, Prague, Bucharest, the United Nations in New York, and the meeting of heads of governments of the Commonwealth countries in New Delhi. Belatedly, at the funeral of Yuri Andropov in Moscow, Trudeau met with Andropov's successor, Constantine Chernyenko.

A number of national leaders supported the Trudeau effort, but the peace mission was not well received in official Washington. Three weeks after the Guelph speech in which he had voiced his alarm at the widening gap between military strategy and political purpose, a group of officials from the United States State Department and the Pentagon openly questioned Trudeau's moral right to pursue world peace on the international stage. They claimed that this right was ruled out because of Canada's too modest contribution to NATO.[23]

The sniping reached its peak in the attack on Trudeau by Lawrence Eagleburger, U.S. Under-Secretary of State for Political Affairs. At a session in Washington attended by more than 100 government officials, journalists, and scholars, the Under-Secretary denounced the Prime Minister's peace initiative as being the ravings of an erratic leftist high on some kind of drug.[24] The off-the-record, unofficial derision in high places formed a pattern. Despite President Reagan's bidding Trudeau "Godspeed" on the White House steps, the Canadian Prime Minister's efforts constituted an unwelcome deviance from the new cold war policies of the Reagan administration: Trudeau had violated the fundamental articles of faith of cold war ideology by questioning the necessity and the morality of the heightened state of East-West confrontation. This was hardly acceptable, coming from the leader of the most important ally of the United States.

There is a stark contrast to this on the other side of the cold war coin. Several months after he had stepped down as Prime Minister of Canada, Pierre Trudeau spoke about the relationship between political leaders and military technocrats in the continuing preparations for nuclear war. He observed that "The politicians who once stated that war was too important to be left to the generals now act as though peace were too complex to be left to themselves."[25]

The anxiety of U.S. policy-makers about their loss of control over large parts of the Third World is translated into a concern with the military balance between the United States and the Soviet Union. During the first two decades after World War Two, the United States easily maintained military supremacy over the U.S.S.R. and every other country in the world. The United States had come out of World War Two with the largest and most powerful military machine in history. In addition to its lead in the technology of modern warfare, including a monopoly on nuclear weapons, it also had a military presence that spanned the globe.

The nations that had been most important on the world stage before 1939 either had been defeated — Germany and Japan — or had suffered serious setbacks from which it would take decades to recover — the United Kingdom and France. The empires of all these powers were effectively destroyed by the war: in the case of Germany and Japan, through military defeat; in the case of Britain and France, imperial domination was weakened by the human and material cost of waging the war. Even more importantly, the war had the effect of accelerating struggles for independence in Asian and African countries.

Emerging from the war with a dynamic economy and unmatched military strength, the United States effectively inherited the imperial role formerly played by the British and, to a great extent, by the other major European powers. At the same time, the Soviet Union was still a relatively backward, semi-industrialized nation that had suffered twenty million dead and vast material destruction during the course of the war.

The launching of the first artificial earth satellite by the U.S.S.R. on October 4, 1957, generated a great deal of concern in the United States about the ability of the Soviets to perfect intercontinental ballistic missiles. But the Cuban Missile Crisis in 1962 demonstrated that, in a military confrontation, the Soviets were no match for the Americans. The fact that Nikita Khrushchev took the gamble of placing intermediate-range ballistic missiles on the very doorstep of the United States constitutes evidence that he did not have a reliable intercontinental missile force available. The development of strategic weapons systems had, however, been a priority for the Soviet military since the mid-1940s.

The Boeing B-29 was the standard U.S. heavy bomber at the end of the war. In late 1944, three B-29s operating out of advance bases in China against the Japanese made emergency landings in the Soviet Union. Soviet engineers saved a great deal of time and expense by developing their own heavy bomber, the Tupolev-4, or TU-4, by examining and copying every detail of the B-29s. It is claimed that even the design flaws of the B-29 were imitated.

The TU-4 did not enter operational service with the Soviet long-range air force until 1949, by which time the wartime B-29 was no longer the principal heavy bomber of the United States Air Force. The Soviets retained the TU-4 in front-line service until 1960, long after the Americans had equipped their Strategic Air Command with much more advanced jet-powered bombers.[26]

The history of the strategic arms race in the late 1940s and 1950s shows clearly that the Soviets were behind in the development of nuclear delivery systems by a factor of several years; yet during the cold war there was a recurrent tendency on the part of U.S. strategists to greatly overstate the technical ability of the Soviet Union to launch an attack on the North American continent.

Throughout both the cold war and the *détente* periods, the Soviets strove to catch up with the Americans in most aspects of military capability. By the mid-1970s they were beginning to achieve rough parity in terms of strategic nuclear forces. As a result,

American leaders became unsure that they would be able to face down the Soviet Union in a crisis situation, as John F. Kennedy had done in the Cuban Missile Crisis of 1962.

Relations between the United States and the Soviet Union had begun to cool early in the Carter presidency. Jimmy Carter warned of a new danger posed by a Soviet combat brigade in Cuba in 1978; it was later revealed that the Soviet troops had been there ever since the early 1960s. The Soviet military intervention in Afghanistan in December 1979 added to the pressure for an end to *détente*. The overthrow of the Shah of Iran and the subsequent hostage crisis in 1980 contributed to the sense of being under siege and helpless that gripped many American people. The Soviet movement of SS20 missiles into Eastern Europe added to the tension. The emergence of the Solidarity Union movement in Poland in the summer of 1980, followed by Soviet pressure to restore the status quo in that country, served to reinforce the widely held American perception of Soviet brutality and Soviet imperialism.

The fundamental principles of Soviet foreign policy had not, in fact, changed during the course of *détente*. Moscow's more open attitude towards the West had resulted from the convergence of a number of factors. Increasing friction with China, culminating in armed border clashes in 1969, had provided an incentive to reduce tensions with the West while attempting to head off the possibility of friendly relations between China and the United States.

The election of Willi Brandt as Chancellor of West Germany was another important factor in encouraging *détente*. His *Ostpolitik* — opening to the East — resulted in, among other things, a Four-Power Agreement on Berlin in 1971. This effectively removed one of the greatest sources of friction from the East-West relationship; this in turn tended to reduce the level of tension throughout most of Europe. An additional factor was the increasing desire of Soviet economic planners to acquire Western technology in order to develop their own industrial capacity.

The humiliation of the Cuban Missile Crisis in 1962 had increased Soviet determination to achieve strategic parity with the United States. This goal was pursued relentlessly throughout the 1960s and 1970s. The Soviet leadership apparently regarded *détente* as an inevitable consequence of their growing power in the world. In their view, parity would force the United States to deal with them as equals. This more respectful relationship would be less likely to lead to confrontation. *Détente* would provide stability in East-West relations, but it would not preclude a continued efort to maintain strategic parity. The Strategic Arms Limitation Talks, which resulted in the SALT I Agreements of May 1972, in effect provided formal recognition of this balance, in that the basic principles of the agreements prescribed "equality, mutual accommodation, and mutual benefit" as the bases for Soviet-U.S. relations.[27]

The rough strategic parity between the superpowers provided the opportunity for the Soviet Union to act on the world stage in ways that had previously been impossible. One Soviet official is quoted as having remarked that it gave them an "equal right to meddle in third areas."[28] And in fact, their intervention in the Third World did play an important part in undermining the *détente* from which they benefited. Soviet and Cuban assistance to revolutionary movements in Angola in 1975 and Ethopia in 1977 demonstrated their ability to project power in the world in a manner that had not previously been possible. This challenge to the dominant position of the United States in the Third World, combined with other factors such as the Vietnam debacle, undoubtedly did much to enhance the influence of American critics of *détente*. Both the Soviets and the Americans wanted *détente* to work in their own interests; when they perceived that it was not doing so, the foundation was laid for the resumption of cold war politics.

The aim of the Reagan administration has been to restore the former strategic advantage through superior technology and massive defence expenditures. One interesting element in this arms race strategy is the idea that the United States has the ability to spend so much that the Soviet economy would be ruined by the effort to compete. According to Nicholas Lemann, a writer for *The Atlantic Monthly*, a view often heard in the Pentagon runs this way:

> Of course we are in an arms race with the Soviets. Of course it won't end at the bargaining table. We can win it. Their society is economically weak, and it lacks the wealth, education, and technology to enter the information age. They have thrown everything into military production, and their society is starting to show terrible stress as a result. They can't sustain

military production the way we can. Eventually it will break them, and then there will be just one superpower in a safe world — if, only if, we can keep spending.[29]

The record United States deficit created by massive defence spending in recent years suggests that this is more than idle speculation. Whether the United States economy itself can endure such expenditures without serious damage is another question.

Perhaps the most publicized beneficiaries of this massive defence spending are the corporations and other organizations engaged in research for the Strategic Defense Initiative; but during the 1980s a great deal has been spent on a wide assortment of other kinds of arms. United States strategic nuclear forces are being strengthened through the addition of new systems such as the supersonic B-1 bomber, the MX missile, and the Trident submarine. Tactical forces, particularly those whose purpose is "rapid deployment" — that is, forces with the capability of quick intervention in the Third World — are also being expanded and modernized, although their possible effectiveness in combat is still a matter of debate within the Pentagon.

The first purpose of these programmes is to enable the United States to reassert its superiority over the Third World, the Soviet Bloc, and its own allies. The pre-eminence of the United States from 1945 to the late 1960s was derived fundamentally from its economic and technological superiority; military power, although overwhelming, was of subsidiary importance. Since the end of the 1960s, the United States has begun to lose some of its economic and technological advantage to Japan and some Western European rivals. To a smaller extent, even some less developed countries, such as Taiwan and South Korea, are becoming formidable industrial competitors. Part of the loss of the competitive advantage must be attributed to the fact that because the United States has invested so heavily in defence-related industries it has been able to devote less capital to the modernization of its basic industrial infrastructure. At the same time, Japan has devoted relatively little capital to the non-productive defence industries and has invested heavily in productive commercial and industrial sectors, with the result that much of its productive technology is more modern and competitive in world markets.

The New Right in the United States has tended to ignore these facts. It has propagated the view that economic and diplomatic problems are less important than military strength. Moreover, the sector of the United States economy that benefits from defence expenditures has gained enormous political influence.

The military build-up has had to be justified by a threat to the nation; the achievement of strategic nuclear parity by the Soviet Union has provided the basis for the assertion that the United States faces a new and immediate danger of aggression from that quarter. Despite its having achieved rough nuclear parity, the Soviet Union remains generally weaker than the United States. Its economy is less than half as large as the American economy. Consequently, in order to maintain rough military parity it has had to devote almost three times as great a percentage of its gross national product to defence as the United States. This undoubtedly places a severe burden on the Soviet economy and depresses its ability to develop new technologies and to raise the standard of living of its population.

Nevertheless, the present position of the Soviet Union is probably more secure than it was during the first round of the cold war. The nuclear balance of terror has, ironically, provided a measure of stability to the geopolitical status quo. Moreover, the Soviet economy, although severely distorted in many respects, has recovered from the devastation of World War Two. The general tendency of Soviet foreign policy has been to adopt a tough stance in relation to countries on its periphery and to maintain dominance over them. It is also frequently prepared to support revolutionary movements and socialist governments in various parts of the world. However, the Soviets are extremely unlikely to risk a nuclear confrontation with the United States for the sake of a minor ally, or indeed for anything except their own survival.

The change in the military balance, the shift in power relations in the Third World, and the growing anxiety in the industrialized countries as a result of prolonged economic crisis and rivalry, are all real factors in increasing world tensions.

The President of the United States is said to be the most powerful man on earth. His relationship to the generals, the admirals, and the heads of the intelligence agencies is different from equivalent relationships in less powerful countries. This was suggested, somewhat wistfully, by Pierre Trudeau, when he remarked that "NATO heads of state and of government meet only to go through the tedious motions of reading speeches drafted by others with the principal objective of not rocking the boat." He added that "any attempt to start a discussion or to question the meaning of the communiqué — also drafted by others before the meeting began — was met with stony embarrassment or strong objection."[30]

The alliance system operates at many different levels. It is an indispensable part of the cold war system. Because the alliances are centred on the two superpowers, they are necessarily not alliances of equals. The power of the President of the United States is enhanced by the alliance systems of which he is at the centre. These alliances at the same time tend to diminish the power of the political leaders of the smaller partner nations. Canada is a particularly unequal partner in the international arrangements of which she is a part.

5

Strategic Considerations

The sea was wet as wet could be
The sands were dry as dry.
You could not see a cloud because
No cloud was in the sky:
No birds were flying overhead —
There were no birds to fly.

C anada's geographic position as a neighbour of both the
United States and the Soviet Union has been of overwhelming importance to the evolution of Canadian foreign
and defence policies since the mid-1940s. The range of options
available to Canadian policy-makers is constrained by both geography and history. The shape of Canadian history has been
influenced by the unavoidable facts of the nation's colonial origins
and its successive dependencies. Accommodating the interests of
greater powers, first the British and then the Americans, has been
a recurring necessity. We see it in the development of trade policies, the management of the economy, culture, and almost every
other major national activity.

Less than a year after he became Prime Minister, Pierre Trudeau expressed his regret that the military alliance of which Canada
had been a member for more than two decades, the North Atlantic
Treaty Organization (NATO), had come to dominate Canadian foreign policy. In a speech in Calgary on April 12, 1969, he lamented
that

We had no defence policy, so to speak, except that of NATO.
And our defence policy had determined all of our foreign pol-

icy. And we had no foreign policy of any importance except that which flowed from NATO. And this is a false perspective for any country. It is a false perspective to have a military alliance determine your foreign policy. It should be your foreign policy which determines your military policy.[1]

Trudeau's unease about this reality was evident on many occasions. Near the beginning of his sixteen years in office he initiated a major review of Canadian defence policy; towards the end he embarked on his peace mission.

Trudeau did not resolve the central dilemma of Canadian defence and foreign policy. In February 1984, the month in which Trudeau decided to step down, the Assistant Deputy Minister of National Defence, John Anderson, described one aspect of the dilemma. He argued that we must adopt a posture that makes us important to the Americans, because "unless we are important to them in a military sense, our capacity to know what they might do that might affect our own fate as a nation would become less and less to the point where we have no influence at all."[2]

The Canadian conundrum to which John Anderson alludes is of no small proportions: if there is no consent to American military use of Canadian territory, then it is likely they will use it without our consent. So Canada must be militarily involved with the Americans in order to retain its sovereignty. It is up to Canada to be involved so that things are done with Canadian consent. This has been the assumption that has supported a great part of Canadian defence policy since 1945. It is the basis of the North Warning System agreement, the North American Air Defense (NORAD) agreement, and many other aspects of current Canadian defence and foreign policies.

Since the early 1940s the United States government has regarded Canadian territory as absolutely fundamental to its own defence interests. In the perception of many U.S. policy-makers, the Soviet Union emerged as the principal threat to the security of the United States even before the end of World War Two. The perceived threat was internal as well as external. The internal threat was posed by the "subversive" intentions of the Communist Party of the United States and its many front organizations. They were a fifth column, waiting to destroy democracy from within. The external threat was presented by the armed forces of the Soviet Union.

At the end of World War Two the United States was the most powerful nation in the world. Its industry was operating at full speed. Its economy appeared to have unlimited potential. United States military forces were the best equipped, and they had proven to be highly effective on the field of battle. Moreover, the United States was in a position to place its forces in a great many of the world's most strategically important locations. At war's end, United States military units were located in almost every part of Western Europe, in the Middle East, Turkey, Iran, Burma, China, the Philippines, Japan, the Pacific Islands, Puerto Rico, the Panama Canal Zone, Alaska — and Canada.

It was the reappearance of overt distrust between the British and the Americans on the one hand and the Soviets on the other that inevitably brought Canada into the geographic middle of relations between East and West. From the early 1940s to the present, the strategic importance of the north polar region has continued to play a decisive part in determining Canada's role in world affairs.

As early as August 1938, President Franklin D. Roosevelt declared in Kingston, Ontario, that "the people of the United States will not stand idly by if domination of Canadian soil is threatened by any other empire."[3] Mackenzie King's characteristically cautious response was that "enemy forces should not be able to pursue their way either by land, sea, or air to the United States across Canadian territory."[4] So it is noteworthy, in view of the superpowers' later interest in the strategic importance of the northern regions, that President Roosevelt personally visited the coast of Labrador a year later on board a United States Navy cruiser. His ostensible purpose was a vacation; but in fact he wanted to interest the officers who accompanied him in the naval and air defence of Canada and Newfoundland.[5]

The implicit alliance between the two countries was remarkable because it was made at a time when Roosevelt's freedom of action was limited by the United States *Neutrality Act* of 1935, and Canada was only one year away from full-scale participation in World War Two at Great Britain's side. Nevertheless, the alliance moved another step closer to being formalized with the establishment of the Permanent Joint Board of Defence in August 1940, when Canada was at war against Nazi Germany and the United States was not. The Permanent Joint Board of Defence did not have decision-making powers; its role was then, and continues to be, to provide consultation and recommendations on defence policy between the two North American neighbours.[6]

The nature of military strategy itself was revolutionized shortly after the Permanent Joint Board of Defence was established. The large-scale use of long-range aircraft was one of the most important military innovations to occur during World War Two; massive strategic bombing campaigns against the Axis powers played a major part in the Allied victory. This development had enormous implications for Canada: the North became immediately useful. A system for ferrying aircraft from the United States to Britain was quickly developed. The "crimson route," as it was called, used a chain of airfields and weather stations from The Pas, Manitoba, to Churchill, then to Frobisher Bay, and on to Greenland and Iceland. An additional route proceeded through northern Quebec via Fort Chimo, and yet another by way of Goose Bay, Labrador. Other major northern projects included the northwest staging route, which extended from Edmonton to Alaska; the Canol pipeline project in the Northwest Territories; and the construction of the Alaska Highway.[7]

The number of United States Army personnel engaged in these projects exceeded the total number of Canadians, both civilian and military, who were involved. The total number of Americans in the Canadian North was kept strictly secret until the war had ended. Neither was the nature of all of the American activity fully revealed to the Canadian public. Indeed, it is not certain that all of it was known even to the Canadian government of the time. Speaking of northern Canada, C.D. Howe once told the House of Commons that "No Canadian has seen certain airports."[8]

Towards the end of the war many of the thousands of American troops were withdrawn from Canadian territory. They did, however, continue to use a number of Canadian facilities, including the strategically located airfields at Fort Chimo, in Northern Quebec, and Frobisher Bay, on Baffin Island in the Eastern Arctic.

The United States continued to operate its major military bases at Goose Bay, Stephenville, and Argentia, Newfoundland, not only after the end of the war but also long after Newfoundland became part of Confederation in 1949. In addition, the Americans continued to occupy bases in Greenland after 1945, in spite of a lack of formal permission to do so.[9]

At the end of World War Two, the Soviet Union had no long-range bomber force and no nuclear weapons. Nevertheless, there was an immediate expression of concern from some military quarters in the United States about the need to protect "the undefended roof of North America."[10] Fears were voiced about Soviet intentions in the Arctic and of the possibility of their using it as a route to attack the United States. Unofficial questions were raised about the legitimacy of Canada's claim to full sovereignty over the Arctic archipelago. The allegation was made that Canada had neglected the Arctic. A fleet of United States Naval and Coast Guard vessels was dispatched to Arctic waters in June 1946, introducing a theme that was to reverberate through Canadian political life right up to the present.

Not surprisingly, the Canadian government was concerned about the direction these developments were taking. In July 1946, Lester B. Pearson, at that time Canadian ambassador to Washington, published an article in which he advocated a multinational approach to Arctic development which would include not only Canada and the United States but Denmark, Norway, and the Soviet Union as well. He decried what he called "an increasing, and in some of its manifestations an unhealthy preoccupation with the strategic aspects of the north: the staking of claims, the establishment of bases, the calculation of risks and all the rest." He went on to assert that Canada did not "relish the necessity of digging, or having dug for her, any Maginot line in her Arctic ice."[11]

But the pressure for a permanent, large-scale United States military presence in the north did not let up. When Mackenzie King visited President Truman at the White House on October 28, 1946, the conversation turned quickly to the question of continental defence. The President spoke of the importance that United States military leaders attached to aviation in the north and of their interest in establishing a major all-weather base at Goose Bay. The Prime Minister responded by expressing the familiar Canadian concern about sovereignty. He recorded that

> I said we had to watch particularly the question of our sovereignty. Not that we entertained any fears on that score, but having regard to the years as they went by and to the view the people would take, large numbers of troops from other countries being stationed out of their own country, or would have to be arranged on the basis of agreement to protect national rights.

Truman spoke about meteorological stations to study the weather. He thought all we might wish to do could be done for several purposes without making any mention of boundaries.[12]

Mackenzie King was perplexed by this attitude. He was also concerned by concurrent pressures from England for Canada to become subordinate to the British in defence matters. On top of that, the Canadian military were causing him to worry. On November 10 he wrote that he felt "a very great and grave concern about the manner in which the services have been pushing their end at the expense of others."[13]

The Prime Minister discussed his displeasure about these American, British, and Canadian military pressures with the Governor-General, Viscount Alexander of Tunis, two days later. He noted with evident satisfaction that Alexander did not think that the American plans for Goose Bay were necessary at all.[14]

But the next day, a remarkable change in King's attitude took place. The Cabinet had a two-hour briefing from the military chiefs of staff. The presentation was directed by the head of the military intelligence branch, Major Anderson. The information, based largely on American sources, was so secret that Mackenzie King would not confide it to his diary; but whatever it was "profoundly impressed" the members of the Cabinet. He noted that "It was interesting to observe how completely surprised some Members of the Government were at what was disclosed; equally amazing in some particulars how little some of the members appreciated the military situation today and what it involves in the way of a complete change in the way in which from now on some old-time conceptions will have to be viewed."[15]

The high-level, military intelligence briefing radically changed the Prime Minister's own mind. Instead of being worried by pressure from the Americans and the Canadian military, he was now convinced that the "world situation is infinitely more dangerous than we have yet believed it to be." He now understood that "we are headed into an inevitable conflict which will mean either civil war or revolution spreading pretty generally through different countries, or open conflict between East and West with Communism versus Capitalism or Atheism versus Christianity. The war will be in the nature of a religious war as well as a class struggle and may result in a sort of Armageddon."[16]

Mackenzie King's prediction was at least partly accurate. The war between East and West that has been under way ever since has indeed at times seemed to have religious overtones. Forty years on, it is still not certain to result in Armageddon, but the likelihood is not to be dismissed lightly.

King's apparent change of attitude about co-operation with the United States in the defence of North America was made public in a major statement in Parliament on February 12, 1947. On the advice of the Permanent Joint Board of Defence, he announced that the armed forces of the two countries would henceforth co-operate in a number of areas, most importantly by "mutual and reciprocal availability of military and naval and air facilities in each country."[17] Before the end of 1947, the desire of the Americans to make use of Goose Bay had been realized,[18] and the airfield was to be a major operating base of the United States Air Force Strategic Air Command for many years to come.

Over the years, the enduring strategic importance of Canadian territory has been intimately bound up with American thinking about the strategic use of military aviation. Until World War Two the use of air power in war had generally been considered to be "tactical"; that is, it served as an adjunct to land or naval forces in achieving the strategic aims of defeating an enemy. Even before the destruction of Hiroshima and Nagasaki by atomic bombs in August 1945, the potential of air power to demolish whole cities had been made fearsomely apparent. In March 1945, U.S. B-29 bombers under the command of General Curtis LeMay dropped some 2,000 tons of conventional bombs on Tokyo; the resulting firestorm killed approximately 100,000 people. This demonstration of the ability of air power to obliterate an entire society qualified it for the status of a strategic force; it now could, in its own right, destroy the very social fabric of the enemy. The atomic bomb confirmed and enhanced this fact.

Throughout World War Two the Air Force had been an integral part of the United States Army. The recognition of its strategic role enabled it to become a separate armed service, fully equal to the Army and Navy, shortly after the end of the war. Almost from the beginning, the Strategic Air Command was the elite force and the most influential component of the United States Air Force. The momentum that the Air Force achieved in justifying and expanding its role through political, financial, and bureaucratic manoeuvring, together with the competitive responses this aroused in the other services, should not be underestimated as a dynamic in the post-war arms race.[19]

74

During the four years after Hiroshima and Nagasaki, the United States enjoyed a monopoly on nuclear weapons. But through much of that period its atomic arsenal was surprisingly small. At the end of 1945, four months after the end of World War Two, the United States had exactly two atomic bombs. By July 1946 it had nine, and a year after that it had thirteen. The situation had changed rapidly by mid-1948, when there were fifty atomic bombs.[20] The acceleration in nuclear weapons production increased throughout the 1950s. In 1953 the U.S. stockpile was 1,000; by 1960 it was 18,000.[21]

In the early years of relative atomic scarcity, war plans and lists of targets in the Soviet Union were drawn up. At first this was done informally by war planners in the United States armed services. By the fall of 1947 the Joint Chiefs of Staff had adopted the BROILER war plan. This was soon followed by FROLIC and HALFMOON. Each of these appropriately named plans emphasized a nuclear offensive to be carried out by the Strategic Air Command. The broad objectives of the United States in a war against the Soviet Union were spelled out in a State Department paper on November 23, 1948. It asserted that the goal in a general war would be to eliminate "Bolshevik" control both inside and outside the Soviet Union.[22]

The atomic planners in this early period of the cold war expected to achieve their goal primarily by striking population and industrial targets. The number of targets grew with the number of available weapons. The BROILER plan of 1947 involved hitting twenty-four Soviet cities with thirty-four bombs. A year later, the TROJAN plan envisioned seventy target cities to be disposed of by 133 nuclear bombs.[23] As additional nuclear weapons and more advanced delivery systems became available, ever larger and more elaborate war plans were developed.

The assumption underlying all this planning was that the Soviet Union might attack the United States with nuclear weapons of its own. This fear was expressed by the Joint Chiefs of Staff as early as September 1945, less than three weeks after the formal surrender of Japan.[24] In fact the Soviet Union did not test its first nuclear device until four years later. It would not have a usable stockpile for some years after that. They were estimated to have fifty bombs by 1952, four years after the Americans had acquired that number.[25]

The fear on the part of American military leaders of a Soviet nuclear attack had consequences that would profoundly affect Canada as well as the rest of the world right up to the present day.

The means available to the United States to defend itself from such an imagined attack were limited. One possibility was to destroy the Soviet Union before it was ready to launch a nuclear attack. This was seriously considered on a number of occasions. In May 1954, for example, the Joint Chiefs of Staff Advance Study Group suggested that the United States consider "deliberately precipitating war with the U.S.S.R. in the near future" before the ability of the Soviets to make use of the hydrogen bomb became a "real menace."[26] Fortunately, President Eisenhower did not accept this advice.

The exact conditions under which BROILER, HALFMOON, TROJAN, and the other nuclear war plans of the 1940s would be activated had not been formally defined in terms of stated policy. But the position of the Joint Chiefs of Staff since 1945 had been that the United States must be prepared "to strike the first blow if necessary ... when it becomes evident that the forces of aggression are being arrayed against us."[27] The Joint Chiefs of Staff subsequently recommended that "acts of aggression" be redefined to include "the readying of atomic weapons against us." This, they implied, should be the basis for a U.S. nuclear assault that would prevent an attack by the Soviets on the United States.

This concept of a pre-emptive strike on the Soviet Union was central to many of the phases through which U.S. nuclear war planning evolved over the years. One of the seminal statements of United States government interests and strategies was NSC-68. It was prepared for the National Security Council in 1950 by a committee of State Department and Defense Department officials under the chairmanship of Paul H. Nitze. (More than thirty years later, Nitze would play a key role in the Reagan administration.) The main focus of NSC-68 was the Soviet threat. U.S. interests around the world were defined primarily in relation to that perceived threat. It asserted that "in the context of the present polarization of power a defeat of free institutions anywhere is a defeat everywhere."[28] In terms of nuclear strategy to deal with the threat, NSC-68 noted that "The military advantages of landing the first blow ... require us to be on the alert in order to strike with our full weight as soon as we are attacked, and, if possible, before the Soviet blow is actually delivered."[29]

The distinction between preventive nuclear war and a pre-emptive strike is a rather fine one. A preventive war, which would be started by the United States, was conceived by the nuclear strategists as one deliberately initiated while the United States still had forces of such overwhelming superiority that it would be able to destroy the Soviet threat once and for all. A pre-emptive strike would in theory be a response to a perceived attack, or preparation for an attack by the Soviets.

Preventive war was finally deemed to be inconsistent with the moral and constitutional principles of the United States. No such inhibition applied to the idea of the pre-emptive strike. It was regarded as justifiable on practical grounds: it would save the United States from suffering a direct nuclear attack and would enable it to prevail in a nuclear war. The implied moral difference was simply that in the case of a pre-emptive war, a clear danger to the United States would have been identified. In either case the military advantage of striking first would lie with the United States.

The sense of moral superiority of the United States was nicely preserved by making the distinction between preventive war and pre-emptive war. The ultimate moral distinction, however, lay in the assumption that the United States was a free and peace-loving nation, while the Soviet Union was a totalitarian society, morally unrestrained in its dedication to world conquest by any means. As one historian of nuclear strategy observes, "American leaders always reacted with considerable disbelief to the suggestion that the Soviet Union might not be as confident of America's good behaviour."[30]

This disbelief might have been tempered somewhat if the appreciation of American history and values held by the head of the Strategic Air Command had been publicly known. During a secret briefing to military officers at SAC headquarters in 1954, General Curtis LeMay was asked how his plans fit in with the stated national policy that the United States would never strike the first blow. The cigar-chomping General replied that he had

> heard this thought stated many times, and it sounded fine. However, it is not in keeping with United States history. Just look back at who started the Revolutionary War, the War of 1812, the Indian Wars, and the Spanish-American War. I want to make it clear that I am not advocating a preventive war; however, I believe that if the U.S. is pushed in the corner far enough, we would not hesitate to strike first.[31]

The American concept of defence by means of such strategies involved Canada in at least three critically important ways: intelligence gathering; access to Canadian facilities for forward basing, that is, locating elements of the Strategic Air Command closer to their targets in the Soviet Union; and continental early warning and air defence. Each of these has at times assumed critical importance in the minds of U.S. strategic planners. Generally, as that importance increases, successive Canadian governments have had less room to manoeuvre.

The ability of the Strategic Air Command to hit targets in the Soviet Union is determined, among other things, by the distance over which its bombers can operate. Limitations in range can be overcome by refuelling in flight from aerial tankers. The range problem can also be diminished by basing either the bombers or the tankers, or both, closer to their targets.

Range limitations represented a potentially serious problem for the Strategic Air Command during the 1940s and 1950s. This was overcome by acquiring air bases in a number of countries on the periphery of the Soviet Union, including the United Kingdom, Libya, the Philippines, and Guam. The Arctic regions were particularly important because of their proximity to the Soviet homeland. The United States established major bases not only on its own territory, but also in Iceland, Greenland, and northern Canada. Harmon Air Force Base near Stephenville, Newfoundland, was an important location for Strategic Air Command refuelling operations. The airfield at Goose Bay was still more vital. Being less than 3,000 miles from such attractive Soviet targets as the port of Murmansk and the Kola Peninsula, it figured prominently in U.S. war planning in the 1950s as a point from which to launch a nuclear strike.[32] Goose Bay also supported refuelling tankers to service bombers on their way from bases in the continental United States to their target areas.

The defence of North America against attack by Soviet forces has also been part of the calculations of the American strategic planners. But the relationship between defensive and offensive actions has often been ambiguous. A United States National Security Council statement in 1953 said that the Air Force was to "defend by both offensive and defensive air operations critical areas in the Western Hemisphere, with particular emphasis on defence against atomic attack."[33]

For decades this persistent ambiguity between offence and defence has characterized both American and Canadian attitudes towards continental defence. The term "defence" is loaded with reassuring connotations; it suggests the image of the brave soldier standing his ground, shield outthrust to defend the weaker beings who huddle for protection behind him. It is not without reason that government departments concerned with military matters in most countries include the word "defence" in their organizational titles. No country has a Minister of National Offence or a Department of Aggression, even though in many cases that would be a more accurate description of the functions of those agencies.

The defence of North America against the possibility of a Soviet attack has been central to Canadian military policy since the 1950s. In the strategic calculations of the United States, air defence has usually been of secondary importance. It has only served as an adjunct to the offensive power of the Strategic Air Command. But the relationship between the two superpowers, and particularly between their military establishments, sometimes means that matters of essentially peripheral importance in the Pentagon take on much greater significance in the political life of Canada. When American military priorities have serious implications for this country, the inclination of Canadian leaders is to acquiesce while finding ways to save face.

Immediately after the Second World War, the Joint Canadian-United States Basic Security Plan had called for the Royal Canadian Air Force to co-operate with the Americans in the development of a warning and control infrastructure for the defence of vital areas against aerial attacks. A study of the feasibility of a northern-based warning system was conducted and, in 1947, concluded that the project would not be worthwhile.[34]

The first Soviet test of an atomic device in September 1949 caused consternation in Washington over the loss of the nuclear monopoly. One consequence was a decision by the government of Canada to collaborate with the Americans in building a series of air defence radar stations across the middle of the continent, instead of in the far north. The Pinetree Line, as it was called, was made up of more than thirty installations that ran roughly along the Canada-United States border. It cost almost half a billion dollars and went into operation in 1954. The cost, as well as the manning of the system, was shared by the two countries.

The Pinetree Line provided radar warning of aircraft approaching from the North to the continental United States and the more heavily populated parts of Canada. How effective any actual air defence based on this warning system might have been was open to speculation. The air defence forces of the two countries co-operated but were under separate national commands.

Some American planners were concerned that the Strategic Air Command bombers based in North America should be given more warning time than the Pinetree Line could provide. In 1951 the United States Air Force contracted the Massachusetts Institute of Technology to conduct a major survey of the means by which a more effective defence could be mounted against a Soviet air strike. In 1951 "Project Charles," as it was called, issued a three-volume report entitled *Problems of Air Defence*.[35] It called for a radar system farther north than the Pinetree Line that would provide additional early warning of a Soviet attack.

The report caused intense debate between advocates of air defence and the entrenched proponents of defence by means of the offensive capability of the Strategic Air Command nuclear bombers. The Strategic Air Command strategists sensed that in the nuclear age offensive forces inevitably enjoy an inherent advantage over any conceivable defensive measures. The unprecedented destructive power of nuclear weapons necessarily means that any defence that is not totally effective is at best useless.

No system that is contrived by human beings ever approaches perfection. As systems become more complex, imperfections multiply. Not many projects could be more complex than a system intended to defend a seven-million-square-mile continent from intrusion by one, ten, or a hundred aircraft approaching at various speeds, altitudes, directions, and headings. During World War Two, the Royal Air Force was able to destroy fewer than ten per cent of the German bombers attacking the United Kingdom. This was in spite of the fact that the country being defended was relatively compact, the technical development of defending fighters was at least as high as that of attacking bombers, and the Royal Air Force already had the benefit of advanced technology in the form of radar. An attempted defence of North America would enjoy few of those advantages.

On another level of strategic thinking, defensive measures in situations involving nuclear weapons are seen to be inherently destabilizing. Any improvement in defensive capability is bound to increase the temptation of a pre-emptive first strike by an adversary because the element of surprise becomes more important: it is necessary in order to diminish the effectiveness of the defence.

By 1953 the apparent contradictions between the proponents

of defence by the offensive forces of the Strategic Air Command and the advocates of a massive continental warning and interception system were about to be resolved. In May, a National Security Council study had concluded that the existing or planned continental defence programmes were inadequate. On October 30 of that year President Eisenhower formally approved NSC-162/2, which was a major statement of his administration's Basic National Security Policy.[36] It recommended an expansion of the already formidable offensive nuclear capability of the Strategic Air Command. It also called for a "reasonably effective" air defence system: the location of the Pinetree Line was too close to the Strategic Air Command bases and the industrial centres of the interior of the United States. The Canadian Arctic was about to come into its own as a potential battlefield.

From 1953 until the end of the decade, the United States government placed great emphasis on developing a continental early warning and air defence system. The top priority was to construct the Distant Early Warning (DEW) Line of radar stations across the northern limit of the continent, from Alaska across the Canadian Arctic to Greenland. This was accompanied by the deployment of several thousand interceptor aircraft, the production of nuclear warheads for anti-aircraft missiles, and the development of sophisticated mechanisms for the integrated command and control of all these forces.

The adoption of this scheme as a matter of high priority by the United States government had inescapable consequences, not only for the Canadian Arctic but also for the Canadian government. · Ministers were confronted with a dilemma that has since become almost traditional for Canadian politicians who must deal with major American military priorities. They could co-operate while trying to make a necessity look like a virtue; or they could follow the improbable course of refusing to collaborate on the basis of the national interest.

The government of Canada chose to co-operate in the DEW Line venture, as it had on the installation of the Pinetree Line. In March 1953, when debate on the idea of the Distant Early Warning Line had been raging in Washington, Canada's Minister of National Defence, Brooke Claxton, had been strongly opposed to it.[37] As the year wore on it became increasingly apparent that the advocates of continental air defence and early warning would have their way. Claxton was well aware of the problems that the

DEW Line would create for Canada. He knew that Canadian interests in the world might be ill-served by it. He accurately predicted that it would become obsolete within a decade. "However," he wrote on October 3, 1953, "it may be very difficult indeed for the Canadian Government to reject any major defence proposal which the United States presents with conviction as essential for the security of North America."[38] Indeed it was. After a decent interval, the decision to proceed was announced by the two governments on November 19, 1954.

The consequences of that decision have reverberated through Canadian political life ever since. The decision to build the DEW Line was followed by integration of the command structures of the air defence forces of the two countries under the North American Air Defence (NORAD) agreement. It provided for the commander of the organization to be an American general, and his deputy a Canadian. This unique bilateral arrangement has been at the centre of some of the most contentious debates in recent Canadian political history. Much of it has had to do with the issue of nuclear weapons.

The original NORAD agreement was signed by John Diefenbaker shortly after he became Prime Minister in 1957. Five different weapons systems intended for use with nuclear warheads were acquired for both the Royal Canadian Air Force and the Canadian Army. But it was the lot of the Pearson government actually to acquire the warheads. The Progressive Conservative Minister of External Affairs, Howard Green, was concerned that Canada's having nuclear weapons would reduce the possibilities of serious world disarmament negotiations and a nuclear test ban. Such second thoughts about Canada's participation in the nuclear arms race, as well as disagreements within the Tory government on the issue, aroused the ire of the Kennedy administration.

The 1963 Canadian general election was marked by a number of events that could be construed as overt meddling by the Americans. United States Air Force General Lauris Norstad denounced the Progressive Conservative government in Ottawa on January 3, 1963, for not accepting nuclear weapons. The American ambassador held private briefings in the basement of the embassy to inform journalists of the dangers of Tory policy.[39] The United States State Department circumvented normal diplomatic procedures by issuing a press release that "corrected" some of the assertions that had been made by the Canadian Prime Minister.[40]

Canadians, as ever, were divided on the question of nuclear weapons, and, as the great Tory historian Donald Creighton described these events,

> Upon this divided people and its divided government, the full weight of American reprimand and injunction now fell with shattering force; the Kennedy administration regarded Canada with a cold fury of impatience. If the Canadians could not make up their minds on this vital subject, they must be taught to do so.[41]

The Liberal Party, under the leadership of Lester B. Pearson, had at first opposed Canada's acquiring nuclear warheads for the obsolescent Bomarc B anti-aircraft missiles that were an integral part of the NORAD system. In the course of the 1963 election campaign this position was reversed, largely for reasons of political expediency. This generated a devastating attack from a future Liberal Prime Minister, Pierre Trudeau. He, along with Jean Marchand, had considered joining the Liberal Party and running as a federal candidate. But in April 1963, at the height of the federal election campaign, Trudeau published an article in *Cité Libre*, in which he was merciless in his criticism of Pearson, the Liberal Party, and the way in which both had been manipulated and intimidated by the United States. Trudeau argued that the Americans wanted above all to undo John Diefenbaker. They had been especially outraged by his alleged three-day delay in putting Canada's armed forces on alert during the Cuban Missile Crisis, as President Kennedy had done with the United States Armed Forces. "Mr. Kennedy's 'hipsters' could not tolerate this," Trudeau wrote. "It could be a bad example to others. Diefenbaker must go."

Trudeau went on to argue that the visit of United States Air Force General Lauris Norstad to Ottawa in January 1963 had been an exercise in arm-twisting. Its purpose had been to force Pearson to change his position on nuclear warheads. In referring to a State Department press release of January 30, 1963, which supported the pro-nuclear position that Pearson by then had adopted, Trudeau asked, "Do you think it's by accident that this communiqué gave the Opposition Leader the arguments with which he larded his speech to Parliament on January 31? You think it is coincidental that this led to events which ended in the fall of the [Diefenbaker] government on February 5th?" He doubted that the United States would treat Canada "any differently than Guatemala when reasons of state demand it and circumstances permit it — but reasons must demand and circumstances must permit." In 1963 it would have been difficult to find a more eloquent description of what, with the revelations of the 1970s, has come to be known as a "destabilization campaign."[42]

In fact, the destabilization campaign was more extraordinary than Trudeau at the time could have known. During the Cuban Missile Crisis Prime Minister Diefenbaker had proclaimed that "This is not a time for panic but for calm resolve." He insisted that Canadian forces not be put on alert right away. The Defence Minister, Douglas Harkness, disagreed. In defiance of the Prime Minister, and without his knowledge, Harkness ordered the Canadian armed forces to go on alert. But he too was fooled: the military had already put itself on alert, with neither the authorization nor the knowledge of either the Prime Minister or the Minister of Defence.[43]

The importance of the controversy over the Bomarc B anti-aircraft missiles did not lie in the obsolescent missiles themselves or their nuclear warheads. The willingness of the Kennedy administration to ensure that the Canadian political process would not disrupt military planning was of far greater significance. Despite the fact that American use of Canadian territory for their own strategic purposes is the single most sensitive area in the national life of Canada, the Bomarc episode made it quite clear that even a component of continental defence that is of secondary importance can be trifled with by Canadian politicians only at their peril.

The Bomarc B anti-aircraft missiles were obsolete by the time they were deployed in Canada. The development of intercontinental ballistic missiles by both the Soviets and the Americans in the late 1950s and early 1960s ensured that active air defence measures would be of minor practical importance. This did not mean, however, that NORAD, the DEW Line, and its associated systems were not of major importance to United States strategists. Today, these — as well as the updated version of the DEW Line, the North Warning System — are integral parts of the United States military Command, Control, Communications, and Intelligence system (C^3I, as it is called by defence specialists). The main purpose of these systems is to provide the United States military and civilian "national command authorities" with information upon which they can base their decisions concerning the deployment of military forces.

Canadian territory and Canadian facilities are also used for other military intelligence purposes. One of the primary missions of the Canadian Armed Forces is anti-submarine warfare. Virtually the entire Canadian fleet, as well as a substantial part of the air element of the Armed Forces, is devoted to this task. Canada is responsible for maintaining surveillance of and control over a large portion of the northwestern Atlantic Ocean known as "Area Elk." Canadian ships and aircraft engaged in surveillance of Area Elk and other parts of the ocean in effect form an integral part of the United States' military intelligence system.

The United States military deploys additional highly classified intelligence and communications systems in Canada. The SOSUS sound surveillance system is made up of chains of highly sensitive hydrophones planted on the ocean floor in various parts of the world. The purpose of these hydrophones is to keep track of nuclear submarines in the ocean depths at ranges of thousands of kilometres. An important SOSUS chain extends down the Atlantic floor off Canada's east coast. A major land terminal for receiving and processing SOSUS data is located at the United States naval station in Argentia, Newfoundland.[44]

Canadian territory is also indispensable to the Pentagon for communicating with its strategic bomber forces. B-52 nuclear bombers are on constant alert in the high Arctic, operating from bases in the United States as well as from the Strategic Air Command bases at Thule and Sondrestromfjord, Greenland. Some bombers are usually in the air in the Arctic region, awaiting signals to proceed along prearranged routes to targets in the Soviet Union.

The B-52s remain in contact with the United States command authorities by mean of several communication systems, including extra-high-frequency (EHF) waves bounced off satellites and high-frequency (HF) signals transmitted from ground stations. The United States Air Force employs two major radio systems for this purpose. "Giant Talk" is a network of fourteen continuously operating high-frequency stations. The "Green Pine" network is operated by Strategic Air Command specifically for the purpose of communicating with nuclear bombers in the Northern Area. Green Pine is made up of thirteen high-frequency radio stations, of which seven are located in northern Canada. Of these, five are at DEW-

Line sites in the Northwest Territories, one at the Melville Air Station in Labrador, and one at the Argentia Naval Station in Newfoundland.[45]

In addition to providing useful real estate for these intelligence-gathering and communications facilities, Canada assists the United States in its military activities in many other ways. Strategic Air Command nuclear bombers fly over Canadian territory in their continuing practice for nuclear war. In the event of real war, carrying nuclear warheads, they would transit Canadian skies on their way over the north polar region to their targets in the Soviet Union. Canadian airfields are available for the dispersal of United States military aircraft in the event of a high-level alert. Canadian ocean ports are frequently visited by nuclear armed ships and submarines of the United States Navy.

No one can imagine exactly what a nuclear war between the superpowers would be like. But it is safe to say that the widespread dispersal of United States military assets in Canada would provide a great number of high-priority targets for Soviet nuclear missiles.

The full extent of American military activity in Canada is virtually impossible to determine. Since 1940, at least 2,500 documents relating to military co-operation between the two countries have been accumulated.[46] Some undoubtedly deal with trivial matters. Others are known to cover such topics as the "Conditions Under Which Storage of Nuclear Anti-Submarine Weapons in Canada, for Use of U.S. Forces, Would be Permitted" and the "Responsibilities for Response to Nuclear Weapon Incidents Involving Canadian Territory." Still others among the 2,500 documents are undoubtedly so sensitive that even their titles have never been revealed.

United States military leaders tend to be cautious in their public statements on the role that they expect Canadian territory and Canadian resources to play in their strategic planning. When he appeared before the Parliamentary Committee on External Affairs and National Defence in late 1985, General Robert T. Herres, the Commander-in-Chief of NORAD, was careful to stress the autonomy of the Canadian decision-making process. But earlier that year, in a specialized United States defence publication, General Herres had made it clear that he would "exercise unilateral operational control of U.S. air defence assets when circumstances do not permit participation by the Canadians."[47]

There is no question that the American authorities will always place matters that they regard as vital to their national interests above other considerations. From a Canadian perspective, the proper question is not whether it is right for the Americans to act unilaterally in such matters. The pertinent question is what course of action Canada should follow in pursuit of its own national interests, particularly when these diverge from those of the Americans. In the world of defence planners, that evidently is the kind of question that is best avoided, at least in public. In an apparent paradox, Trudeau's Assistant Deputy Minister of National Defence, John Anderson, has said that to fail to seek opportunities to co-operate with the Americans would reduce Canadian independence. This arises, in his view, out of the fact that "we are inevitably and inextricably, as far as security in the modern world is concerned, tied in with the United States."[48] In this most sensitive area of public discourse paradoxes abound. It is often necessary to look for more than one level of meaning in such discussions. The lines separating perception, deception, and accommodation are sometimes indistinct.

In its 1985 Report on Canada's Air Defence, the Special Senate Committee on National Defence observed that "Whatever Canada's own perceptions of the world, this country has to aim at maintaining mutually satisfactory arrangements with the United States. In the air defence area, this means dealing with American perceptions of the threat as much as with the threat itself."[49]

When it went into operation in 1957, the DEW Line was welcomed because it was widely believed that it would enhance the air defence of both the United States and Canada. Its fundamental purpose was not so much to make possible the interception of Soviet bombers by Canadian and American fighters; it was rather to provide enough warning of an attack to enable Strategic Air Command nuclear bombers to depart for their assigned targets in the Soviet Union. In 1957 extensive secret tests were conducted that showed that even with the three to six hours' warning provided by the DEW Line, most of the Strategic Air Command bomber force in North America would not be off the ground and on its way. A number of American strategic planners were alarmed by this revelation, as it appeared to directly undermine the basis upon which the security of the United States was supposed to rest. General Curtis LeMay, the head of the Strategic Air Command, was neither surprised nor worried, however. For some time the United States intelligence agencies had been able to maintain sufficiently close surveillance of the Soviet Union that General LeMay assumed he would have at least thirty days' advance notice of any attempted Soviet attack. This fact was known only to a very small number of people. The intention of the Commander of the Strategic Air Command was to launch a devastating pre-emptive strike well within the thirty-day warning period. The colourful General is reported to have said, "If I see that the Russians are amassing their planes for an attack I'm going to knock the shit out of them before they can take off the ground."[50]

The widely held view that nuclear deterrence involves nuclear retaliation for a Soviet attack is mistaken. The actual purpose of the Strategic Air Command is to pre-empt such an attack. There is no point in planning to destroy a Soviet airfield after the bombers have left or to destroy a missile silo after the missiles have been launched.

The publicly stated purpose of the DEW Line, to give warning of a surprise Soviet attack so that it could be intercepted, may be somewhat fanciful. But nevertheless, Canadian territory clearly plays a vital part in United States nuclear strategy. Much of the intelligence that created General LeMay's thirty-day warning period is collected from Canadian territory. Canada's geographical location is useful not only for detecting Soviet aircraft and missiles on DEW Line or North Warning System radar; through the technology of signals intelligence, Canadian geography is also ideal for determining exactly what Soviet operators are seeing on their own radar scopes. By this and related techniques, the movements and communications of Soviet forces are known long before an aircraft or missile could conceivably approach North America. It is for this reason, more than any other, that Canada has been deeply but secretly involved in the Western intelligence community for more than four decades.

6

Canada and the Western Intelligence Community

"O Oysters, come and walk with us!"
The Walrus did beseech.
"A pleasant walk, a pleasant talk,
    Along the briny beach:
We cannot do with more than four,
    To give a hand to each."

C anada's security and intelligence agencies are very closely
linked with similar organizations in other Western countries. A particularly close relationship connects Canada with
the United States, Britain, Australia, and New Zealand — often
referred to as the UKUSA countries within the Western intelligence
community. The security and intelligence agencies of the five UKUSA
nations are estimated to have a combined annual budget of not
much less than twenty billion dollars, and to employ a total of
more than a quarter of a million full-time personnel.[1]

These organizations are bound together by a number of factors.
For one thing, they share a great deal of history: intelligence
agencies in some countries were created by those of an allied
country. They co-operate on a daily basis, and frequently exchange
personnel. Their operations are shrouded in great secrecy, but
security and intelligence activities in one country are often better
known in sister agencies than they are by the home government.
Most of the organizations maintain permanent liaison officers with
the other agencies; in some cases full-scale operational units of one
UKUSA country are permanently stationed in another.

The agencies of each country can be divided into three categories that are functionally defined. Collecting and analysing foreign intelligence in general is the responsibility of the Central Intelligence Agency in the United States, of MI6 (also called the Secret Intelligence Service or SIS) in the United Kingdom, of the Australian Secret Intelligence Service (ASIS), and the External Intelligence Bureau in New Zealand. Canada does not have a comparable organization.

The second category, signals intelligence (SIGINT), is in many respects a more important source of intelligence collection than the more traditional methods used by the foreign intelligence agencies just mentioned. Canada is heavily involved in SIGINT collection through the Communications Security Establishment (CSE). The equivalent organizations are the National Security Agency (NSA) in the United States, the Government Communications Headquarters (GCHQ) in Britain, the Defence Signals Directorate (DSD) in Australia, and the Government Communications Security Bureau (GCSB) in New Zealand.

The third major component of the Western intelligence community is the internal security organization of each country. This function is carried out primarily, but not exclusively, by the Federal Bureau of Investigation (FBI) in the United States, by MI5 (also called the Security Service) in Britain, by the Australian Security Intelligence Organization (ASIO), and by the New Zealand Security Intelligence Service. Internal security has been the responsibility of the Canadian Security Intelligence Service (CSIS) since it took over from the RCMP Security Service in 1984.

The Western intelligence community is dominated by its American members. The United States is estimated to contribute approximately ninety per cent of the twenty-billion-dollar budget of the community.[2] Its massive organizations are unparalleled in manpower, advanced technology, and a global presence. The agencies of the smaller countries tend largely to supplement and assist the activities of their American counterparts. Joint projects are frequently carried out. One well-known example was the combined CIA-MI6 operation that overthrew the Mossadeq government of Iran in 1953. Americans and British agreed that Prime Minister Mohammed Mossadeq's moves to nationalize foreign oil companies were not acceptable. He also attempted to purge the Iranian police of its pro-American leadership, which led to fears that Communist influence was increasing. After a dispute with Mossadeq, the Shah fled to exile in Italy. Using a network of MI6 agents, headed by George K. Young, and CIA money and direction, a coup was organized, which resulted in the return of the Shah as absolute dictator of Iran. There he remained until finally toppled by the Khomeini revolution in 1979. The cost of the CIA-MI6 operation was estimated at ten million dollars, a paltry sum considering the oil fortunes that were at stake.[3]

Most co-operation within the Western intelligence community is much less dramatic, but is nonetheless highly secret, made up mainly of a continuous flow of massive amounts of information.

International intelligence exchanges involve information on almost every conceivable human activity. They include, among many other subjects, such matters as military and naval deployments in every part of the world, interpretations of political events in every country, details about the characteristics, contacts, habits, and movements of thousands of persons of interest, stories told by defectors from "unfriendly" countries, the suspected intentions of political or terrorist groups, technological developments and economic performance in other countries, and so on. Obviously, such intelligence varies greatly in accuracy, reliability, and usefulness. Inevitably, much of it is misleading, either intentionally or, more usually, because of an inability within the intelligence community to analyse and comprehend the meaning or importance of raw information.

Among the members of the Western intelligence community, the United States has by far the greatest ability to collect information. It also has the greatest ability to consume it. Its ability to analyse and interpret the information far exceeds that of the other partners in the community. Consequently, most of the material collected throughout the world by other partners flows into the headquarters of the CIA and NSA. It has been estimated that the Canadian government is able to process and use less than one per cent of the data collected by Canadian security and intelligence agencies.[4]

In the interest of maintaining secrecy, the "need to know" rule is applied to the distribution of information throughout the intelligence community. This is based on the assumption that if information is restricted to people who need to know it to carry out their tasks, it is less likely to find its way into unauthorized hands. Because of their more limited interests abroad, the smaller partners in the community are generally deemed to have a smaller

91

requirement for information than does the United States. The flow of finished intelligence a country such as Canada tends to receive is not necessarily determined by its own perceptions of its own interests. It is partly the extreme secrecy that surrounds these matters that has created the situation in which the public and in many cases the sovereign governments that nominally employ the security and intelligence agencies have little or no knowledge of the ties among them.

Among the most secret, and the most secretive, organizations in the Western world are the SIGINT agencies. Canada, the United States, the United Kingdom, Australia, and New Zealand are parties to a series of secret agreements that have linked their respective signals intelligence organizations since the 1940s.

The term "signals intelligence" refers to the monitoring and interception of electromagnetic signals. These signals are in the form of energy emitted by all electronic devices: for example, radio communications, telephone messages, data transmission, the electronic waves from radar sets, the telemetry signals from tests of missiles and rockets, and transmissions of data from orbiting satellites. Signals intelligence activity is directed towards listening to, recording, and interpreting these electromagnetic signals.

A closely related activity involves encrypting, or placing in code, important messages so that their meaning cannot be understood by the SIGINT agencies of other countries. This, of course, results in a considerable part of the effort of SIGINT agencies being directed towards breaking the secret codes of other countries — friendly and unfriendly countries alike.

SIGINT is valuable in determining the intentions, plans, and strategies of other countries. Such knowledge is particularly useful in time of war. Since World War Two, SIGINT has assumed greater importance than more conventional forms of intelligence collection, such as the espionage carried out by human agents. The rapid development of electronic communications and the vast increase in the use of electronic devices such as radar have resulted in SIGINT activities expanding at an enormous rate. It is reliably estimated that in the early 1980s, eighty to ninety per cent of the usable intelligence collected by the United States government came from SIGINT activities.

Most major powers have engaged in some form of SIGINT activity since the era of World War One. The first SIGINT facility in Canada was a British Admiralty intercept station established in

Esquimault, B.C. in 1925.[5] The first specifically Canadian efforts in this field occurred during World War Two, when Canadian naval and military units developed an Operational Intelligence Headquarters which made extensive use of intercepted enemy radio signals, and which was particularly useful, for example, in locating German naval movements in the Atlantic. The Radio Division of the Federal Department of Transport provided the British government with additional information.[6]

The National Research Council (NRC) ultimately provided the organizational home for Canada's SIGINT operations. Its "Examination Unit" — a bland-sounding name intended to obscure its true purpose — was formed for this purpose in Ottawa in June 1941.[7] The NRC was chosen for this purpose on the assumption that secret activity involving technical apparatus would not arouse undue suspicion if it was being conducted under the auspices of Canada's main scientific establishment. The Examination Unit performed valuable service in intercepting diplomatic messages to and from the embassy of Vichy France in Ottawa. Some Japanese diplomatic traffic was intercepted by a SIGINT station in Vancouver.[8] The NRC Examination Unit handled messages from nineteen Canadian intercept stations.[9]

A special Intelligence Section was formed in the Department of External Affairs in September 1942, for the purpose of analysing NRC Examination Unit information and turning it into finished intelligence reports. The Special Intelligence Section was headed by Herbert Norman.[10] According to some historians, the Office of Strategic Services, the U.S. wartime predecessor of the CIA, was "an avid consumer of Norman's work."[11] It is a bitter irony that Norman later became the victim of witch-hunters in the United States Congress.

Towards the end of the war, consideration was given to the idea of dismantling the NRC Examination Unit. But with the early frost of the cold war already making itself felt, the government reconsidered this plan, and by December 1945, three months after the defection of Igor Gouzenko, the decision had been made to continue Canada's SIGINT activities.[12] The name of the Examination Unit was subsequently changed to the Communications Branch of the National Research Council (CBNRC). Thenceforward, its attentions were directed primarily, but not entirely, at the Soviet Union.

The wartime co-operation that had developed among the SIG-

INT organizations of the United States, Britain, Canada, Australia, and New Zealand was formalized in a series of extremely secret treaties signed in the late 1940s. The most important of these were the UKUSA agreements of 1947.[13] The agreements ensure that almost the entire globe is monitored by the SIGINT agencies of the UKUSA countries. Canada is primarily responsible for coverage of the Northern Soviet Union and parts of Europe.[14] The agreements are structured in such a way that the United States is designated the "first party" and the other four nations are "second parties."[15] Thus the United States is in the pivotal position; its NSA has a special relationship directly with the SIGINT agencies of each of the second-party nations. The agreements provide that security arrangements, code words, indoctrination procedures, and terminology are standardized among the five SIGINT agencies. All of this is set out in a large volume called *International Regulations on SIGINT*.[16]

The existence of the UKUSA agreements has been surrounded by exceptional secrecy on the part of all of the governments involved. In addition to being a party to the UKUSA agreements, Canada has bilateral SIGINT agreements with other UKUSA nations. The existence of the UKUSA agreements has been confirmed by a man who has been at the very centre of SIGINT activity in Canada since the end of World War Two. Kevin O'Neill is a dapper, sophisticated Anglo-Irish gentleman. His sense of the absurd is manifested in an encyclopaedic knowledge of limericks. His sonorous baritone and rugged good looks bring to mind the image of a mature British stage actor rather than the major player in the international intelligence world that he actually is.

Kevin O'Neill learned about SIGINT as a young officer in the British Army during World War Two. At the end of the war, he was sent first to New York to work briefly with Sir William Stephenson, then to Ottawa to help establish Canada's SIGINT organization on a permanent basis. O'Neill was a senior officer throughout the history of the CBNRC, became Director-General in 1970, and retained his position when the identity of the agency was changed to the Communications Security Establishment (CSE) under cover of the Department of National Defence on April 1, 1975.

Since retiring in 1980, Kevin O'Neill has been writing a history of Canada's SIGINT organizations. No one could be better qualified to do this. Yet the massive document will remain secret, despite the undoubtedly fascinating material it contains. According to O'Neill, the UKUSA agreements directly link the United Kingdom and the United States. Canada is involved in a less formal way. The agreements to which Canada is a party do not exist on paper. There is no one document spelling out their terms. But they do nonetheless exist as an understanding among the SIGINT organizations of the five English-speaking nations.[17] Canada's part in the UKUSA agreements was also obliquely confirmed by the Minister responsible for the CBNRC on March 24, 1975 in a session of the House of Commons Committee on Miscellaneous Estimates. C.M. Drury was Minister of Science and Technology at the time. In discussing the estimates for the National Research Council, for which he was responsible, Mr. Drury was asked by Perrin Beatty, "Is there, to the best of your knowledge, Mr. Minister, an agreement referred to as the U.K.-U.S.A. agreement, which would affect the activities of the CBNRC?" Mr. Drury replied that "There is an agreement, a security agreement, involving a number of countries including Canada and the U.S.A., but it is not a bilateral agreement solely." Mr. Drury then went on to confirm that the United Kingdom is also a party to the agreement, and he added that ". . . the purpose of the agreement is to ensure effective collaboration between these three countries in security matters."[18]

The management of national security is ultimately the responsibility of the Prime Minister. The Clerk of the Privy Council is in effect the Deputy Minister in the Privy Council Office and is therefore the civil servant who is ultimately responsible for all national security and intelligence organizations, including the CSE. Michael Pitfield, who filled that position for a number of years, has observed in relation to the UKUSA agreements that "There are agreements ... and they are important, not for what they say but for what they mean."[19]

The agreements may not explicitly say that the United States, through its SIGINT organization, the National Security Agency (NSA), dominates and controls the SIGINT organizations of the other member nations, but that is clearly what the agreements mean. The NSA is by far the largest organization in the U.S. intelligence community. It probably employs about 100,000 people; its budget has been estimated at ten billion dollars.[20] Yet it has no statutory existence. It was created on November 4, 1952, by a secret order issued by President Truman. The existence of the NSA did not become known to the public until a former employee, Winslow Peck, revealed its existence in a long interview with *Ramparts* magazine in 1972.[21]

The existence of the CBNRC and its close relationship with the NSA were revealed to the public in a documentary film entitled *The Fifth Estate — The Espionage Establishment*, which was broadcast on CBC television on January 9, 1974. The programme caused a sensation because of its revelation that the CBNRC operates in secret, under the terms of the UKUSA agreements and in close co-operation with the NSA. When questions were raised in the House of Commons following the telecast, the government, not surprisingly, tried to skate around them. Prime Minister Trudeau and External Affairs Minister Mitchell Sharp were critical of the programme but neither stated categorically that the statements made in it were false. John Diefenbaker asked Mitchell Sharp about the "alleged revelations that the National Research Council of Canada is being used as a secret intercepting and bugging agency working directly with United States national security agencies." Mr. Sharp replied, "I would like to say to him [Mr. Diefenbaker] that there has been no change in the arrangements regarding the activities talked about on the program since he was Prime Minister of this country." Mr. Diefenbaker angrily shot back, "Any suggestion that anything of that kind was done when I was Prime Minister I say is false!"[22] Either the former Prime Minister had not known of Canada's extensive SIGINT activities or else he did not wish to be associated with them in public. The most likely explanation is that he did not want to know about it. According to Kevin O'Neill, Diefenbaker never had any comprehension of the activities of the CBNRC. When a briefing on the CBNRC was arranged for Diefenbaker during his time as Prime Minister, he expressed no interest in learning about the organization.[23] The Chief was, however, curious about the details of the personal histories of the senior staff.

On the question of the UKUSA agreements, Prime Minister Trudeau was extremely cautious. When asked about it by future Prime Minister Joe Clark, who was then a young Opposition MP with three years of parliamentary experience, Mr. Trudeau denied that Canada was a party to such a treaty. On further questioning, the Prime Minister acknowledged that there is "exchange of information with our friends and allies on intelligence and security matters. We hope that we are the beneficiaries of such an exchange when it does take place."

When questioned by reporters outside the House, the Prime Minister said, "I don't want to comment on questions of security. It's much too delicate. The danger is that you will drag out confidences from me and I'll say things that I'll regret."[24]

But the following day in Parliament the Prime Minister made a statement that could be interpreted as implying that the international SIGINT arrangements have not always been beneficial to Canada. David Lewis, the leader of the New Democratic Party, had asked whether the government had considered the propriety of Canada's being involved "in intercepting and decoding foreign information not so much for its own use but for the use of one of the superpowers? Is such an activity of value to Canada's own interests or does it merely underline Canada's satellite position in international affairs?"

The Prime Minister replied cautiously, "We have assessed it from time to time and we have decided to continue any security and intelligence activities which are of benefit to Canada and to discontinue any which might be of benefit merely to a foreign power."[25]

The Prime Minister may well have been giving veiled acknowledgement to the suggestion that, since the beginning of the UKUSA arrangements, Canada had occupied a position of secondary importance in the decision-making process among the participants.

Canada was not a party to the BRUSA agreement which covered signals intelligence co-operation between the British and the Americans. It was concluded before the UKUSA agreement of 1947. In 1948 another agreement between Canada and the United States, the CANUSA agreement, covering Communications Intelligence, was negotiated in extreme secrecy. During the spring of 1948, proposed drafts of the agreement were exchanged between military intelligence officers of Canada and the United States. The Americans were concerned to ensure that the language of the agreement would duplicate that of the BRUSA agreement. But at the same time they were anxious to restrict the flow of information to Canada.[26] The Acting Director of Intelligence of the United States Air Force, Brigadier General Walter Agre, was particularly concerned about the security of information should it fall into Canadian hands. In a memorandum to the Co-ordinator of Joint

Operations, referring to the proposed U.S.-Canada agreement, he stated that

> Paragraph 6 is not considered sufficiently restrictive. In effect it provides for the complete exchange of information. Not only is it considered that the Canadians will reap all the benefits of complete exchange but wider dissemination of the information could jeopardize the security of the information.[27]

In due course the CANUSA agreement was concluded to the satisfaction of the Americans. The CBNRC continued to monitor Soviet signals and various other signals and routinely pass along the results to the National Security Agency headquarters in Fort George Mead, Maryland. The Canadian SIGINT operation has utilized facilities in at least four provinces, the Yukon, the Northwest Territories, and in Bermuda. The facilities in the Arctic, with their geographical proximity to the Soviet Union, are of unique value. The station at Alert, on the tip of Ellesmere Island, is the most northerly permanent military facility in the world. The NSA or its military components have had guest detachments at Communications Security Establishment facilities in Canada, often on a long-term basis.[28]

Despite this, the Americans at various times have been reluctant to include Canadians in the higher-level deliberations of the intelligence community. An early example of this reluctance is the hesitation of the United States Army G-2 (intelligence) staff to allow Canadian representatives to attend long-term planning conferences with the British Joint Intelligence Committee in London in 1950. The United States Joint Intelligence Committee had advised the British that Canadian participation in the U.S.-U.K. Intelligence Conference would be "neither essential nor appropriate."[29] The British disagreed. The Americans subsequently decided not to object to Canadian participation "if such an invitation is issued by the British to the Canadians."[30]

These were not isolated instances of the United States' military and intelligence authorities adopting a superior attitude towards Canada and the other UKUSA partners. They are simply early manifestations of an approach that has characterized the relationship throughout its history.

The problem does not consist simply of an arrogant attitude on the part of the United States intelligence authorities towards the sensibilities of their colleagues in allied countries. A more disturbing aspect of the UKUSA relationship is the quite different kind of institutional loyalty that has developed within the international intelligence community. The SIGINT agencies of the UKUSA countries work closely together, and in extreme secrecy. This has led to a situation in which some personnel in the SIGINT agencies tend to identify more closely with the international SIGINT community than with their own governments. This phenomenon is not surprising considering their shared insider's knowledge of the secrets of SIGINT operations and security measures.

The *International Regulations on SIGINT* prescribe the security procedures and methods of indoctrination agreed to by the UKUSA members. Any employee who is briefed for communications intelligence must sign a declaration that "COMINT and all information relating to COMINT may only be discussed with persons whom I know to be COMINT-indoctrinated."[31] Such persons are more likely to be other COMINT-indoctrinated members of the Western intelligence community than other Canadians who are not so privileged. It is inevitable that this kind of procedure should lead to the prevalence of a sense of estrangement from many of one's fellow citizens.

In contrast, successive Canadian Prime Ministers failed to become acquainted with the operational details or even the very existence of the CBNRC and its relationship with the NSA and GCHQ.[32] The MPs who created the commotion over the CBC-TV programme on the intelligence community in January 1974, failed to address one of the central questions raised in the broadcast. Winslow Peck, the former NSA intelligence officer who had first revealed the existence of the NSA in *Ramparts* magazine two years earlier, asserted flatly that

> Now the information that is coming to the United States comes not only from the United States' monitoring stations but also from the monitoring stations of the other countries. Information all comes to the United States, but the United States does not totally reciprocate in passing all the information on to the other powers. At the same time, for security reasons, whatever that means, the United States does monitor the communications of the other parties of this treaty. Whether or not these other powers are aware of the United States' monitoring of their own communications, I don't know. It is a daily practice, it happens constantly, and it's something that everyone

in the American intelligence community assumes is standard practice, standard operating procedure.... I doubt if they [other governments] realize the scope of the problem, that virtually every means of communication that your government has is monitored by the United States government.[33]

When asked about this practice, the former Director-General of the RCMP Security Service, William Kelly, was not as naive as Peck seemed to expect. He commented that

I think it would be rather stupid of any Canadian authority to think that if NSA covers the rest of the world they would make an exception of this country. I think that you have to work on the assumption that they do. Now whether they do or not, I don't know.[34]

The United States intelligence agencies, operating under the umbrella of the UKUSA agreements, do not simply monitor the communications of governments whose SIGINT agencies are also members of the pact. There is also evidence suggesting that they have on occasion interfered in the internal affairs of some of those nations when their SIGINT interests are perceived to be at risk.

The firing of Gough Whitlam, Prime Minister of Australia from 1972 to 1975, suggests a remarkable revelation of how far that interference might go. Australia is an important member of the UKUSA group. Her SIGINT organization, the Defence Signals Directorate (DSD), her foreign espionage organization, the Australian Secret Intelligence Service (ASIS), and her internal security agency, the Australian Security Intelligence Organization (ASIO), all cooperate closely with their British, Canadian, and American counterparts. In addition, the United States maintains a number of important and secret military and intelligence facilities in Australia.[35]

There are more than two dozen American installations involving military communications, navigation, satellite tracking and control, and various types of SIGINT activities.[36] Only the United Kingdom, Canada, and West Germany host greater numbers of U.S. military and intelligence sites. The most critical and sensitive of the facilities in Australia is the SIGINT station in Pine Gap, near the town of Alice Springs in South Australia. Pine Gap became operational in 1969. It is used by the CIA to control several highly secret "Rhyolite" SIGINT satellites that are in permanent orbit over the equator.

Pine Gap and the other U.S. installations have caused a good deal of political controversy in Australia. Many Australians worry that they will invite nuclear attack from the Soviet Union in the event of war. Another area of concern has to do with the inability of the Australian government to control the uses to which the facilities are put, or even to have full knowledge of those activities. For a time some of the installations were operated solely by the Americans. More recently, Australian personnel have been permitted by the Americans to be present at each of them. But at the most important stations there are special areas set aside for exclusive American use. Notwithstanding UKUSA co-operation, the signals analysis section at Pine Gap is accessible only to American CIA and NSA personnel.[37] The same is true of other sensitive areas of the Pine Gap operation, as well as a number of other U.S. installations. Consequently, many Australians suspect that their own domestic communications are being surreptitiously monitored by the CIA and the NSA on Australian soil.

The U.S. installations played a major role in one of the most serious political crises in recent Australian history. In what has come to be called the "Whitlam coup" in Australia, Labour Prime Minister Gough Whitlam was summarily dismissed by Governor General Sir John Kerr on November 11, 1975. Since the election of his Labour Party government in 1972, the first in twenty-three years, Whitlam had been a source of great concern to the Australian security and intelligence services and to the CIA. ASIO officials felt that the left wing of the Australian Labour Party (ALP) was too powerful. They also thought that Communists had too much influence in the ALP.

As Prime Minister, Whitlam made a number of moves that appeared to confirm the worst fears of both ASIO and the CIA. Various Communist governments were recognized for the first time: Cuba, North Korea, and the German Democratic Republic. Conscription was ended and Australian troops were withdrawn from Vietnam. The Christmas 1972 bombing of Hanoi by the U.S. Air Force was criticized. The proposal by the Movement of Non-aligned Nations to make the Indian Ocean a "zone of peace" was supported. The Australian government even applied for observer status at the summit meeting of the Non-aligned Movement. All the while, the left wing of the ALP continued to press for additional reforms.[38]

But the Australian security officials were most offended by

Whitlam's decision to allow his staff to submit to ASIO security clearance procedures on a voluntary basis, rather than the traditional mandatory basis. Despite the fact that classified materials in the new Prime Minister's office were being handled by persons who did have security clearance, ASIO immediately communicated Whitlam's proposed decision to the CIA, without Whitlam's assent or knowledge.[39] The CIA threatened to cut off the flow of intelligence to Australia. The Whitlam Labour Government was at loggerheads with the CIA, as well as with its own security service, ASIO, within two days of taking office.

The CIA was to make similar threats on two subsequent occasions during the three years that Whitlam served as Prime Minister. In March 1973 a dispute erupted between the Australian Commonwealth Police and ASIO. The issue was an impending visit to Australia by the Prime Minister of Yugoslavia. According to the Commissioner of the Commonwealth Police, the safety of the Yugoslav visitor might be jeopardized because of threats by right-wing Croatian terrorists. A dispute erupted over an ASIO report that appeared to distort the meaning of a discussion of the matter by a high-level interdepartmental committee. Members of the government felt that ASIO was withholding vital information. On March 16, 1973, the Attorney-General of Australia, Senator Lionel Murphy, accompanied by twenty-three members of the Commonwealth police force, visited ASIO headquarters in Melbourne, where Senator Murphy personally scrutinized the security files on the Croatians.[40]

The incident touched off an uproar in the Australian press and in the CIA. James Angleton, who was head of CIA Counter-Intelligence at the time, later recalled his consternation about the conduct of the Whitlam government in an interview on Australian television. He lamented that "Everything worried us. You don't see the jewels of counter-intelligence being placed in jeopardy by a party that has extensive historical contacts in Eastern Europe...."[41]

The final act in the drama of Gough Whitlam and the Western intelligence community occurred in November 1975. A Labour government supply bill was being blocked in the Opposition-controlled Senate. Scandals involving close associates of Prime Minister Whitlam were making headlines. Whitlam himself was again in potential confrontation with ASIO and the CIA. The Americans' lease on the Pine Gap SIGINT base was due to expire on December

10, 1975. In April of that year Whitlam had stated that he might insist that the terms of the lease be changed, or that he might not renew it.[42] Whitlam was also raising awkward questions about the uses to which Pine Gap and other U.S installations in Australia were being put.

On November 10, 1975, the Director-General of ASIO received a top-secret cable from his liaison officer in Washington. The cable conveyed a formal démarche from Theodore Shackley, chief of the East Asia division of the CIA. The message enumerated a long list of grievances against the Prime Minister; most of them had to do with criticisms Whitlam had been making about CIA activities in Australia. The message stated that

> CIA feel that everything possible has been done on a diplomatic basis and now on an intelligence liaison link they feel that if the problem can not be solved they do not see how our mutually beneficial relationships are going to continue.
>
> The CIA feels grave concern as to where this type of public discussion may lead.
>
> The DG [Director-General] should be assured that the CIA does not lightly adopt this attitude.[43]

The next day, on November 11, 1975, Governor General Sir John Kerr summoned Prime Minister Gough Whitlam to his official residence and dismissed him from office. The Vice-Regal prerogative had never before been used in this way in a Commonwealth country.

Sir John Kerr had been appointed on the advice of Gough Whitlam in 1974. He is known to have had a long association with both British and American intelligence agencies. The day before he sacked Whitlam, the same day the CIA message was received by the Director-General of ASIO, Sir John Kerr had been briefed by the Permanent Secretary of the Australian Department of Defence. The briefing had to do with American concerns about Whitlam and with the CIA message.[44]

Exactly what the Governor General's motives were in firing the Prime Minister is not known. A CIA coup against the Prime Minister of Australia has never been proven conclusively; but it has continued to be a matter of intense debate among Australians.

Gough Whitlam is not the only Prime Minister of a UKUSA member nation to come into conflict with his own Security Services. For years rumours have persisted that, when he was Labour Party Prime Minister of the United Kingdom, Harold Wilson was placed under surveillance by the British Security Service, MI5.

In 1977 Chapman Pincher reported in the London *Daily Telegraph* that Harold Wilson's fear that he had been under electronic surveillance "was fully justified."[45] Pincher's published work displays a classic, cold war view of the world. He dwells at great length on the conspiratorial practices of the KGB. Pincher is also known to be extremely close to leading figures in the British security and intelligence establishment, and often to act as a mouthpiece for certain factions within it. In spite of this, he has stuck to his story that the Prime Minister of Britain was bugged. He argues in effect that it was made necessary by the UKUSA agreements, and implies that the bugging might well have been carried out by the American intelligence agencies. On this subject Chapman Pincher is worth quoting at length:

> Britain is totally dependent on the U.S.A. for intelligence from orbiting satellites — now the major source. Most of the radio monitoring establishments in Britain have been built with American money and are manned by NSA staff working jointly with GCHQ. Dependence is so great and co-operation so close that I am convinced that the security and Intelligence chiefs would go to any length to protect the link-up and that they would be right to do so.
>
> So if the CIA or the NSA, which is responsible for planting the listening devices it calls "sneakies," overstepped the mark in Britain I am sure that MI5 and MI6 would cover up for them. One prime MI6 source, who admitted that representations had been made by Washington about some of the ministers appointed by Wilson, assured me that, "Anything and everything would be possible if it was considered necessary to protect the Anglo-American joint Intelligence arrangements. They are priority number one."[46]

The NSA and its sister SIGINT agencies undoubtedly have enormous potential power. If it can be used against Prime Ministers, it is most assuredly used against ordinary citizens. Senator Frank Church, former chairman of the U.S. Senate Intelligence Committee, stated in 1975 that at any time the massive capability of the NSA "could be turned around on the American people and no American would have any privacy left, such is the capability to monitor everything: telephone conversations, telegrams, it doesn't matter. There would be no place to hide."[47]

Indeed, the NSA was used by the Nixon administration in operations MINARET and SHAMROCK to spy on American citizens. The FBI, the CIA, the Drug Enforcement Agency, and other branches of the U.S. government provided it with "watch lists" that included the names of thousands of Americans, ranging from Jane Fonda to Dr. Benjamin Spock. The NSA obligingly intercepted and recorded all communications to and from these citizens. The total number of Americans subjected to this intrusion exceeded seventy thousand. The practice was supposedly ended by the Carter administration; it is impossible to know if it has been resumed since. In view of the inclination of the Reagan administration to give free rein to U.S. intelligence agencies, such a development would not be surprising.

In Canada there is no direct evidence of the CSE having been used for gathering domestic intelligence. During the Quebec October Crisis in 1970, the Privy Council Office did indirectly request assistance from the CBNRC, as the CSE was then known, in searching for James Cross and Pierre Laporte. The CBNRC is said to have declined to assist, arguing that it was beyond its technical capability to be of any help.[48] But there is, in fact, little doubt that the CSE has the technical capability to eavesdrop on virtually any kind of electronic communication that takes place in Canada. In debating the new Security Service Bill in the House of Commons in March 1984, former Progressive Conservative Solicitor General Allan Lawrence warned that "There is a terrible potential for abuse in the CSE and its allied and international agencies in other countries. They can, and I am convinced they do, listen in, break into, decodify and store conversations of people in this country with no independent control, supervision, or monitoring."[49]

This assertion was not denied by the government. It subsequently stated that even though the CSE has this potential, it does not use it because it would be a violation of the *Protection of Privacy Act* of 1974. The historical record does not inspire great confidence that secret intelligence organizations are always scrupulous in adhering to the letter of the law, especially when the possibility of their being caught breaking the law is non-existent.

Senior figures associated with the Trudeau government took a more realistic position later that year. In the summer of 1983, the proposed new Security Service legislation, Bill C-157, had been under review by a special Senate Committee chaired by the former Secretary to the Cabinet, Senator Michael Pitfield, established for that purpose. For the first time the question of bringing Canada's SIGINT agency, the CSE, under statutory control was placed on the public agenda. Pitfield felt that communications intelligence activities in Canada should be brought strictly under the control of the highest authorities in the federal government. He was determined that the NSA should not operate in Canada, and that the CSE should not do so on its behalf without the explicit approval of the Cabinet. He visualized an arrangement whereby CSIS itself would be made responsible for ensuring that such activities would not occur. He stated that

> What in essence I'm talking about is you make the CSIS not only responsible for watching the foreign spies, but for watching the foreign "friends." [If an allied power required intelligence that could only be gathered in Canada] you'd require them to go to the responsible Minister but you would have the CSIS monitor that in fact they do.[50]

Pitfield developed a formula for amending the CSIS legislation in such a way that it would apply also to the CSE. He suggested that the law should state that CSIS would have a monopoly on all domestic eavesdropping in Canada. This would make it positively illegal for the CSE or for its American partner, the NSA, to engage in such activities.[51] On September 22, 1983, acting Minister of External Affairs Jean-Luc Pepin testified about the activities of the CSE before the Pitfield Senate Committee. In discussion following Pepin's initial statement, Pitfield criticized Bill C-157 for failing to deal with the SIGINT problem. He argued that the CSIS should have a monopoly on "gumshoe activity in Canada, and in doing so ensure through the provision of the law that it is not targeted on Canadians.... It [sic] that it is the intent of the legislation, then my question is: Should the section not say something like that? It implies that, but it really does not say that."[52] Mr. Pepin's reply was vague, but he seemed to allow that such an amendment might be possible.

The report of the Pitfield Senate Committee, which was released in November 1983, made the same suggestion. Its recommendation regarding collecting foreign intelligence, including SIGINT, stated that the CSIS "should have a monopoly on all operational work. This would ensure that all such activity comes within the regime of review and accountability which will accompany the CSIS."[53] The report goes on to explain that "the 'monopoly' aspect of this procedure would ensure that the Security Intelligence Review Committee would consider the conduct of such operations, and attempt to verify their propriety."

The version of the new Security Service legislation that was eventually passed by Parliament in June 1984 did not follow those recommendations. As was proposed in the original version of the legislation, CSIS may "assist" in the collection of foreign intelligence. Far from having a monopoly in the field, CSIS is an adjunct to the CSE whenever it is invited. The SIGINT monopoly is still intact in Canada, free of legislative control or oversight. The UKUSA agreements have not been breached.

The SIGINT agreements represent only a fraction of the total number of arrangements among the security and intelligence agencies of the UKUSA countries. The existence of such arrangements has been surrounded by secrecy, but there is no doubt that they number in the thousands. Some are written agreements; others are verbal understandings.[54] In 1970 the RCMP carried on liaison with at least several dozen U.S. federal government departments and agencies. This included not only many agencies concerned with law enforcement, but also, for example, the State Department Agency for International Development, the U.S. Senate Permanent Subcommittee on Investigations, and the "Intelligence Division (Unions) of the U.S. Department of Labor."[55] In the field of security and intelligence, liaison was "maintained with a number of U.S. Agencies, and with Washington and New York based Intelligence groups."[56] The official attitude of the RCMP was summarized in the direction to officers in the field: "Personal liaison with U.S. Federal Agencies is to be developed and maintained at the local level wherever possible."[57]

The Canadian security services have depended heavily on their allied counterparts, and especially on the American security and intelligence agencies, for information, expert advice, and access to new technology. They have, in turn, been generous in their cooperation with their American friends in providing information that is available only in Canada. On many occasions this has involved the security services suggesting to foreign agencies that specific Canadians, including senior members of the federal public service, are involved in "subversive activities." This has often been done despite the subjects having no idea that they were even suspected of any kind of disloyalty.[58]

These widespread practices have a number of unfortunate consequences. The most obvious is that individual Canadians may suffer grievous harm, as the case of Herbert Norman demonstrated all too clearly. But even more serious for Canada as a whole is the distortion in our perception of the world that is bound to occur as a result of dependence on the secret agencies of another government for information and for interpretations of that information.

The McDonald Royal Commission on the RCMP was aware that the CSIS would face this danger; for the RCMP, it had been an important factor in the orientation of their Security Service over the years. The Royal Commission warned of "the risk of the security agency's becoming an appendage of foreign agencies, particularly in relation to those agencies from whom it borrows information frequently."[59] The various national agencies that make up the Western intelligence community are bound together, not only by formal and informal arrangements, but by shared attitudes that are in important ways distinct from those that prevail in the larger societies around them. This becomes particularly apparent when policy differences arise between the U.S. government and the governments of the other UKUSA partners. The McDonald Commission's warning was based on the most thorough investigation of this problem that has ever taken place in Canada. Like the UKUSA agreements, it meant far more than it stated.

7

Political Violence

"If seven maids with seven mops
Swept it for half a year,
Do you suppose," the Walrus said,
"That they could get it clear?"
"I doubt it," said the Carpenter,
And shed a bitter tear.

In the entire range of national security concerns, terrorism is the most widely publicized and one of the least understood. Because terrorist activity and its victims are so highly visible, it has become a subject that has enormous emotional and political impact. Protecting citizens from terrorism is a legitimate and in fact essential responsibility of governments. At the same time, however, because of its emotional power, the issue of terrorism can provide governments with a pretext for political activity that far exceeds the reality of the actual battle against terrorism. The propaganda, intelligence, and military offensives by the United States against Nicaragua, and against Libya in the spring of 1986, are typical examples of this kind of activity.

All of Canada was traumatized by the October Crisis of 1970, in which civil liberties were suspended under the *War Measures Act* in response to terrorist activities by the Front de Libération du Québec (FLQ). To most Canadians at the time, the kidnappings in Montreal of British Trade Commissioner James Cross and Quebec Labour Minister Pierre Laporte, following seven years of bombings and other crimes by the FLQ, seemed to justify the imposition of the *War Measures Act*. The detention of more than

400 citizens, most of whom were totally innocent, without warrants or other customary legal protection, seemed of little consequence compared to the unknown threat posed by the FLQ. In the atmosphere of the time, virtually any measures construed as being against the FLQ would have been accepted by the public. The atrocities committed by the FLQ were real enough.

But as the years have passed, the fact that three levels of government overreacted, as well as the public, the media, and the police, has become evident. It was not necessary to suspend the constitutional rights of all Canadians, arrest hundreds of innocent people, and create a situation of near panic in the country in order to resolve the crisis; indeed, the draconian measures probably contributed to the death of one of the two hostages.

In the 1980s, the atrocities committed by international terrorists are very real. Television viewers everywhere are familiar with the sickening images of helpless hostages held at gunpoint, burned-out airliners, and all too often, the mangled corpses of the innocent. The excruciating tension of the unfolding dramas of hi-jackings, bombings, and hostage-takings is communicated directly to every part of the globe. The victims of terrorists are ordinary human beings; almost anyone can identify readily with them. When cabinet ministers and generals are held hostage, they too are soon reduced by the circumstances to their essential humanity. Fear and revulsion at the actions of terrorists, no matter what cause they claim to be serving, are virtually universal. Measures that are intended to combat the scourge of terrorism are almost always welcomed widely; to be opposed to anti-terrorist measures would be politically disastrous in almost any country.

It is this aspect of the situation that holds potential dangers and the possibility of the misuse of powers. Whenever any cause acquires a status that places it above skepticism and questioning, there is bound to be enormous temptation to use it as a pretext for other, largely unrelated activities. During the October Crisis, both politicians and police exploited the situation to settle old scores that had nothing to do with the Cross and Laporte kidnappings. The present cycle of international terrorist brutality and public outrage has also created a situation in which governments are tempted to deal with other problems in the name of fighting international terrorism.

But terrorism is in fact different from other forms of political violence. If its unique characteristics are not understood, then it cannot be isolated and prevented from being repeated. Although Canada has been relatively free of the problem, it is nonetheless important that its nature be understood; a failure to understand it contributed to the national crisis that gripped Canada after the kidnappings by the terrorist FLQ in October 1970.

A good deal of the contemporary confusion about terrorism has arisen because of the imprecise statements about it on the part of political leaders in a number of countries. In some cases, this imprecision has been caused by carelessness; in others, it has been deliberate.

Terrorist incidents often involve the interests of the United States because of its global presence. This has prompted some members of the United States Congress to demand, after terrorist incidents, that the U.S. intelligence community be strengthened and the budgets of its member agencies increased. Former CIA Director James Schlesinger noted that terrorist activity has caused a dramatic shift in American public attitudes towards the Agency. "Just a short time ago, we were talking about the CIA as a rogue elephant whose wicked acts had to be reined in. Now," he said in 1985, "some say we must have a mechanism for inflicting punishment on America's foes."[1]

Terrorist actions have prompted members of the United States Congress to demand new resources for the intelligence community. Following one hostage crisis in the Middle East, for example, a Democratic senator from Texas called for a thirty per cent increase in the counter-terrorism budget of the CIA. The Reagan administration has urged the CIA to redouble its efforts to identify and locate terrorist groups. It has recognized that technical means of intelligence collection, such as SIGINT, are not well suited to the task of finding terrorists. As an alternative, the administration has called for strengthening human intelligence efforts.[2] It has also made extensive plans to deal with the problem militarily.

Their evident inability to suppress international terrorism causes leading members of the administration enormous frustration. President Reagan has referred to terrorists as "cowardly, skulking barbarians."[3] He has warned that "Terrorism must not be allowed to take control of the lives, actions, or futures of ourselves and our friends."[4] At issue, according to the President, is "freedom itself."[5] Secretary of State George Shultz has said that terrorism "threatens the very foundations of civilized life."[6]

Whatever their political goals may be, contemporary terrorists usually seek a platform from which to make their programmes and their grievances known to the world. The rhetorical response to them by the Reagan administration and some of the Western media has unhappily lent them the status of major actors on the world stage. The Secretary of Defense, Caspar W. Weinberger, stated in the summer of 1985 that the United States was engaged in "the beginning of a war" with Middle East terrorists.[7] Shortly after that, the President spoke of "acts of war against the government and people of the United States" being waged by "a confederation of terrorist states."[8]

This new "war" has a good deal of similarity to the more traditional cold war. It not only features the United States in a titanic struggle against an evil force, but when the mask is ripped off, the same familiar villain is revealed. The "confederation of terrorist states" that is said to be behind the terrorist conspiracies is in turn made up of "surrogates" of the Soviet Union. The implication that virtually all terrorist incidents are the result of the Soviets controlling and manipulating an "international terrorist network" has been advanced by right-wing journalists, writers, and "terrorism experts" for a number of years.

At his first press conference as Secretary of State of the newly elected Reagan administration, Alexander Haig claimed that the Soviet Union, as part of a deliberate policy, trained, equipped, and provided financial support to international terrorists. At the same time, the CIA was ordered to conduct a study and submit a report on the question of the relationship between the Soviet Union and international terrorism.[9] Alexander Haig was by no means the only member of the administration convinced that the Soviets were the controlling force behind the terrorist scourge. Secretary of Defense Caspar W. Weinberger has been one of the most consistently powerful and influential members of the Reagan cabinet. He has been a close associate of Reagan since the mid-1960s. He has presided over the greatest peacetime increase in defence spending in the history of the United States. Weinberger's Pentagon office is bigger than a good-sized ranch house, as befits a man who heads such an enormous empire. The decor is subdued, as is the persona of the Secretary himself. One is in fact just slightly taken aback that a man who is so personally unprepossessing controls such unimaginably vast destructive machinery. The Secretary is passionate in his denunciation of every aspect of the Soviet threat. He had occupied his blue and mahogany office for only two months when he allowed in a matter-of-fact way that the evidence of Soviet control of international terrorism is overwhelming.[10] Yet within a matter of weeks, the CIA's National Foreign Assessments Center produced a draft report that said there was not sufficient evidence to support the assertions of the administration and Secretary Haig. It concluded that such evidence was either "murky" or "non-existent." The report angered key figures in the government. Secretary of Defense Weinberger, for example, stated that any suggestion that the CIA had not agreed with the administration's claims about Soviet involvement would be very premature and "quite wrong." CIA Director William Casey returned the report to its authors and asked that they review their conclusions.[11]

Much of the controversy about the international terrorist conspiracies has arisen because of deliberate or careless imprecision in the use of the word "terrorist." In his rejection of the 1981 CIA report, Weinberger referred to "groups, that for want of a better term, can be called terrorist groups."[12] Four years later, as part of the Reagan administration's continuing attack on Nicaragua, Secretary of State George Shultz claimed that as a "brutal tyranny that respects no frontiers," the Sandinistas are, among other crimes, "linking up with the terrorists of Iran, Libya and the PLO, and seeking to undermine the legitimate and increasingly democratic governments of their neighbors." To underline the point, he went on to claim that it was "clear that the comandantes were bent on Communism not freedom, terror not reform, and aggression not peace."[13]

In the first cold war period, language was corrupted to create invidious equations among terms such as "radical" and "subversive," "Communist" and "spy." The process now under way leads to a similarly spurious confusion of words such as terrorism, national liberation, Communism, and aggression. As in the 1940s and 1950s, this verbal obfuscation causes complex historical realities to appear falsely simple. In the process, moral and political issues are blurred and distorted beyond recognition.

An additional consequence, ironically, is that those who commit these linguistic atrocities defeat their own purpose. The only serious possibility of ending actual terrorism lies in international co-operation. Such co-operation is out of the question as long as the word "terrorism" is used as a bludgeon against certain nations or groups of nations. It is irrational to expect widespread international co-operation in any effort to curb or eliminate terrorism when the word is used to describe more than a narrowly circum-scribed and precisely defined kind of activity.

Since the late 1960s terrorist groups have taken a fearsome toll in innocent human life. Hijackings, bombings, and kidnappings have traumatized countless individuals as well as disrupting local, national, and international communities. The vast majority of the world's people agree that the plague of terrorism must be ended.

Terrorism is taken here to mean the use of force against in-nocent persons to achieve a political end. Its victims are often randomly selected. Intimidation is seen by the terrorist as a means of coercing those who hold political power. This is accomplished in a number of ways: by holding hostages ransom for political demands, by selective political assassinations, by committing ran-dom shootings or bombings to frighten a whole population, or by simply threatening to commit acts of massive destruction.

These tactics are not the exclusive domain of the advocates of any one political ideology. They have been pursued extensively by extremists at both ends of the political spectrum. Attention has largely been directed at left-wing terrorism, but Fascists, neo-Nazis, and other groups on the extreme right have also been re-sponsible for a substantial number of terrorist acts. Political vio-lence, in fact, has been practised by the extreme right for decades. Fascist seizures of power in Germany and Italy, as well as in a number of other European countries, were accomplished by the widespread use of brutality and intimidation. Fascist groups have reappeared in Europe in recent years under names such as the Black Order, Year Zero, and the Mussolini action squads. Such groups have been responsible for some of the most destructive terrorist acts. The bombing of the railway station in Bologna, Italy, on August 1, 1980, took eighty-five lives. Responsibility for the massacre was claimed by a neo-Fascist group, the Armed Revo-lutionary Nuclei.[14]

At least one of the right-wing terrorists who was indicted (but not captured) in the Bologna bombing has also been implicated in large-scale drug smuggling, murder, and political collaboration with Nazi war criminal Klaus Barbie in South America.[15] It is possible that members of this group were also involved with Meh-met Ali Agca, the Turkish Fascist who was convicted of shooting and wounding Pope John Paul II in Rome in 1981.[16] The allegation that Agca had been acting on behalf of the Bulgarian and Soviet secret services was widely touted as proof that the international terrorist conspiracy and the international Communist conspiracy were one and the same. The case disintegrated when an Italian prosecutor called for the acquittal of three Bulgarian officials who had been on trial for conspiring with Agca in the assassination attempt.[17] The effort to build the case against the Bulgarians had been under way for several years. It had received a great deal of publicity and had served as the basis for several efforts to construct a theory of a world-wide, left-wing terrorist conspiracy.[18]

Numerous terrorist groups do claim to be acting in the name of left-wing ideology in the contemporary world. The Baader-Meinhof gang in West Germany, the Red Brigades in Italy, and the Provisional Wing of the Irish Republican Army are merely some of the better known among a much larger number of groups that conduct bombings, shootings, and kidnappings in the name of socialist revolution or national liberation, or both.

In the 1980s the Middle East is the source, although not always the location, of a great deal of terrorist activity. The complex history, tangled territorial claims and counter-claims, and prevalence of strong religious convictions have combined to turn the region into a political and social cauldron. Not only have Israelis and Palestinians battled one another with the desperation that is bred by a sense that national survival itself is at stake; moderate Arabs themselves are often the targets of Palestinian terrorists determined to prevent any non-violent political process from succeeding. This, together with the Israeli doctrine of massive reprisals for all terrorist acts, has led to a cycle of violence that not only threatens to engulf the Middle East region but presents a danger to the entire world.

Those who employ the tactics of terrorism share in common a cynicism about human nature and human society that is often the result of despair. Many advocates of terrorist tactics have been people who are inclined to hold an exaggerated view of the importance of the individual in history. Heroic or spectacular acts by individuals or small groups are regarded by them as having the potential to influence the course of history in the face of adverse factors. Moreover, such views often carry a heavy burden of moral absolutism: virtue is thought to reside in the act itself — or in the intention behind the act — rather than in its human consequences. Western standards of political rationality are often not applicable to terrorists motivated by religious fanaticism, in the same way that they could not be applied to the violent acts of the nineteenth-century nihilists.

Terrorism is part of a spectrum of political violence that ranges through armed resistance, guerrilla warfare, conventional warfare, and ultimately, in the modern world, nuclear war. It is easily distinguishable from full-blown warfare because of its much smaller scale, if not always for its different moral character. On the other hand, terrorism is frequently confused, either deliberately or through ignorance, with various other manifestations of political violence. In the context of cold war perceptions, terrorism is often regarded in the West as being virtually identical with revolutionary activity in general and Marxist politics in particular. This perception is enhanced by the fact that since the 1960s many terrorist groups have made use of the rhetoric of Marxism in attempting to explain and justify their actions. A number of groups have derided more humane approaches to left-wing politics and have claimed that their violent practices represent the only truly revolutionary activity.

The relationship between political violence and the state is central to any serious discussion of the nature of democracy. The subject of the cold war has a great deal to do with political violence on a massive scale. Fortunately that violence is threatened more often than it is realized.

The existence of security and intelligence establishments in most countries, including Canada, is justified by governments essentially on the basis that their primary purpose is to protect society from political violence. The democratic process involves continual change in society. In order to place terrorism in its proper context in relation to democracy and to the national security agencies, it is necessary to examine the wider phenomenon of revolutionary politics in relation to violence as well as the responses it evokes. It will then be possible to evaluate the extent to which Canadian democracy is endangered by both the threat of and the response to political violence in general, and terrorism in particular.

Few political subjects have caused greater confusion than has the relationship between Marxism and violence. The notion of a necessary connection between Marxism and terrorism is particularly widespread in the cold war context.

In both theory and practice terrorism has very little to do with Marxism. In fact, historically the terrorist obsession with violence and spectacular individual actions has most often been connected

116

with political currents such as anarchism and Fascism that are profoundly opposed to Marxism. The question of whether violent means are necessary to achieve a revolutionary transformation of society has, however, been a matter of serious disagreement among Marxist thinkers for the better part of a century. But this debate has had virtually nothing to do with terrorism. The central question has been whether fundamental social change can be accomplished within the constitutional framework of existing states or whether a popular uprising or insurrection is ultimately necessary. Both the constitutionalist and the insurrectionist currents within Marxism agree that the existence of a mass political movement is a necessary pre-condition for social change in any case. Building such a movement traditionally involves the creation of popular organizations with specific goals, engagement in articulating widely held grievances, and the dissemination of revolutionary ideas. The debate has to do with how these political organizations interact with the existing state.

The disagreement between constitutionalist and insurrectionist strategies centres on whether the state can accommodate the kind of political change that is being sought. Can a popular movement whose programmes are revolutionary (in the sense of intending to alter the nature of society fundamentally) proceed legally, or would the state resort to force in order to prevent it from achieving its ends? The question has frequently been debated in terms of the particular nature of a specific society. In the nineteenth century, for instance, Marx thought a peaceful revolution would be possible in countries such as Britain, Holland, and the United States because of their long-established traditions of constitutional democracy.[19]

On the other hand, the insurrectionist current in Marxist theory and in Communist practice developed in the early part of the twentieth century in societies where democracy was weak or non-existent, and in which there was virtually no possibility of revolutionary change within a constitutional framework. Russia, with its total lack of democratic tradition, was the most important case of this kind. Here too, though, Lenin's emphasis was on political organization. But the "vanguard" nature of the Bolshevik party emphasized a smaller, more disciplined organization that would lead the uprising and seize power from the Russian state. Although this strategy included the use of force, it did not envision acts of spectacular destruction meant to generate support or to lead to a

117

spontaneous uprising. In fact, both spontaneous action and isolated acts of violence, which had been commonplace in nineteenth-
century Russia, were looked upon disapprovingly by the Leninists.
In contrast, their position was that armed insurrection must involve a large number of people who would act in a disciplined
manner.

The fact that the first successful socialist revolution took place
in backward Russia added great weight, in the debate within Marxism, to the argument of the faction favouring insurrection. In the
period immediately after 1917, revolutionary stirrings occurred in
a number of European countries. Unsuccessful insurrections took
place in Germany, Austria, and Hungary. Lenin believed that
successful uprisings would occur rapidly in most of the industrialized world. Thus the politics of insurrection that are known as
"Leninism" became central to the formal ideology of most Communist parties. Not all Marxists, however, accepted this theoretical
development.[20]

By 1920 it was clear that Lenin had been wrong; armed insurrection was not on the agenda in the advanced countries. Stalin
used the rhetoric of Leninism to justify his own policies, which
in fact were principally concerned with establishing socialism in
one country — Russia. The policies of the Communist parties in
other countries in the Stalin period were directed in support of
this effort. The result was that these parties were for the most
part isolated from the mainstream of political life in their own
countries.

Faced with overwhelmingly strong governments and lacking a
significant base of support of their own, the Western Communist
parties were in no position to seriously attempt revolution by
insurrection. For the most part, they refrained from doing so, and
therefore in fact functioned as "reformist" parties, in spite of their
continuing use of the language of Leninism. On the rare occasions
when insurrection actually seemed possible in a liberal democratic
country, the Communists refrained from taking part. Thus, for
example, the large-scale uprising in Paris of May 1968 was not
supported by the French Communists. They denounced it as
"adventurist."[21]

Many other Marxists in Western countries have rejected the
Communist perspective for a variety of reasons. Some have criticized it as being too cautious. Others have rejected its support of
the Soviet Union. Today, the main currents of Western Marxist

thought are concerned with the problem of analysing historical development in a way that will lead to a theory of social change consistent with current political realities. This scarcely includes violent activity in liberal democracies.[22]

There has, nonetheless, been a great deal of armed revolutionary activity in the world since the 1920s. But it has not been of a terrorist nature. In Europe, the anti-Nazi resistance effort of World War Two represented a major insurrectionary struggle. In nearly every country the resistance was made up of a number of groups representing a range of political opinion. The international alliance between the Soviet Union and the Western countries was in some cases replicated in the resistance movements. In other cases there was bitter rivalry between left and right.[23]

Participation in the wartime resistance constituted the only major instance in which the orthodox Communist parties departed from their constitutionalist political strategies in liberal democratic countries after the 1930s. But of course the resistance was not against liberal democratic governments, but rather against the Nazi occupation regime that had usurped such governments.

The constitutionalist strategy of change within the existing legal framework of the state has not been duplicated in the many parts of the world governed by despotic regimes of one kind or another. In many such areas revolutionary struggles and national liberation movements have been conducted by means of guerrilla warfare. Like all warfare, it is extremely violent. Random acts of destruction are occasionally committed. But guerrilla warfare is fundamentally different from terrorism both in its political assumptions and in the way it is conducted.

The Chinese revolution took the form of a massive armed struggle that lasted from the early 1920s until 1949. The strategy upon which that guerrilla struggle was waged was fundamentally different from that of the Soviet and Western Communist parties. The Chinese Communist Party was based in the countryside; the great majority of its members were peasants. They made up a "people's army," which waged a guerrilla war, a war of resistance against the Japanese invaders in World War Two, and ultimately a full-scale civil war against the Chiang Kai Shek regime.

The practice of guerrilla warfare did not originate with Mao Tse Tung and the Chinese People's Liberation Army. But many people striving to free themselves from local oppression or foreign domination in other countries were undoubtedly influenced by certain aspects of the Chinese experience, and particularly by Mao's formulation of the principles of guerrilla warfare. Mao's writings on this subject stressed its political nature. According to Mao, the education, mobilization, and support of the people are the basic prerequisites for successful armed struggle. Military operations are important but are secondary to political considerations at all times. The military tactics described by Mao (and by other theorists of twentieth-century guerrilla warfare) are characterized by flexibility and by a determination to take full advantage of the unique characteristics of the terrain, both physical and social, on which the battle is being fought. The guerrilla army must respect the people, must never subject them to abuse, and indeed must embody their aspirations; otherwise it is bound to fail.[24]

Many guerrilla wars have been fought since 1945. Some guerrilla movements, such as those in Malaya and the Philippines in the 1950s, were defeated. But the victory of the Cuban revolution at the beginning of 1959 had far-reaching consequences. Fidel Castro's entry into Havana was the culmination of several years of guerrilla warfare in mountains and countryside. The rebel army had started as a group of a few dozen people in 1953. In spite of tactical defeats, it slowly drew the support of a great number of Cubans who wanted to be rid of the Batista dictatorship, and who came to share the belief that this could be accomplished only through force.

In the early 1960s armed insurgencies also began or were resumed in a number of other Third World countries. The defeat of the French Army in Algeria in 1962 represented a victory for a population that had waged a protracted battle against an occupying force. The Vietnamese also resumed their long-standing revolutionary effort by organizing the National Liberation Front in 1960.

These and similar developments helped inspire revolutionaries in other underdeveloped countries to build insurgent movements. But they also stirred apprehension in the developed world. Washington in particular was not long in devising plans to move against the new round of Third World unrest.

The operative assumption was not that people who had long suffered under oppressive political systems were struggling to find a way to free themselves, much as the Americans themselves had done two centuries earlier; Third World liberation movements were, instead, interpreted in a cold war context. They were seen as part of a direct Communist threat to the security of the United States itself. In early 1961 President John F. Kennedy asserted that "The message of Cuba, of Laos, of the rising din of Communist voices in Asia and Latin America — these messages are all the same ... that our security may be lost piece by piece, country by country, without the firing of a single missile or the crossing of a single border."[25]

The counter-insurgency plan devised by the United States was based on an evident appreciation of the principles of guerrilla warfare set out by Mao Tse Tung and other revolutionary theorists. It recognized that guerrilla warfare is essentially a form of political struggle, and that the success or failure of a guerrilla army depends heavily on the extent to which it is able to generate popular support. According to Robert McNamara, Secretary of Defense in the Kennedy administration, the purpose was "to provide the means for local military establishments, with the support and co-operation of local populations, to guard against external covert intrusions and internal subversion designed to create dissidence and insurrection."[26]

The main focus of the counter-insurgency programme was on isolating the guerrilla forces from the general population. Implicitly recognizing the difficulty of accomplishing this when the insurgents were part of the indigenous population, the strategy of "resettlement" was employed. United States military planners were aware of historical precedents for taking rural populations into custody to "protect" them from insurgent forces. During World War Two the occupying Japanese Army had used this technique against the resistance in central China in what it called the "Rural Purification Movement."[27] A resettlement plan had been used against rural guerrillas in the Philippines in the 1950s, and in Malaya against the Chinese-backed Communist insurgents.[28]

American planners in the early 1960s were aware of the delicate nature of resettlement operations. For example, one military writer counselled that the population should be convinced to give up their homes through "speeches and patient discussion," but as that might not work,

> it will be wise literally to capture the audience for this briefing and then immediately follow up with the implementation of the program. The reason is that if advance notice is given, many inhabitants in these villages will be gone when the gov-

ernment officials arrive. They will hide in the forest until the operation is completed and then will return to rebuild a home on their ancestral land.[29]

The writer recognized that "the removal of peasants from their traditional home sites and the destruction of their dwellings [so the guerrillas cannot use them] automatically cause these people to experience serious social and physical stresses." But for every problem there is a solution. In this case he pointed out that "It is important that the government's project team include medical personnel and social workers to assist the people in solving personal problems raised by the resettlement process."[30]

Resettlement, "psychological warfare," and other related techniques of attempting to separate rural populations from guerrilla forces were widely applied in the Third World in the 1960s. Much as Secretary McNamara had promised, the medium through which American counter-insurgency warfare techniques were applied was usually the local military establishment. In several Latin American countries the local military forces were able to thwart revolutionary movements with the help of U.S. advisors, training, equipment, and funds. One of the consequences of this strategy was that traditionally powerful military influence on the political life of Latin American countries was further enhanced. The military assistance programme so weakened the civil political structure in many countries that it simply could not survive. Governments that were formally democratic were replaced by military dictatorships in Brazil in 1964, in Argentina in 1966, in Peru in 1968, and in both Chile and Uruguay in 1973. During the same period military influence was also greatly increased in Venezuela, Colombia, Bolivia, and most of the Central American countries. In most cases the threat of "subversion" and "Communist aggression" was the pretext for limiting or abolishing democratic institutions. Instead of democracy being strengthened by the military, as Robert McNamara had declared, it was destroyed. The widespread Latin American military view that "politics" must be ended in the name of authority, order, and national security was put into practice with fearsome consequences not only for revolutionaries but for entire populations.[31]

Counter-insurgency doctrine was applied on a massive scale in Vietnam in the 1960s. An elaborate "pacification" strategy was developed in the early 1960s. The United States military supplied advisors as well as massive quantities of arms and material to the South Vietnamese government. The United States Agency for International Development dispensed economic assistance and political advice to Saigon. The United States Information Agency developed programmes designed to undermine and discredit the insurgent National Liberation Front. The CIA was extremely active not only in collecting intelligence but in training and advising the South Vietnamese police and military forces in such arts as prisoner interrogation and security procedures.[32]

Hundreds of thousands of villagers were resettled in strategic hamlets in an effort to isolate them from their fellow countrymen, the Viet Cong. Massive firepower was then brought to bear on the countryside on the assumption that anyone remaining there was by definition "the enemy." By 1964 it was clear that the Saigon government could not successfully prosecute the war even with substantial American assistance and advice. During the following seven years the United States military waged a full-scale war of attrition against the insurgent National Liberation Front and its North Vietnamese allies. Attempts at "Vietnamization" — replacing United States troops with friendly Vietnamese — were futile. American forces were withdrawn in 1972; the Saigon government fell three years later.[33]

The problem was with the fundamental assumption of counterinsurgency warfare: that the struggle of a determined people to free itself from an oppressive regime can be blocked by foreign military and political intervention. The notion that a morally and politically bankrupt government can be propped up and reformed through such intervention is grievously mistaken. This conundrum has been recognized by United States military commentators, one of whom has elegantly summarized it by observing that:

> Withholding U.S. aid from the South Vietnamese in exchange for reform or a purge of corrupt officials pointed to an inherent dilemma of leverage and pacification. Withholding aid could be self-defeating because it would give the Communists an opportunity to strike at our weakened ally. Forcing the South Vietnamese government to reform could jeopardize its own interests, because swiftly and vigorously pursuing social justice might influence the very politics and social structure supporting the government. If U.S. policy was to promote security before reform, there was a danger that the government elite

would have no incentive to reform. If the United States insisted on reform first, it was possible that the government might fall from internal conflict.[34]

Despite such stark recognition of the "inherent dilemmas" of supporting corrupt and unpopular governments, the practice has continued. The United States military has, however, been very reluctant to engage in foreign hostilities on anything like the scale of the Vietnam war.

The defeat of the Saigon government was not the only victory for a Third World national liberation movement in the 1970s. The pro-American governments of neighbouring Cambodia and Laos fell to Communist insurgents almost simultaneously with the fall of Saigon. Guerrilla armies defeated Portuguese colonial forces in five African nations between September 1974 and November 1975. The Shah of Iran was deposed in February 1979. A month later the left-wing government led by Maurice Bishop took power in Grenada. The Somoza dictatorship in Nicaragua was deposed in July 1979. In April 1980 the guerrilla movement led by Robert Mugabe was formally recognized as the government of independent Zimbabwe.[35]

A good number of United States military officers understand that most conflicts in Third World countries occur fundamentally because of social conditions in those countries. This is particularly true of the many officers who had direct experience of the war in Vietnam. This understanding of the essentially futile nature of the American effort in Vietnam has contributed towards a reluctance to commit United States forces in other similar situations. Ironically, to some extent the Pentagon has acted as a restraint on the more ideologically motivated civilians in the Reagan administration.

However, like President Reagan, Secretary of State Shultz, and Defense Secretary Weinberger, some American military officers persist in regarding Third World conflicts as functions of the cold war contest between the United States and the Soviet Union. In reference to the Sandinista victory in Nicaragua, for example, one United States Army analyst explained that "Castro has finally convinced Moscow that revolution in Central America is possible without waiting for *all* objective conditions to exist."[36]

The same assessment has been made at the highest levels of the Reagan administration. Emphasis has been placed on strengthening and expanding U.S. military Special Operations Forces (SOF).

These are specifically trained to engage in guerrilla warfare, covert operations, and counter-terrorism. Between 1981 and 1985 the funds allocated to such forces increased by more than 300 per cent. The number of Special Operations troops increased by thirty per cent in the same period.[37] In justifying this increased capability for military intervention, Secretary of Defense Caspar W. Weinberger has explained that "The high priority we have assigned to SOF revitalization reflects our recognition that low-level conflict — for which SOF are uniquely suited — will pose the threat we are most likely to encounter throughout the end of this century."[38]

The term "low-intensity conflict" has replaced "counter-insurgency" in current military usage, as it is apparently considered to be less controversial and have fewer unpleasant connotations from the past.[39] The proponents of a doctrine that emphasizes low-intensity conflict argue that the United States must be capable of intervening militarily anywhere in the world because of the inherent nature of the Soviet Union and its political system. "Because they believe that it is their historical and ideological duty to resist imperialism and support Marxism-Leninism," according to one military analyst, Colonel James B. Motley, "Soviet leaders will continue to use military force, directly and indirectly, to advance policies aimed at the disruption of international order, fomenting destabilization and revolutionary conditions worldwide."

Because the Soviet Union is behind such political developments around the world, Motley argues the United States should prepare to

> better influence politico-military outcomes in the resource-rich and strategically located Third World areas. This global approach will mean shifting some resources and program emphasis from the short, intensive European war scenario to power projection and Third World intervention capabilities while continuing and, in some instances, increasing security assistance and arms transfers to critical allies and Third World countries.

This is necessary because "The expanded threat confronting the United States extends across a full spectrum of conflict ranging from terrorism and unconventional warfare, through minor and major conventional war to, ultimately, the risk of theatre and strategic nuclear war."[40]

The large-scale preparations for low-intensity conflict are justified by a set of assumptions that are not new. The idea that civil unrest and revolutionary upheavals around the world are caused by Soviet manipulation rather than by unique sets of social, political, and economic factors in each country represents a reassertion of the traditional cold war view of history. The suggestion of a political equation among all forms of violence, from terrorism to nuclear war, because they all threaten the United States, implies an unfortunate inability to comprehend the complex nature of the contemporary world.

The theorists of counter-insurgency in the 1960s recognized that revolutionary warfare, whatever tactics it may employ, is essentially political in nature. The doctrine failed in Vietnam because it was combined with a war of attrition, and because the solution to the political problems of one country can ultimately never be solved by intervention from abroad. The new version of counter-insurgency warfare has dropped the previous recognition of the political dimension of revolution in favour of a single-minded emphasis on a military answer to all challenges.

In a characteristically forthright way, the conservative United States military expert Edward N. Luttwak has asserted that "the United States must stand ready to resist aggression even though the interests thereby affirmed can scarcely be deemed 'vital' except in the rarest cases. A protective quasi-global empire cannot merely fight when 'vital' interests are at stake." If this obligation is rejected, he points out, "then in logic one can no longer claim an imperial-sized budget for the armed services, whose quasi-global scope must then be a mere facade, dangerously deceptive to all concerned."[41]

Luttwak approves of the American "quasi-global empire." His interest is in making it more effective, and his main criticism is that the orientation of the United States military has always been towards fighting wars of attrition: bringing into play advanced technology and massive destructive power. Such military forces, he argues, "tend to be focused on their own internal administration and operations, being correspondingly less responsive to the external environment comprising the enemy, the terrain, and the specific phenomena of any one particular conflict."[42]

This set of attributes is well adapted to a world seen through the prism of the cold war. If the apparently bewildering array of threats and problems in the contemporary world is simply a variety of tactics deployed by one enemy, then the distinctions between one country and another, or between guerrilla warfare and terrorism do not matter a great deal.

But in fact terrorism is fundamentally different from other forms of political violence. The Chinese revolution, the Vietnam war, and other similar events have demonstrated that guerrilla armies succeed only when they have the political support of a very large number of people. Guerrilla failures such as that in Malaya in 1951 and the defeat of Che Guevara in Bolivia in 1967 support the same point. Those national liberation movements that have adopted terrorism as their primary tactic have been weak and have failed. Terrorism is an inherently unpopular activity. No significant group of people approves for very long the random victimization of the innocent, no matter in what cause it is supposedly being done.

In the practice of terrorism, the distinction between left and right becomes meaningless; it can lead neither to the building of a mass movement nor to any form of democratic politics. Despite its rhetoric, "left-wing" terrorism is a grotesque parody of revolutionary activity. Unlike the guerrilla army, the terrorist group attempts to intimidate the population through fear rather than seeking to work with it and be part of it. The rationalization for this approach has taken a number of forms. Some have argued that the increased police and military activity that is provoked by violent acts will cause widespread resentment and rally popular support to the cause of the terrorists.

The work of Carlos Marighella, a Brazilian theorist of terrorism, had considerable impact on the development of American and European terrorist groups in the 1960s and early 1970s. He argued that the actions he advocated would mean that "The government has no alternative except to intensify repression. The police networks, house searches, arrests of innocent people and of suspects, closing off streets, make life in the city unbearable." This would result, he claimed, in a situation in which "The people refuse to collaborate with the authorities, and the general sentiment is that the government is unjust, incapable of solving problems, and resorts purely and simply to the physical liquidation of its opponents."[43]

In practice, of course, terrorism has had the opposite effect. Police and military repression have often been effective. In most cases the majority of the people have deplored terrorist actions, and the terrorists themselves have been isolated. In spite of their subjective identification as leftist revolutionaries, terrorists have tended to weaken the cause for which they profess to fight. More-over, in their emphasis on the importance of spectacular individual acts and their devaluation of democratic opinion, they share a good deal with terrorists whose motivations arise out of nihilism or religious fanaticism.

In the final analysis, terrorism, like every other political phe-nomenon, emerges from the historical circumstances in which individuals find themselves. However unpopular, deluded, and brutal terrorist acts may be, they do reveal other ways of seeing the world. If the explanations for terrorist phenomena are distorted to conform to a rigid set of political preconceptions or to an ar-tificially constructed conspiracy theory, then the realities out of which they spring will not be understood.

The attempt to integrate and identify terrorism with the cold war paradigm of global competition and conflict between the su-perpowers is bound to be simplistic and misleading. Certain states (Iran and Libya top the list of suspects) undoubtedly do harbour international terrorists and support them with arms and money. Some of those states in turn acquire military equipment from the Soviet Union or other Communist bloc nations, as well as from other countries. International traffic in arms is so widespread that the relatively simple weapons in the terrorist arsenal can be ac-quired by almost any determined group from a number of sources. Terrorists, mercenaries, and international criminals all make use of these black-market sources.

The complex geopolitical reality of the contemporary world involves relationships of various kinds between the superpowers. It also includes relationships between them and a large number of other states, some of which are clients and others of which are autonomous. Relations are also conducted with political move-ments in the smaller states. These other states in turn have a multiplicity of relationships amongst themselves, each pursuing its own political interests. Most of these inter-relationships are conducted through such familiar modes as trade, commerce, and diplomacy. A smaller number of international transactions are clandestine. In the context of intricate world-wide interrelations, myriad interests are pursued. Some are complementary; some are in direct conflict; most fall somewhere in between. In spite of its deadliness, international terrorism represents only a tiny fraction of this global activity. It can be defeated only if it is isolated. That can not be accomplished with sweeping generalizations and inducements to hysteria; it is more likely to be achieved through explicit recognition of how it differs from other forms of political activity.

International terrorist groups have not been active on a large scale within either the United States or Canada. But in the late 1960s and early 1970s the United States suffered an appalling spasm of politically motivated bombing, arson, and shootings. One contemporary estimate placed the number of such incidents perpetrated by self-styled revolutionaries at 503 in 1969 and 546 in 1970.[44]

During the 1960s massive protest movements against participation in the Vietnam war had developed in the United States. The main organizational focus for this activity was Students for a Democratic Society (SDS), which specifically advocated non-violent tactics. But as the intensity of the war and the magnitude of the protest against it increased, violent confrontations between young people and police inevitably occurred. The Democratic Party convention in Chicago in 1968 provided an occasion for large protests in which scores were injured and hundreds of youths were arrested. The members of SDS soon fell to bitter dispute over the kinds of tactics that should subsequently be employed. The result was the breakup of the organization and the emergence of a number of rigidly dogmatic factions. One of these, the Weather Underground, specifically advocated violent political activity in the form of bombings, arson, and assaults on police personnel. In theory, this was supposed to lead to an upsurge in revolutionary activity by growing numbers of Americans. In practice, it resulted in deaths, injuries, and widespread property damage, along with the total isolation and destruction of the terrorist groups and their supporters.

During the 1960s the Student Union for Peace Action (SUPA) had emerged in Canada as an organization whose purposes and strategies were quite similar to those of the SDS in the United States. SUPA too dissolved at the end of the decade. Some of its veterans joined the government-sponsored Company of Young Canadians to continue their efforts towards organizing the socially disadvantaged. Others became active in the more conventional politics of the NDP and its left-wing Waffle movement. A small number joined dogmatically sectarian left-wing groups. But no organization even remotely similar to the Weather Underground developed in anglophone Canada. The gun and the bomb did not hold the same attraction for youthful Canadians at the end of the turbulent 1960s that they did for a relatively small but nonetheless potent number of their American counterparts. The fact that Canadian society was not bitterly polarized by involvement in a distant and morally repellent war undoubtedly represented an important difference. Canadian society has also tended to display a greater inclination to avoid violence in general, as is evident in such indices as the homicide rate in comparable urban areas, or in the Canadian willingness to accept gun-control legislation.

This relatively tranquil pattern did not apply in Quebec during the 1960s. The October Crisis was a major event in the recent history of Canada. The crisis had been preceded by seven years of sporadic terrorist activity by the Front de Libération du Québec (FLQ). The 1970 kidnappings and the strong reaction they provoked from the federal government set in motion events that had far-reaching implications for internal security policy in Canada.

On October 16, 1970, the day the *War Measures Act* was put in force by the government of Canada, Justice Minister John Turner stated, "It is my hope that some day the full details of the intelligence upon which the government acted can be made public, because until that day comes the people of Canada will not be able fully to appreciate the course of action which has been taken by the government."[45] Six days later Mr. Turner said that "it might not ever be possible to disclose to the public the information on which the government made its decision."

The kidnapping of British Trade Commissioner James Cross in Montreal on October 5, 1970, and of Quebec Labour Minister Pierre Laporte in a Montreal suburb five days later took the RCMP and the federal government by surprise. The *War Measures Act* was imposed on the grounds that a state of "apprehended insurrection" existed in Quebec. On October 18 the body of Pierre Laporte was discovered in the trunk of a car parked near the St. Hubert Canadian Armed Forces Base outside Montreal. It was not until December 3 that James Cross was located and set free. The members of the "Chenier cell" of the FLQ that had murdered Pierre Laporte were finally arrested on December 28, almost three months after the beginning of the crisis.

The federal government did not have an adequate base of intelligence on which to make its decisions in managing the crisis. It is astonishing (as it was in 1970) that the civil liberties of all

Canadians had to be suspended, several thousand troops deployed and many thousands of homes raided over a period of more than two months before James Cross could be found and the kidnappers of Pierre Laporte arrested.

The lack of reliable intelligence on the FLQ in the fall of 1970 contributed to a situation in which rumours became more dramatic every day. Federal cabinet ministers were unable to make statements that might have clarified the situation and restored calm. Indeed, some ministerial remarks had the effect of compounding a widespread sense of panic in the country. Politicians at each level of government conjured up visions of conspiracies to justify their use of the *War Measures Act*. In retrospect, it is difficult to believe that all the politicians believed what they were saying. But the atmosphere in the country at the time encouraged credulousness.

Jean Marchand, the Minister of Regional Economic Expansion, claimed that people in the rest of Canada could not possibly know the gravity of the Quebec situation. The day the *War Measures Act* was invoked, Marchand claimed that there were 3,000 armed FLQ terrorists in Quebec. He warned that "those who are well protected behind the Rockies or even in the centre of Toronto don't know what is happening in Quebec right now." He was sure that conspirators had "infiltrated all the vital places of the province of Quebec, in all the key posts where important decisions are taken." There were at least two tons of explosives, thousands of rifles and machine guns and bombs, according to Marchand. "For whoever knows the FLQ right now, whoever knows this organization well cannot do otherwise than recognize that the provincial state of Quebec and the federal state are really in danger in Canada."[46]

On the same day as Jean Marchand made this statement, Justice Minister John Turner told the House of Commons that "they will stop at nothing to subvert democratic government in this country. While their prime target today may be the Government of Quebec there is every reason to assume — indeed I think there are many clear indications — that other governments and indeed the central government of this country fall within the purview of their efforts."[47]

The danger posed by the FLQ was soon supplemented in the statements of federal Liberals by what was claimed to be imminent danger of a *coup d'état* in Quebec. On October 14, a group of prominent citizens, including René Lévesque, Claude Ryan, and the leaders of the three major labour federations in Quebec, issued

131

a statement calling upon the provincial government to accede to some of the demands of the FLQ and thereby defuse the crisis. Some members of this loosely knit group within the Quebec elite held discussions with Premier Robert Bourassa in an effort to bolster his faltering government. They were concerned to avoid any pretext for federal intervention.

On October 26, the *Toronto Star* ran a front-page unsigned article claiming that a group of leading Québécois had been planning a coup against the Bourassa government and that this had been the real reason for the imposition of the *War Measures Act*.[48] Subsequently, on October 30, Prime Minister Trudeau charged that an attempt had been made to form a "provisional government" in Quebec in the preceding weeks. The conspirators, he claimed, had been Claude Ryan and other signatories of the October 14 statement that had called for concessions to be made to the FLQ.[49]

That such assertions could have been made by Canada's top political leadership suggests an appalling lack of understanding of what was taking place in Quebec. The key members of the Cabinet who were making decisions and public statements must have had little confidence in whatever information was given to them. In the years since the October Crisis, no evidence has been revealed to support the wild claims made by cabinet ministers during the crisis. Indeed, senior public servants who were in the Privy Council Office during the October Crisis have stated that neither they nor the senior members of the Cabinet had any precise knowledge of the organizational structure, strength, or intentions of the FLQ. Decisions were being made on the basis of guesses, which often as not were wide of the mark.[50]

There is no question that the FLQ was a troublesome phenomenon from 1963 to 1970. The two kidnappings in October 1970 presented a difficult situation for the federal and Quebec governments and for the various police forces. However, there was never the remotest possibility of a seizure of state power by the FLQ.

The stated fear, by the politicians, of a *coup d'état* was bizarre but revealing. The claim for the existence of such a plot had no basis in fact. United States military expert Edward Luttwak, in his study on the coup, defines the phenomenon as "the infiltration of a small but critical segment of the state apparatus, which is then used to displace the government from its control of the remainder."[51] Although discussions of the idea of forming a provisional government of "national unity" apparently did take place between Bourassa and Ryan at the height of the October Crisis, this would hardly qualify as evidence of clandestine infiltration of the state apparatus, as the Premier himself was one of the "plotters." Moreover, it is hardly possible for a coup to occur in a provincial government in a federal system. Actual power cannot be seized if the major locus of political power and legitimacy resides in the federal capital.

The events of October 1970 became a national crisis for two principal reasons. First, none of the three levels of government involved had sufficient intelligence upon which to evaluate the situation properly. Second, exaggerated assumptions about the nature and capability of the FLQ were made, and quickly led to a state of virtual panic on the part of some political leaders. Ironically, this was caused to a great extent by governments taking a number of bravado-filled statements made by the FLQ itself literally. The federal government suffered not only from a shortage of raw information, but also from an appalling inability to analyse and assess the data it did have properly. The sledgehammer of the *War Measures Act* enabled the police forces to detain and question anyone they chose and to search any premises. What they lacked in skill and insight they made up for in sheer scale of operations. The operation was, in a sense, like a war of attrition. This approach to the problem of the FLQ was continued for several years after 1970. The excesses that were committed by the RCMP Security Service in this period were the principal factor that led to the establishment of the McDonald Royal Commission in 1977.

One of the fundamental weaknesses of the Security Service was an institutional culture that was so imbued with the primacy of the "Communist" or "Soviet" threat that it was largely incapable of finding an appropriate means of comprehending the social and political changes that occurred during the 1960s and early 1970s. This failure led, in the words of Pierre Trudeau, to the government's directing the Security Service "to pay a little more attention to internal subversion caused by ideological sources in Canada and not only concentrate on externally-sponsored types of subversion.... They did not have inside information on the terrorists."[52] The result was the expansion of a clumsy and wide-ranging hunt for and harassment of "subversives." Among the targets were not only terrorists, but political parties, anti-war groups, trade unions, and many individual Canadians who were involved in perfectly legitimate political activity. The exposure of these activities and the public indignation they caused led ultimately to the dissolution of the RCMP Security Service. The process of reform began in the mid-1970s. It was a period in which Canada was free of terrorist activity, and at the international level cold war tensions were at their lowest point. It was a uniquely propitious time for the conduct of the Security Service to be subjected to the political will of the country.

8

The Reform of the Security Service

But four young Oysters hurried up,
All eager for the treat:
Their coats were brushed, their faces washed,
Their shoes were clean and neat —
And this was odd, because, you know,
They hadn't any feet.

T he *Canadian Security Intelligence Service Act* was the last substantial piece of legislation enacted by the government of Pierre Trudeau. Its proclamation into law by the Governor General took place only hours before Trudeau's resignation on June 30, 1984. Although he rarely spoke about it in public, Bill C-9 had been a matter of much interest to Trudeau. He was keenly interested in seeing it through the Cabinet, the Liberal Caucus, and Parliament during his final months as Prime Minister. The reform of the Security Service and its relationship to government was the most important matter of public policy that Trudeau wished to deal with before retiring from politics.[1]

During his sixteen years as Prime Minister, Trudeau had seldom displayed much interest in security and intelligence matters; generally, he appeared to deal with such matters only when forced to do so by circumstances. In reality, however, Trudeau had a serious appreciation of the potential power of the security and intelligence services either to support government objectives or subtly to obstruct them.

Trudeau had been interested in the state's role in the repression of the rights of citizens long before he became Prime Minister. His own battles against the authoritarian Duplessis government in Quebec in the 1940s and 1950s undoubtedly made him aware of the potential for oppression inherent in political police forces. Much of his writing from the Duplessis period is concerned with the dangers posed by unfettered state power.

The need to separate the security service from the RCMP had been recognized by some people in the federal government since the 1950s. In 1955 Mark McClung, at the time a civilian employee of the RCMP, had prepared a massive report that argued in favour of civilianization, but it had been rejected by the RCMP Commissioner of the day, Leonard H. Nicholson.[2] The Commissioner, like several of his successors, saw no reason why policemen could not hunt subversives as well as they could hunt ordinary criminals.[3]

By the time he became Prime Minister in 1968, Trudeau appreciated the need to reform the Security Service. He was familiar with the arguments that the internal security of the country could be undertaken more effectively by specially recruited and trained civilians than by the police. Moreover, he also knew of the special relations between the RCMP and its American and British counterparts, which at times tended to raise doubts about the ability of the government of Canada to be fully informed and in complete control of security and intelligence operations on Canadian territory.

The new Prime Minister undoubtedly was aware of the lingering suspicion with which his predecessor, Lester Pearson, was regarded by the more extreme elements in the Western intelligence community. The witch-hunting of the McCarran subcommittee was receding into obscurity. Nevertheless, in their continuing effort to trace what they believed were the most deeply buried possibilities of high-level treachery, the zealots of counter-intelligence had kept their files on political leaders open. What history had determined to be reckless scandal-mongering by United States congressional committees in the 1950s was thus secretly kept alive long afterwards in the institutional memories of the CIA Counterintelligence Division and the RCMP Security and Intelligence Branch.

Elements within these agencies had also maintained an interest in Trudeau himself for some time. Many of his attitudes and interests would have been categorized as "subversive" by the conventional standards of the intelligence community. His battles on behalf of striking workers, criticisms of police power, visits to Communist countries long before such excursions became fashionable, and attacks on U.S. meddling in Canadian politics, were sufficient to arouse the interest of those whose job is to watch out for subversion.[4] Indeed, for a time Trudeau had been barred from entering the United States on the grounds of being an alleged "security risk."

When Trudeau became Prime Minister in June 1968, a Royal Commission had been reviewing the Canadian internal security policies and practices for more than two years. On March 7, 1966, a Royal Commission, headed by Maxwell W. MacKenzie and including Yves Pratte and M.J. Coldwell, had been mandated by Lester Pearson to "make a full and confidential inquiry into the operation of Canadian security methods and procedures."[5] The Commission submitted its report in October 1968, just four months after Trudeau became Prime Minister. Its key recommendation was for "the establishment of a new civilian non-police agency to perform the functions of a security service in Canada. This agency should eventually be quite separate from the RCMP."[6] The recommendation was based mainly on the argument that a civilian organization would be more effective than the RCMP in coping with the security and intelligence functions that had traditionally been the responsibility of the RCMP. The Commission emphasized that police responsibilities and security functions are quite different. Collecting evidence for use in a criminal prosecution is not at all like collecting intelligence for purposes that are ultimately political in nature. The Commissioners pointed out that security work requires "imagination, tact, high professional standards and complex decision-making." They found it difficult to believe that "officers with the background and training of those in the RCMP will be able to meet the increasingly complex challenges in the field of security that are to be expected in the future."[7] The RCMP high command was outraged by the suggestion and lost no time in denouncing it. The head of the RCMP Security and Intelligence Branch, W.L. Higgitt, claimed that a civilian security service would be "a travesty of justice" and that "the Soviet intelligence would be jubilant. They could never hope to duplicate the accomplishment."[8]

The RCMP high command insisted that the recommendations concerning the Security Service not be published at all, because, they argued, it would result in severe damage to the Canadian security community. The Cabinet Committee on Security and Intelligence did seriously consider not publishing even an abridged version of the MacKenzie Report. Eventually, however, on June 26, 1969, an edited version was tabled in the House of Commons.

The resistance of the RCMP and the Western intelligence community was so determined that Prime Minister Trudeau backed down on the question of separating the Security Service from the RCMP. It would be more than a decade until the next opportunity to reform the Security Service would arise. Trudeau offered the compromise that the Security Service would remain within the RCMP organization but would become "increasingly separate in structure and civilian in nature."[9] Within a year, John Starnes, a veteran diplomat with wide experience in security and intelligence matters, was appointed first civilian Director-General of the RCMP Security Service. John Starnes has the urbane demeanour of the professional diplomat that he is. The opinions he expresses tend to be understated and conservative. Even the most hard-nosed veterans of the cold war in the RCMP would not have been able to find the slightest fault with his anti-Communist credentials. Starnes spared little effort in attempting to fulfill the Prime Minister's mandate to alter the paramilitary nature of the Security Service. He did succeed in increasing the number of civilian employees in the organization. But ultimately his efforts were thwarted by the entrenched power of the RCMP, and John Starnes resigned in quiet frustration in 1973. Apart from the Starnes appointment, Trudeau's promise, as well as MacKenzie's principal recommendation, were to be largely unrealized.[10]

By 1981, when the McDonald Royal Commission issued its final massive report on RCMP wrongdoing, opinion on the issue of civilianization, or "separation" as it was called, had changed. The move was opposed by many officers in the RCMP and their friends in the international intelligence community. Elements in the hard-line, pro-cold-war faction tended to be particularly supportive of the Mounties. James Angleton, the ex-CIA Counterintelligence Chief, for example, argued that a civilian Security Service would be a boon to the Soviets. He asserted that the great advantage of a Security Service made up of policemen was that its members' political loyalty would be thoroughly tested through their years of hard work in law enforcement.[11]

Many of the more astute officers in the Security Service, however, recognized that the establishment of a civilian agency was inevitable. They were determined to ensure that it be designed to function in the most effective way possible.

The work and the recommendations of the McDonald Royal

Commission constituted a truly significant event in the history of Canadian democracy and Canadian independence. One of the hoariest truths in Canadian political life is that Royal Commissions are often devices used by governments to dispose of inconvenient controversies. This motive might have played some part in the decision to establish the McDonald Commission, but it was done at a uniquely opportune time for a major reform of the Security Service. East-West *détente* was still intact; the Watergate scandals were fresh in the minds of Canadians and had created a relatively high level of awareness of the dangers to democracy posed by uncontrolled or irresponsibly used security and intelligence agencies; the American agencies themselves were on the defensive as the Carter administration attempted to restrict their activities and impose various reforms. Moreover, the late 1970s were marked by an increasingly strong assertion of Canadian independence in most aspects of public life. And, in a relatively relaxed international atmosphere, it becomes more difficult for liberal democratic states to find plausible justification for a severe attitude towards political dissent. In civil society there is less willingness in such periods to accept the proposition that dissent is tantamount to subversion than in times when there is widespread fear of open conflict with foreign powers. The convergence of these related factors was vital in creating a context in which it was possible for reforms to be made in the intelligence services of a number of countries.

During its four years of work, the McDonald Royal Commission was not limited to investigating incidents of wrongdoing by the Security Service. It considered the fundamental questions of the role, structure, and function of security and intelligence agencies in the context of liberal democracies. The massive reports of the McDonald Royal Commission reflect a deeply held concern for those liberal democratic values. They contain little cold war posturing.

The present Canadian Security Intelligence Service (CSIS) arose directly out of the work of the McDonald Commission. The *Canadian Security Intelligence Service Act* went through several stages of drafting. The first version of the act, known as Bill C-157, was not well received. It was withdrawn, and was replaced by Bill C-9. The final proclamation of the *CSIS Act* on July 16, 1984, was achieved after much manoeuvring, debate, and rewriting had taken place.

The Royal Commission of Inquiry Concerning Certain Activities of the RCMP was established in July 1977 by the Trudeau government in response to the rapidly growing number of revelations about scandalous and apparently improper and illegal activities by members of the RCMP Security Service during the early 1970s. These actions had taken place mainly in Quebec, and had been part of a concerted effort to combat the Front de Libération du Québec (FLQ) in the wake of the October Crisis of 1970. Unease inside the Security Service and among its critics grew after the first suggestion of scandal was made in March 1976, in a Montreal courtroom. Robert Samson, a former RCMP constable facing criminal proceedings arising out of the bombing of a private home two years previously, made the remark that he had done much worse things in the line of duty.[12]

The inquiry was headed by Justice David McDonald of the Alberta Supreme Court. His fellow commissioners were Guy Gilbert, a Montreal lawyer, and Donald Rickerd, President of the Donner Canadian Foundation. Formal hearings were started in December 1977. One hundred and forty-nine witnesses were heard and 805 items exhibited during 333 days of hearings. The final reports of the McDonald Commission are in five volumes and run to 1,784 pages. The picture of the RCMP that emerged in the reports was of an organization that was rigid and authoritarian in its internal management and its attitude towards the public. The McDonald Commission found that the RCMP Security Service had been routinely conducting illegal operations for decades.

When the federal government had become aware of the inadequacy of the information upon which it had based its actions during the October Crisis, it had pressured the RCMP for better intelligence on threats to internal security. This pressure was not entirely unwelcome to the policemen in the Security Service, many of whom were inclined to use aggressive techniques to acquire intelligence on left-wing political groups.[13]

Among many other violations of the law and of the rights of Canadians by the Security Service, the Commission cited the use of intimidation in attempts to recruit informers; the systematic use of confidential files from other government departments in order to build up dossiers on "subversives"; the spreading of false information in order to disrupt or discredit left-wing groups; burglaries of the premises of left-wing groups in order to inspect documents or plant surveillance devices; illegal mail-opening, a practice that had been going on at least since the 1950s; and, of course, the famous episodes of stealing dynamite in order to discredit a subversive group, and burning a barn in an effort to prevent a meeting of suspected "subversives."[14]

The McDonald Royal Commission discovered that the Security Service kept files on approximately 800,000 Canadians. It is, of course, inconceivable that even a small fraction of these people could constitute a threat to the security of the state. Many were on file for frivolous reasons, such as having been impolite towards a member of the RCMP, but most of the files were kept because of the obsession of the Security Service with having a vast data bank just in case someone might some day do or say something that might be "subversive."

The assumption of possible subversive intent was found to be directed almost exclusively at the left. As was the case during the classic period of the cold war, suspicion of holding left-wing views or of associating with persons known to hold such views was sufficient reason to place a person under surveillance.

One of the clearest examples of a political organization being the target of surveillance simply on the grounds of its left-wing political position, is that of the Waffle group that developed within the NDP between 1969 and 1972.[15] The Waffle was an expression of left-wing social-democratic ideas combined with a sentiment strongly in favour of Canadian nationalism. The Waffle was strongest in Ontario and Saskatchewan. Its membership included trade unionists, intellectuals, and other rank-and-file members of the NDP. New Left organizations such as the Student Union for Peace Action were beginning to disintegrate by the end of the 1960s, and a number of activists from the New Left saw the Waffle as a means to continue the political struggles in which they had been engaged.

A small number of additional supporters were former members of the Communist Party of Canada. Nikita Khrushchev's revelations and denunciation of the crimes of Stalin at the Twentieth Congress of the Communist Party of the Soviet Union in 1956 had surprised and shocked Communist Party members around the world. The Communist Party of Canada had been badly divided by the crisis in 1956 and 1957. One faction wanted to break the traditional ties with the Soviet Communist Party and to establish an independent Canadian socialist party. After a great deal of struggle, the Communist Party of Canada remained loyal to the Soviets, but most of the reformers, as well as a great many other

141

disillusioned members, left the Party during 1956 and 1957. Some of the ex-Communists rejected their former socialist ideals; others, however, maintained a vision of socialist justice and equality. During the late 1950s and the 1960s they had no organizational focus. A number of these people perceived the Waffle group as offering potential for the democratic socialist politics for which they longed.

Members of Trotskyist organizations also became involved with the Waffle movement for a time. Trotskyism has never been a particularly influential stream of thought in the Canadian left, but for decades there has been a small Trotskyist movement. Many of its adherents have clung to the NDP, as they had to its predecessor, the Co-operative Commonwealth Federation (CCF), in the hope of recruiting members or influencing policy. Generally, Trotskyists have not embraced an insurrectionary ideology but have argued that the struggle for reforms would lead to the politicization of increasing numbers of people. The Trotskyists have been notable for their persistence, if not for their ability to accomplish their purposes. The advent of the Waffle movement simply provided the Trotskyists with another locus in the NDP for their efforts. They were in effect an opposition group within the Waffle, and wielded no influence over the Waffle leadership.

After an initial period of rapid growth, which lasted until early 1972, the Waffle movement came into increasing conflict with the NDP leadership, particularly in Ontario. The most apparent reason for this was the Waffle's advocacy of autonomy for the Canadian sections of international unions. To a great extent these unions, through the Canadian Labour Congress, have been quite influential in the NDP since its founding in 1961. When, in the view of the union leadership, the Waffle began to meddle in internal union affairs, the union leaders forced a confrontation that resulted in the Waffle being expelled from the Ontario NDP in June 1972.

The Waffle continued to exist for another two years as an independent socialist grouping. It ran three unsuccessful candidates in the 1974 federal election and shortly afterwards disintegrated. One of the principal reasons for its demise was increasing conflict between the Waffle leadership and a growing number of members of Trotskyist and Maoist groups who had infiltrated the organization. The leaders of the Waffle decided in September 1974 that the organization was no longer viable, and they proceeded to disband it. The full extent to which disruptions may have been caused by *agents provocateurs* is still not definitely known, but such activity was suspected in a number of cases at the time by the leaders of the movement.[16]

The McDonald Royal Commission discovered that from its beginning the Waffle group had been the object of intensive surveillance by the Counter-Subversion Branch of the RCMP Security Service. A memorandum from the Counter-Subversion Branch to field divisions, dated December 29, 1970, exhorted operatives to increase their surveillance of the Waffle:

> because of its socialist nature, the NDP has always attracted subversive and radical elements in society. However, it has now become increasingly apparent that these elements are now polarizing around the Waffle Group in even greater numbers, particularly in view of the willingness of the Waffle leadership to accept dissident Communists, Trotskyists, and "leftists" in an attempt to "unite the left". Consequently, the Waffle Group is of particular interest due to the number of persons of subversive interest involved, especially on the National Leadership Committee and the National Steering Committee.[17]

The Counter-Subversion Branch of the Security Service maintained its intense interest in the Waffle in subsequent years. Quite clearly there was no thought that the Waffle might foment insurrection or other kinds of violent political activity. The Waffle was of interest simply because in that period it was a modestly successful, left-wing political formation.

This was stated quite explicitly in a 1972 memorandum from the Counter-Subversion Branch of the Security Service to its local divisions. It said that

> Commencing from the premise that our interest in the movement is made obvious by the extreme left posture it has adopted, and because so many persons of interest to us have gravitated towards its ranks, it does not follow that we are interested in all that the Waffle Group does....
>
> By way of broad parameters, we are interested in determining National aims, strategies and planned tactics of the Waffle leadership, especially when insights we develop go beyond their open, public announcements. That is, do they have designs which exceed their publicly declared aims and, if so, by what means [strategies] do they hope to attain them and, where possible, some estimate of their probability of success

in effecting those ends would certainly place areas of concern in a more balanced perspective.[18]

The McDonald Commission characterized the surveillance of the Waffle by the Security Service as

> an illustration of some of the major problems that have plagued Canada's security intelligence function over the past decade: the lack of vigorous review and monitoring of Security Service activities by government; the lack of a clearly defined mandate for the Security Service; and insensitivity on the part of the Security Service about what constitutes legitimate dissent in a liberal democracy and about the dangers inherent in any surveillance of a non-violent political party.[19]

The McDonald Royal Commission found that the surveillance of the Waffle was only one example of this kind of RCMP activity. Its 1,700 pages of reports contain much evidence of the inclination towards political repressiveness that was characteristic of the RCMP Security Service. The Commission ascribed the problems to the paramilitary nature of the RCMP, the lack of a clear mandate for the Security Service, and an absence of willingness on the part of the Cabinet to take full political responsibility for the management of internal security.

The illegal and improper activities were usually carried out with the implicit or explicit approval of the senior officers of the RCMP. The relationship of the government to these activities was more ambiguous. Senior managers of the Security Service asserted that they had repeatedly sought guidance from the Cabinet regarding the kinds of operations that would be acceptable. During the 1960s and early 1970s, they claimed, their operational guidelines had to be gleaned from regulations and Cabinet Directives (which provide instructions to government employees) dating from the original cold war period, and were concerned mainly with the presumed need to prepare for war with the Soviet Union. This orientation was consistent with their traditional preoccupation with the left in general and with Communists in particular. But, as McDonald pointed out, by the 1960s

> the perception of threats to security and the concept of subversion were gradually extended to encompass a wide spectrum of groups associated with radical dissent, political, social, and constitutional change and the use of demonstrations and confrontations for political purposes. Security Service surveillance

of those groups was not directed by any explicit government policy or guidelines.[20]

Warren Allmand, the Solicitor-General of Canada for much of the early 1970s, thought that clear guidelines for the Security Service were needed because

There was sometimes a tendency to consider a left-wing activist group as subversive even though they did not believe in carrying out their work contrary to the law or in a violent way, and I felt that was wrong, even though we may disagree with the purpose of those groups.[21]

The leadership of the Security Service had its own reasons for wanting written guidelines from government. General Michael Dare, John Starnes' successor as Director-General of the Security Service, claimed that the Security Service took the initiative in seeking a formal mandate because of the effect that the Watergate revelations were having on the security and intelligence organizations in the United States.

On March 27, 1975, the Cabinet approved a set of guidelines for the Security Service entitled "Role, Tasks, and Methods of the RCMP Security Service." The Directive stated that the Security Service was to

maintain internal security by discerning, monitoring, investigating, deterring, preventing and countering individuals and groups in Canada when there are reasonable and probable grounds to believe that they may be engaged in or may be planning to engage in:

(I) espionage or sabotage;
(II) foreign intelligence activities directed toward gathering intelligence information relating to Canada;
(III) activities directed toward accomplishing governmental change within Canada or elsewhere by force or violence or any criminal means;
(IV) activities by a foreign power directed toward the commission of terrorist acts in or against Canada; or
(V) the use or the encouragement of the use of force, violence or any criminal means, or the creation or exploitation of civil disorder, for the purpose of accomplishing any of the activities referred to above.[22]

These guidelines did not prevent the Security Service from

continuing to operate much as it had done. There were two main reasons for the failure of the Cabinet Directive to constrain the activities of the Security Service. The first was that the guidelines themselves were so vaguely worded and so broad that virtually any clandestine police activity could be justified within their limits. The wording of the Cabinet Directive was strikingly similar to that of an amendment to the *Official Secrets Act*, Section 16, which had come into force on July 1, 1974. Section 16 authorized the federal Solicitor-General to intercept or seize communications "for the prevention or detection of subversive activity,"[23] both for the security of Canada and for the purposes of gathering foreign intelligence. This legislation defined "subversive activity" as including the traditional categories of espionage, sabotage, terrorism, as well as "activities directed toward accomplishing governmental change within Canada or elsewhere by force or violence or any criminal means."[24]

This definition of subversion is sufficiently broad that the legality of many kinds of traditionally acceptable political activity in Canada is thrown into doubt. For example, advocacy of and organization for the support of political forces attempting to overthrow repressive regimes abroad could be interpreted as falling under the meaning of this section. And the 1975 Cabinet Directive could be interpreted in an even broader fashion. In particular, the addition of the phrase referring to "the exploitation of civil disorder" for "subversive" purposes suggests that activities such as strikes and political demonstrations could be considered subversive activities. Moreover, the fact that the 1975 Cabinet Directive directed the RCMP Security Service to "deter," "prevent," and "counter" subversive activities in effect gave the force *carte blanche* not only to monitor and watch the activities of various political groups — it was a virtual invitation to engage in dirty tricks, or "covert action," as it is called in security and intelligence parlance.

If the Cabinet Directive served to legitimize, or at least sanction, questionable activities on the part of the Security Service, it did little to resolve the ambiguous relationship that had existed between the Security Service and its political masters. The McDonald Royal Commission discovered that the Security Service had maintained surveillance on, infiltrated, and in some cases disrupted not only left-wing organizations in addition to the Waffle group in the NDP, but also the Parti Québécois, the Quebec Liberal Party under the leadership of Robert Bourassa, and at least some members of

146

the Federal Cabinet. Some former Solicitors-General have stated at various times that they either suspected or knew that they were being kept under surveillance by the RCMP.[25] In one case, this suspicion was confirmed by the RCMP operative who carried out the bugging of the Solicitor-General.

Warren Hart was an American black who for years had worked for the FBI. In the early 1970s, the RCMP Security Service was worried about what it regarded as the threat to national security posed by the Black Power movement in Canada. Unable to recruit a black agent of its own, the RCMP turned to the FBI. Help was provided in the form of Warren Hart. Hart successfully infiltrated a number of black groups in Canada, posing as a very militant American activist. Using these groups as cover, he acted as an *agent provocateur* with other dissident organizations.[26] One of his more notorious exploits was an attempt in 1968 to convince several native groups to arm themselves and to engage in terrorist activities against government officials. By this time, however, Hart was not being taken seriously by many native leaders, and he was not successful in persuading any of them to go along with his intrigues.

Warren Hart was successful, however, in surreptitiously bugging Solicitor-General Warren Allmand with a hidden tape recorder in the early 1970s. By Hart's own account, he did this on the specific instructions of the RCMP. Hart stated in 1981 that "there was a feeling of the RCMP officers at that time that Mr. Allmand had Communist tendencies. He was leaning a little too far to the left."[27] Hart attended a meeting between black leader Roosevelt Douglas and Solicitor-General Warren Allmand. He related that he "was told to tape it, and so subsequently I taped it ... I had a body pack on in a three-piece suit and I had the mike tucked neatly under my tie and there was a little switch in my right-hand pocket so I had a four-hour tape on so subsequently I taped it."[28]

The McDonald Royal Commission discovered and reported scores of incidents essentially similar to the Warren Hart episode in their disregard for constitutional authority. These adventures tended to suggest a marked inclination on the part of the RCMP to make political judgements on the basis of what can only be described as stunning ignorance. A political orientation that would lead to the RCMP assertion that Solicitor-General Allmand was "leaning a little too far to the left" and that he should therefore be surreptitiously bugged was at the root of much of what the

147

McDonald Royal Commission reported was wrong with the organization. The Commission's key recommendations were meant to ensure that in a future security organization such views could not prevail, or that if they should prevail, they could not be translated into unfettered action.[29]

Despite McDonald's dedication to eradicating these problems, his project met with a number of formidable obstacles. These problems became evident during the drafting of the legislation that would realize McDonald's key recommendation, the establishment of the civilian Canadian Security Intelligence Service (CSIS) to replace the RCMP Security Service.

The second and third reports of the McDonald Royal Commission were made public on September 5, 1981. They contained 285 recommendations. On the day that the reports were published, Solicitor-General Robert Kaplan appointed a "transition team," whose mandate was twofold: to draft the legislation that would establish CSIS, and to become the nucleus of the new organization. The transition team was headed by Fred Gibson, a former Deputy Minister of Justice, who had little previous experience in the field of security and intelligence. With his slight stature and prematurely greying beard, Gibson conveys the impression of a scrupulous and thoroughly decent man. On his first day on the job, he openly admitted that he had little idea of how the arcane business of security and intelligence works.[30] It is difficult to imagine him ever countenancing the kind of excesses in which security services tend to indulge. Indeed, when he later was switched to the post of Deputy Solicitor-General, at least one Minister complained that Gibson's insistence on adhering to the letter of the law could be an unfortunate impediment to the kind of aggressive tactics that CSIS should be using.

Gibson was assisted by two principal members of the transition team. T.D. (Ted) Finn had been Assistant Secretary to the Cabinet for Security and Intelligence. Finn was regarded in Ottawa as a protégé of Michael Pitfield, who was then Secretary to the Cabinet and Prime Minister Trudeau's closest and most influential advisor. It is probable that Pitfield had some say in the early stages of the drafting of the *Canadian Security Intelligence Service Act*, the first version of which was known as Bill C-157. But after less than a year of work on the bill, the influences on what would be its final configuration had changed. Michael Pitfield was moved from the Privy Council Office to the Senate; Fred Gibson was removed as head of the Security Intelligence Transition Team and made Deputy Solicitor-General. Ted Finn took Gibson's place as head of the transition team and future Director-General of CSIS. Ted Finn is the son of a legendary Ottawa police reporter, Joe Finn. The elder Finn was known for his iconoclastic sense of humour. The private Ted Finn has the kind of wit and charm one would expect of his father's son. But in public his inclination towards irreverence is well hidden. He is proper in every way. One senses that he tries hard at everything he does, whether it is working efficiently or living correctly. He does not smile readily; the attitude that he affects is one of determination that at times appears to border on being downright grim. One cannot help but wonder if Finn will always be able to make the distinctions between the serious and the nonsensical that are not always very clear in the world of security and intelligence.

The third key member of the Transition Team remained in his position throughout the drafting process. Chief Superintendent Archie Barr was a career officer in the RCMP Security Service. He had survived the storms of the 1970s unscathed and had been influential in the decision of the RCMP to request a Commission of Inquiry. Indeed, according to the McDonald Royal Commission, the key instrument leading to its own creation was a memorandum to the Director-General of the RCMP Security Service, written on June 27, 1977 by four senior officers. The group included Superintendent Archie Barr. The memorandum urged "a co-ordinated and total review of former Security Service operational techniques." It stressed the harm that its authors feared would be done to the Security Service from more revelations about its activities in parliament, the criminal courts, or in the media. One of the more interesting points in the June 27 memorandum was that

> if the RCMP took the initiative "we could perhaps have some influence in drafting terms of reference which could limit the inquiry to the Security Service" and so "avoid the prospect of the entire Force being subjected to the tortuous procedure and consumption of time that such investigations could impose.[31]

And in response to the memorandum, the RCMP did indeed take the initiative. The head of the Force, Commissioner Maurice Nadon, asked Solicitor-General Francis Fox to appoint a commission of inquiry.

Archie Barr occupied the vital position of head of the counter-espionage branch of the RCMP Security Service; while on the transition team, he retained his rank as a Chief Superintendent in the RCMP. Barr had two important resources to bring to the transition team. He had years of operational experience as a Security Service officer; therefore he could give compelling advice as to which legal restrictions might seriously hinder the work of CSIS. His many years of work in counter-intelligence also provided him with excellent contacts throughout the Western security and intelligence community. He therefore knew what would be acceptable to the sister security and intelligence agencies. Given the intimate and secret relationships among these organizations, the ability to bring their influence to bear on the process of drafting the mandate for CSIS inevitably had considerable effect.

Barr's influence within the transition team and ultimately within CSIS was also enhanced by his own reputation. He was known in Ottawa as an efficient and competent counter-intelligence officer; but within the intelligence community, there was also a certain aura of subtle glamour attached to Archie Barr: it was known that he sometimes travelled to Bermuda to consult with the legendary Sir William Stephenson, "the man called Intrepid."[32]

In his long retirement, Stephenson carefully cultivated his image as the wisest and most insightful senior statesman of the spy world. He had not been actively involved in intelligence work since the end of World War Two, but for years he has been touted by his admirers as a man with profound insights into the intricacies of contemporary international politics, particularly the intrigues of the Soviets.[33]

On September 22, 1983, the 87-year-old Sir William Stephenson left his Bermuda retreat for the first time in many years. He travelled to New York to accept the William J. Donovan medal from the veterans of the Office of Strategic Services (OSS). The ceremony was aboard the aircraft carrier U.S.S. *Intrepid*, which is now an air and space museum anchored off mid-town Manhattan in the Hudson River. In his speech at the black-tie dinner, Stephenson opined that

> One of the chief objectives of the Soviet Union since the War has been to create a division among the allied forces of the West. The enemy is not only at our door, but inside our house, in practically every room.... The West is fortunate in having

in the United States of America the most important, knowledgeable and visceral leaders against their enemy in the persons of Ronald Reagan and Vice President George Bush. Standing firmly alongside them are Prime Minister Margaret Thatcher of Great Britain and Canada's Conservative Party leader Brian Mulroney — Canada being fully involved with you in NATO.[34]

Stephenson's speech took place when the debate about Bill C-157 was at its height in Ottawa. The speech was notable not only for its clichés but also, as the *Toronto Star* observed, for pointedly omitting any reference to the Prime Minister of Canada, Pierre Trudeau. On the same occasion, Stephenson discussed the Communist threat in Canada and the future of CSIS with some of his admirers. He is reported to have said that there was only one man who could save Canada from Communism by running CSIS, and that man was Stephenson's friend, Archie Barr.[35]

Barr has neither the appearance nor the manner of the stereotypical Mountie. His build is trim, his speech measured and understated. His mind is agile. He listens with patience. He rarely seems to direct a conversation. Indeed, patience must be the dominant aspect of his personality. He gives the impression of savouring the thought that the world is full of puzzles, each with a vast number of pieces; some day they will all come together and the picture will be completed for the player with enough wit and patience. A case starts with a lead. It might be a vague reference from a defector that the side he has deserted is receiving information, which might come from any of fifty sources. Years might go by before the possibilities are reduced by half. More years and more defectors narrow it further. Someone patiently shuffles the bits of information. Some day they will fit. To Archie Barr, this is how the game of catching spies is played. It is also the way the greater game of moving bureaucracies and governments is orchestrated.[36]

When the transition team was formed in 1981, its leader, Fred Gibson, was sanguine about the prospects for framing legislation that would for the first time bring the secret activities of the Security Service under responsible political control. Looking back two years later, he recalled that "There was no particular threat in the environment at that time that lent to this task a sense of urgency or necessity, but rather a body of evidence and an environment of public debate and concern that appeared to provide a unique opportunity, at least in Canadian history, to carry out the formalized establishment of a Security Service in a rational and thoughtful and politically stable environment."[37]

But Bill C-157 received a disastrous reception from the public. It was tabled in the House of Commons on May 18, 1983; within days it had generated a storm of controversy. The bill was attacked not only by civil libertarians, but also by labour leaders, church leaders, and provincial Attorneys-General. Roy McMurtry, the Progressive Conservative Attorney-General of Ontario, summed up the views of many of his colleagues when he said that "The federal government has produced a legislative monster which places freedom in actual jeopardy by threatening to stifle the ordinary debate and discourse which is at the very foundation of freedom itself."[38]

Peter Russell had been Director of Research for the McDonald Royal Commission. His reaction to Bill C-157 was that the government had responded to the Commission's recommendations by expanding the powers of the Security Service while decreasing political control over it.[39]

Three aspects of Bill C-157 posed serious problems: first, the definition of threats to the security of Canada; second, the scope of the powers that would be granted to CSIS; and third, the proposed mechanisms for control and oversight of CSIS.

Bill C-157 stipulated that CSIS was to investigate "activities that may on reasonable grounds be suspected of constituting threats to the security of Canada."[40] To carry out such investigations, the bill provided for CSIS to obtain warrants that would enable its agents to intercept communications, obtain information, records, documents, or "things," as well as "to do any other act or thing that is reasonably necessary...."[41] The effect of this wording would have been to render legal the list of improper and illegal activities that had been practised by the RCMP Security Service over the years and had been so painstakingly described by the McDonald Commission.

The scope of CSIS operations is determined by the legislative definition of threats to the security of Canada. Consequently, the most fundamental question is whether the definition contained in the CSIS legislation is repressive or whether it is consistent with the concepts of liberty that are implicit in the principles of liberal democratic government. Bill C-157 described four categories of threats to the security of Canada. These included espionage and sabotage; "foreign influenced activities" that are "clandestine or deceptive"; activities relating to political violence; and finally, "subversion," which was defined as "activities directed toward undermining by covert unlawful acts, or directed toward or intended ultimately to lead to the destruction or overthrow of, the constitutionally established system of government in Canada."[42]

This definition of threats to the state contained fundamental difficulties and contradictions. In the first three categories — espionage and sabotage, foreign-influenced activities, and political violence — "threats to the security of Canada" were deemed to include not only threats against the Canadian state but also threats against "any state allied or associated with Canada."

Canada is "allied" with many other states through its formal treaties or informal arrangements. It is "associated" with almost every other country through the United Nations and other international organizations. The wording of Bill C-157 would have mandated CSIS to keep watch on virtually anyone working for political change, not only in Canada but in other countries as well. This possibility was obvious to church workers, human rights advocates, and other Canadians interested in assisting those who are the victims of oppression in other countries. This added significantly to the opposition to Bill C-157 in the spring and summer of 1983.

A democratic state is undoubtedly justified in keeping watch on persons who attempt to engage in espionage or sabotage on behalf of a foreign power. Similarly, it is clear that the state must protect society from those who might practise political terrorism, although there is no definition of that term that is universally accepted. But the word "subversion" and how it should be regarded in a liberal democracy raises much more difficult questions. The right to engage in political dissent is essential to the existence of any democratic political process. Whenever the issue of "subversion" is raised, the difficulty lies in making a distinction between subversion and dissent.

Skepticism about the validity of the idea that there is such a thing as "subversion" is not new. For example, in 1940, U.S. Attorney-General (later Supreme Court Justice) Robert H. Jackson wrote that

Activities which seem helpful or benevolent to wage earners, persons on relief, or those who are disadvantaged in the struggle for existence, may be regarded as "subversive" by those whose property interests might be affected thereby; those who are in office are apt to regard as "subversive" the activities of any of those who would bring about a change of administration. Some of our soundest constitutional doctrines were once punished as "subversive."[43]

Bill C-157 stated that an activity did not necessarily have to be illegal, violent, or "foreign" to be subversive. It merely had to be "directed toward or intended ultimately to lead to"[44] the destruction or overthrow of the government. One of the improvements found in the csis Act as it was passed in 1984 is that the word "violent" has been added as a necessary part of the description of activities deemed to be subversive. But even with the addition of the test of violence, activities are still considered to be subversive if they are deemed to be "intended" to have a given result, namely the overthrow of the government. To be merely intended, an act need not have taken place. It need not even have been attempted. To be subversive, an uncommitted act needs only to have been considered by the authorities to have a certain ultimate purpose. The danger in this formulation, of course, is the possibility that certain modes of thought or ideologies might in themselves come to be construed as "subversive." Subjected to this reasoning, a person could be considered "subversive" simply for being suspected of holding certain beliefs.

The word "intended" as it is used in the *Security Service Act* also poses problems. Critics regard it as being too ambiguous for use in statutes precisely because its meaning is derived from the political context in which it is used. The problematic nature of "intention" was summarized elegantly by one of the leading theorists on the meaning of democratic rights, Ronald Dworkin, Professor of Jurisprudence at Oxford University. In relation to Bill C-157, he said,

It's very hard to separate someone's intention from someone's expectation from someone's hope. If somebody writes a tract, for example, a Utopian tract describing an ideal society and saying the only way we'd ever get there is through revolution, the question is whether someone who obviously *hopes* that his work in the long run will have some influence, whether he intends to do it. These would be questions of a philosophical

154

nicety bordering on semantic questions. Now, when you introduce ... the idea of intending to endanger the security of a country then all the difficulties ... are magnified exponentially, because the concept of security of a nation and what would endanger it is itself a network of contested ideas. Unfortunately those ideas mean different things to people who hold different kinds of political convictions.[45]

The position of the McDonald Royal Commission had been that the only legitimate purpose for a security service in a democracy is, ultimately, the protection of democratic rights. The Commissioners were concerned that democratic rights are jeopardized when citizens or non-citizens are subjected to surveillance simply because of their ideas, regardless of the nature of those ideas.

The McDonald Royal Commission emphasized the need for a statutory definition of threats to the security of Canada. The Commissioners' nearly four years of investigation of the wrongdoing of the RCMP Security Service had made them well aware of the problems created by such an organization when it operates without statutory limits on its scope of action. The McDonald Commission reports draw attention to the inadequacy of the definitions of "subversive activity" that had previously been set out in an amendment to the *Official Secrets Act* that had been made in 1974 (Section 16(3)) and in the Cabinet Directive of March 27, 1975, on the "Role, Tasks, and Methods of the RCMP Security Service."[46]

The Commission proposed its own definition of threats to the security of Canada. These included espionage and sabotage, foreign interference, political violence and terrorism, and "revolutionary subversion."[47] But McDonald insisted that "revolutionary subversion" should be treated differently from the other categories of threats. The Commission formally recommended that for revolutionary subversion

> *only non-intrusive techniques be used to collect information about individuals or groups whose known and suspected activities are confined to this category.*[48] [emphasis in original]

In other words, individuals and groups were not to be subjected to bugging, phone-tapping, mail opening, break-ins, or infiltration simply because of their supposed or actual adherence to a "subversive" ideology. The recommendation goes on to say:

So long as political organizations which espouse totalitarian

155

ideologies stick to the methods of liberal democracy to promote their cause, they should not, simply by virtue of their beliefs, be subject to intrusive investigations by the security intelligence agency.[49]

Exactly what a "totalitarian ideology" might be is not clear; the description "totalitarian" may be applied to the practices of certain states but hardly to sets of ideas. In any case, both Bill C-157 and its final version, the *CSIS Act*, have ignored McDonald's advice regarding subversion. Despite the impossibility of defining subversion, they construe it to be fully equal with foreign espionage and terrorism as threats to the security of Canada. Consequently, persons suspected of subversive activities could be subject to the same intrusive techniques of investigation as suspected terrorists or spies.

Solicitor-General Robert Kaplan defended this important departure from the McDonald recommendations against intrusive investigations when he argued that he "was satisfied that the security service couldn't do its job without them — the job that McDonald himself recognized needed to be done. I felt that that job could not be done without the availability of these techniques, like wiretapping."[50]

What evidence convinced Kaplan that there are activities in this country so potentially dangerous that McDonald's safeguard would prevent the security service from coping with them effectively? On July 16, 1984, the day CSIS was formally established, Kaplan stated that the most pressing problem facing the service would be "international terrorism." This was followed, he said, by unauthorized transfer of technology to other countries. He did not mention the danger of subversion.

The argument was used, by Kaplan and by other defenders of the CSIS legislation, that the forces of the state must be able to gather preliminary evidence of activities threatening to the state in order to be able to determine if further action, whether prosecution or further surveillance, might be warranted. It was on these grounds that the provision for the use of intrusive investigative techniques against suspected subversives was justified.

If these assumptions are accepted by a liberal democratic state, a paradoxical situation is created. As long as there is fear that citizens might think subversive thoughts, the state should be aware of them so as to be able to prevent such ideas from spreading or becoming popular and dangerous. In this case the detection of such incipient subversion does require state scrutiny at an early stage. Therefore the task of keeping the state informed of possible subversion necessarily requires surveillance not only of real actions but also of contemplated actions. The paradox is that the kind of state that would systematically attempt to monitor the intentions of its citizens could hardly be characterized as a liberal democracy.

Deciding who is to be the subject of surveillance by CSIS is largely the prerogative of the director of the organization. The person occupying this office is charged with the responsibility of deciding which persons or groups of persons constitute possible threats to the security of Canada and who therefore will be investigated. The only guide that the director will find in the *CSIS Act* is in Section 2. This section includes the reference to (paragraph (d)) ultimate intentions providing reason to bring a person or group of persons under surveillance. The director therefore enjoys considerable latitude in deciding who the targets of his organization should be. Ted Finn, the first Director of CSIS and a cautious, serious lawyer, had spent much of his career in the Privy Council Office, and before joining the Security Transition Team in 1981 had been Assistant Secretary to the Cabinet for Security and Intelligence. The ambience of the Trudeau-Pitfield Privy Council Office in the 1970s was undoubtedly quite different from the world of ex-RCMP officers in which Ted Finn subsequently went about directing CSIS.

When asked whether he thought that subversion poses a real threat to the security of Canada, Finn replied, choosing his words carefully, that he thought it would be wrong to assume "that it is beyond either the imagination or the ability of Canadians to develop in a wholly domestic way, either plans of proposals or actions which would be deemed, I think by anyone, to be subversive within either the first or the second part of the definition in paragraph (d)."[51]

Finn was then asked if there are ideologies that are in themselves subversive by that definition, and that therefore would render any person who subscribes to them subject to surveillance by CSIS. He replied, "The definition talks about activism. If one can say that thought is an activity which is brought in under the definition, then I suppose the answer ... would be yes, but it's a qualified yes. For my own part, I would say that free thought, which is guaranteed by the Charter of Rights and Freedoms, apart from anything else, would not fall under the definition as being an activity which is directed by covert unlawful means to undermine the constitutionally established system. Nor would I say that it is an activity directed toward the destruction or overthrow of that system."[52] It is difficult to know how much comfort can be taken from this view.

Because of the unprecedented range of criticism directed at Bill C-157 in the summer of 1983, unusual steps were taken to salvage it. A special committee of the Senate was struck to review the controversial bill and to make recommendations for improvements. The committee was chaired by Michael Pitfield, who had moved from the Privy Council Office to the Senate in late 1982. The committee's deliberations began in July 1983, and its report was issued the following November.

The question of the definition of threats to the security of Canada, and of the nature of subversion in particular, came up repeatedly in the Senate Committee's deliberations. Two of the government's three star witnesses, Robert Kaplan and Ted Finn, were not optimistic that the wording of the section on subversion could be improved. The third member of the trio, Archie Barr, was silent on this matter. On August 18, 1983, apparently almost by chance, a solution to the problem was found. Liberal Senator Royce Frith somehow thought of a time-honoured device by which Canada had been kept free of subversive elements.

> SENATOR FRITH: Under the old section 7(b) of the Immigration Act, an immigration officer would refuse admission to someone because he or she was a member of the Communist Party; but he did not say that that was the reason; rather, he said that it was because he or she was a member of an association or organization that advocated the *violent* overthrow of the constitutionally established system of government. The word "violent" is not included here.
>
> Yes, it is reverting to the same issue — and maybe all we are doing is underlining it. What we are finding, Mr. Chairman, it seems to me, is that we are gradually starting to highlight or put in neon the issues that are going to concern us with regard to many of these things.
>
> SENATOR GODFREY: It is a drafting problem, isn't it?
>
> SENATOR FRITH: Do you find the word "violent" troublesome, Mr. Finn?

MR. FINN: No, I do not, senator. In fact, I would argue that if one goes to a dictionary definition of "destruction or overthrow" one will find a clear expression of violence. It may be a drafting problem. It would not worry me if the word "violent" were part of it.

SENATOR FRITH: Without supporting the suggestion, if it read "the violent overthrow" or "the overthrow by violence" — which is what I think the wording was — you would not view that as something that would be an undesirable imposition on your powers if you were the director?

MR. FINN: No, I would not view it as such, provided of course that the first part of the definition remained either intact or suitably amended; that is, that part of it which talks about the covert unlawful activities.

SENATOR FRITH: Oh yes, that has to stay; absolutely.[53]

Thus in its final report the Senate Committee duly pointed out that under the original wording of Bill C-157

> . . . it would be open for the CSIS ... to investigate the activities of a peaceful, legal political party, for example, which seeks to alter Canada's constitutional system. This would not be acceptable. Accordingly, the Committee would modify this ... by including reference to destruction or overthrow "by violence." Peaceful and lawful agitation for constitutional change should not be considered a threat to the security of Canada.[54]

The government accepted this recommendation, and the phrase "by violence" appeared in the revised version of Bill C-157, which was known as Bill C-9. The Senate Committee recommended a total of thirty-two changes in the Bill. The government incorporated most of them in Bill C-9. The major exception was the move to bring the signals intelligence-gathering activities of the CSE under the same control and review procedures as those governing the CSIS. For its own reasons, even the Trudeau government could not go that far.

For a time, it seemed that Bill C-9 might arouse sufficient controversy that it too would not be passed. Some elements of the right in the Western intelligence community continued to oppose it. In their view, any statutory limitations on the activities of a member organization would be undesirable. Moreover, Bill C-9 provided the means for overseeing the activities of CSIS; this

159

"oversight" provision — that is, continuing inspection of the agency's activity by a government-appointed Security Intelligence Review Committee — held the danger that the secrets of the community might be discovered by outsiders. The fact that the McDonald Royal Commission's recommendations that this review be conducted by a parliamentary committee had been dropped in favour of review by government appointees mattered little; to the Western intelligence community, any outside inspection might be a foot in the door that would lead to further democratic intrusions.

On the other side, objections were again raised that Bill C-9 still contained far too many loopholes that would allow CSIS to in effect become a kind of secret police. But these criticisms did not generate the kind of passion aroused by Bill C-157. The process of amending the legislation had calmed the fears of some critics. For some people, also, there was the stark realization that if Bill C-9 did not pass, Canada would be left with the RCMP Security Service, free as always of statutory restraints.

The *Bill to Establish a Canadian Security Intelligence Service* was passed on Thursday, June 21, 1984. It was the next-to-last day in the life of Canada's thirty-second parliament, the last parliament in which Pierre Trudeau would sit as Prime Minister. It was Trudeau's last law.

The preceding night the House of Commons had sat until six a.m., debating one of the most contentious pieces of legislation in years. The Progressive Conservative opposition members had wavered in their support of separating the Security Service from the RCMP. In principle, Opposition leader Brian Mulroney and most of his chief advisors wanted Bill C-9 passed. Elmer MacKay, the future Solicitor-General of Canada and at that time a senior advisor to Mulroney, had said in late 1983 that the Tory caucus faced a dilemma: whether to do what it regarded to be best for the country, or what would be politically expedient.[55]

The top leadership of the federal Tories had several reasons for wanting Bill C-9 to be enacted. They were well aware of the deficiencies in the existing arrangement. Moreover, expecting as they did to form the next government, they wanted the Trudeau Liberals to be responsible for establishing CSIS. Creating spy organizations of any kind, they reasoned, is inherently not politically popular. Having the Liberals pass Bill C-9 gave the Tories a double advantage. They did not have to pay the political price, particularly in the Western provinces, of appearing to gut the RCMP by removing its most prestigious function: the protection of national security. And when they assumed power that September, they inherited a new security service.

The process that began with the appointment of the McDonald Royal Commission in June 1977 ended with the establishment of CSIS in July 1984. During those seven years some progress towards reform had been made: some of the darker secret practices of the Security Service had been revealed. A large part of the Canadian component of the Western intelligence community had been given a legislated mandate. Its conduct would henceforth be subject to scrutiny by a Review Committee that would include representatives of the three federal political parties. There would be an appeal procedure available to persons who might believe that they had been treated unfairly by the new Security Intelligence Service. The relationship between the Service and the government was now spelled out in the law. The Solicitor-General would be responsible, but would not be permitted to intervene in the day-to-day operations of CSIS.

To this extent, the project of Trudeau, Pitfield, and the reform-minded elements in the security community had been successful. And yet, in the summer of 1984, Michael Pitfield was still somewhat uneasy about the adequacy of the reforms. Sitting in his third-floor office across Wellington Street from the West Block of the Parliament Buildings, almost next door to the United States Embassy, he spoke at length about the problems of managing the security and intelligence machinery in Canada. Four days after CSIS had been formally established, he conveyed the impression of a man who was relieved, intrigued, and yet concerned. He was worried about the size of the intelligence-collecting apparatus, and the sheer volume of material it collects. "It is a problem ministers can't deal with," he said. "It is too complex. Most of the security and intelligence product is dealt with at a lower level. Ninety-nine per cent of what reaches ministers is in a highly generalized form. Perhaps one-tenth of one per cent of what is collected even reaches the Deputy Minister. Some of it is collected under international agreements, much more is not. But the security service and the CSE go on producing far more than we can process in this country.... For what purpose?"[56]

He and Pierre Trudeau were acutely aware that their agenda

in the international arena was at substantial variance with that of the Reagan administration. The difference had come to a head with the Trudeau peace mission of the preceding nine months. In 1974, three years before the appointment of the McDonald Commission, because of uncertainty about the RCMP, the federal government had turned to the Department of National Defence to provide experts to sweep the offices of MPs and Ministers for electronic listening devices. Now, ten years later, Pitfield gestured around the room. "We still can't be sure," he said. The newly legislated reforms to the security service could only succeed if they were administered by a government with the political will to make them work. There was a bureaucrat's satisfaction at having navigated the uncharted course from the failure to implement the MacKenzie Commission recommendations in 1969 to the creation of CSIS. But it was tempered by the overpowering awareness that in political terms the world of 1984 was very different from that of 1969.

9

Legacy of Fear

"O Oysters," said the Carpenter,
"You've had a pleasant run!
Shall we be trotting home again?"
But answer came there none —
And this was scarcely odd, because
They'd eaten every one.

A ll governments want to be informed of threats to themselves and to their vital interests. As we know, the threats can take a variety of forms: they can be legal or illegal, parliamentary or extraparliamentary, internal or external, real or imaginary. Similarly, governments have an endless appetite for information about their adversaries that will enable them to thwart the hostile efforts of those adversaries, and to exploit weaknesses to their own advantage. The acquisition, storage, and selective dissemination of such information in itself often produces results that benefit either the government or, more particularly, those institutions whose special responsibility it is to deal in information. The management of information — its collection, its storage, and its distribution — is inevitably a political activity.

Virtually any government has at its disposal a variety of means to gather information. These means include the activities of diplomats, journalists, scholars, certain public servants, political party activists, and public opinion pollsters. Security and intelligence agencies exist ostensibly to provide information that is not available through other, more ordinary, means. This activity is valid in a liberal democracy to the extent that it actually contributes to the protection of society from the dangers of violence and interference by foreign governments. But the evolution of these agencies in the cold war context has allowed them to exert a powerful influence on the operative distinction between the kinds of political thought that are considered by governments to be acceptable and the kinds of views that are deemed "subversive."

This process is both subtle and effective. The public in general and government functionaries in particular tend to intuitively grasp the essential nature of acceptable political orthodoxy: the practice of self-censorship then becomes widespread. The cycle is self-reinforcing and self-perpetuating. It is strengthened not only by the national security agencies themselves, but also by the wider circle of people who share their assumptions. This includes their allies in related organizations such as the military, the individuals throughout society who need their blessing in the form of a "security clearance" in order to pursue their own interests, and security and intelligence agency veterans who are ensconced in various institutions in both the public and private sectors.

The stated purpose of CSIS is "to provide the government with intelligence and advice relating to activities suspected of constituting threats to the security of Canada,"[1] those threats being essentially defined in the CSIS legislation as espionage, sabotage, foreign-influenced activities, terrorism, and subversion.[2] CSIS itself has no law-enforcement powers; "countering" threats is specifically not within its statutory mandate. The information that it provides to government is to be used by police forces for prosecutorial purposes, at the discretion of the Crown. The government more often takes "preventive measures" on the basis of the information in ways that are not spelled out in the law.[3] These measures generally involve deceiving or attempting to recruit espionage agents, making preparations to physically protect repositories of secret information, and making plans to subdue disorderly or violent activity.

Two additional and more specific uses are made of security intelligence. The first involves planning for national emergencies, particularly war or insurrection, real or apprehended. The *War Measures Act* empowers the federal government to arbitrarily detain citizens without a warrant, and to suspend for long periods of time their constitutional rights to be charged with an offence and tried in court. Canadians are all too familiar with the way in which these powers were used against citizens of Japanese origin during World War Two and again in Quebec during the October Crisis in 1970.

For decades the RCMP compiled and maintained lists of persons to be detained in time of emergency. Since World War One, the RCMP has provided to successive governments lists of "subversives" who might be interned. During the original cold war period in 1948, a major priority of the RCMP was to identify persons to be arrested should war with the Soviet Union break out. For the next two decades, this programme was pursued enthusiastically by the force.

The continuous updating of the list provided the pretext for many of the improper or illegal investigations discovered by the McDonald Royal Commission; yet the programme had been concealed from the highest governmental authorities. According to the Commission, the most senior government official responsible for security matters between 1964 and 1977, Gordon Robertson, was unaware of the "essentials" of the programme and he did not know that "the Security Service regarded it as one of the major sources of authority for some of the Service's most sensitive investigations."[4] In 1981 the Security Service was still busily preparing its lists of potential internees, without the approval of the government.[5]

The obsession of the Security Service with the possibility of interning large numbers of citizens is strikingly similar to the cold war internment programmes that flourished in the United States. Also beginning in 1948, the FBI maintained a list of "dangerous" persons who were to be detained without legal rights, not only in the event of war with the Soviet Union but also in time of a "threatened invasion." The list, known as the FBI Security Index, reached its peak in 1955, when it included more than 25,000 names.[6] The FBI practice had been reinforced in law when the United States Congress passed the *Internal Security Act* in 1950. The legislation, sponsored by Senator Karl Mundt and Representative Richard Nixon, contained sweeping provisions for surveillance, deportations of "aliens," and the mass round-up of dissidents on the basis that they might be expected to engage in "disloyal" conduct.

The provisions of the *Internal Security Act* of 1950 were somewhat more restrictive than the standards upon which the FBI had been basing its Security Index; but the FBI continued to apply its own standards in identifying "subversive" organizations and individuals, rather than abiding by the Congressionally-defined criteria. FBI Director J. Edgar Hoover conducted ongoing skirmishes with the Department of Justice and the White House on this issue through most of the 1950s.

The *Internal Security Act* was finally repealed in 1971, but not before detention camps had actually been set up across the United States. The camps were in Arizona, California, Florida, Oklahoma, and Pennsylvania. They never had to be used.[7]

Another major preoccupation of security services in both Canada and the United States has been the conduct of security screening programmes for government employees. The ostensible purpose of these programmes has been to ensure that public servants would not engage in espionage, sabotage, or "subversive" activities of any other kind. There is an undeniable logic to the argument that any state must ensure that its employees will not destroy it from within; but security screening programmes inevitably have effects that are broader than their stated purposes imply. They provide a major opportunity for security and intelligence agencies to conduct large-scale surveillance programmes. Ultimately, they also have a profound ideological effect; they necessarily tend to legitimize one set of political ideas while implicitly rendering other views unacceptable.

If the background check carried out by the security service is thought to reveal a tendency on the part of an individual to express subversive views or to keep subversive company, then that person should not be *cleared*: cleared to work in "sensitive" areas of the public service, or to know state secrets, or to use them as the basis for participation in public debate. This process has an additional dimension of ideological control: the knowledge that some day one will have to be "cleared" has a remarkable ability to induce intellectual self-censorship. The inevitable consequence is that basic assumptions about international relations and about the political process tend to remain unchallenged. Thus the scope of public discourse is narrowed, and the dominance of cold war ideology is enhanced.

Federal loyalty and security programmes in the United States have been carried out under the authority of every president since Franklin Roosevelt. The historian Athan Theoharis has pointed out that investigations under these programmes

were not confined to incumbent employees — the Civil Service commission, the FBI, the CIA and the NSA also maintained extensive files on American citizens on the premise that at some future date these individuals might apply for federal employment. The FBI in particular exploited its investigative responsibility under these programs to initiate far-ranging investigations of dissident organizations.[8]

The American loyalty and security programme came into its own under President Harry Truman during the early years of the cold war. It was implemented with increasing severity after the election of President Dwight Eisenhower in 1952. The Eisenhower security programme was launched on April 27, 1953. It provided for the summary dismissal of federal employees not only for "disloyalty" but also for lack of "suitability." This meant that they had to be "reliable, trustworthy, of good conduct and character, and of complete and unswerving loyalty to the United States."[9] In a number of cases, the last known of which was that of J. Robert Oppenheimer, the nuclear physicist, security clearances were denied to persons who had previously been cleared, even though the denial was based on no new information. During the 1960s, security investigations of government employees were broadened to include new categories of dissident political activities.

The Canadian government security investigation programme for its employees was also started in the early days of the cold war. The essentials of the system of security screening were set by Cabinet Directive 4 in March 1948. Persons who were considered to be "members or associates of Communist or Fascist organizations"[10] were prohibited from being employed in sensitive positions in the public service. The distinction between "loyalty" and "reliability" was introduced in Cabinet Directive 24 in 1952. The definition of loyalty continued to turn on a person's not being a member of the Communist Party and not believing in "Marxism-Leninism or any other ideology which advocates the overthrow of government by force." The single-minded, cold war concern with Communism was evident in this formulation.

Cabinet Directive 24 also made a distinction between "loyalty" and "reliability." The latter term referred to personal characteristics that might, in the view of the government, cause an employee to be dishonest, indiscreet, or vulnerable to blackmail. The reliability criteria were to provide the pretext for an intensive, country-wide hunt for homosexuals during the late 1950s and early

1960s. Some of the more sordid episodes in the history of the RCMP Security Service occurred in this context. A special unit was established for the sole purpose of attempting to locate and remove homosexuals in the public service. Extensive use was made of informers and interrogations, and an elaborate and of course futile effort was made to devise a mechanical device for the detection of hidden homosexual impulses in suspects.[11]

During the turbulent years of the Diefenbaker government, there was little time for officials in the Prime Minister's Office or the Privy Council Office to review the basic assumptions on which security screening policy rested.[12] Lester Pearson, however, was seriously interested in security policy, and understood its importance. Shortly after he became Prime Minister in April 1963, he acted firmly to prevent the more extreme manifestations of cold war paranoia from taking root in Canada. He initiated a thorough review of policies and procedures for the security screening of federal government employees, and the Privy Council Office began a process of re-examining its practices in this area.

Don Wall, then Assistant Secretary to the Cabinet for Security, spent most of that summer drafting a new document that would form the basis of security screening policy for the following two decades. Wall, a man who is deeply humane as well as having a highly developed sense of the ironic, spent much time atop his boat-house on Big Rideau Lake wrestling with the concepts of dissent and subversion, loyalty and treason, espionage and revolution.[13] His efforts resulted in the first draft of a new policy that was described in a major speech in the House of Commons by Prime Minister Pearson on October 25, 1963. The new policy was formalized in Cabinet Directive 35 (CD 35) on December 18, 1963. It embodied substantial reform and moderation of the system.

CD 35 remained the basis for security screening procedures until after the CSIS Act was passed by Parliament in 1984. Its major advantage over its predecessors had been that it provided review procedures for individuals who failed to receive a security clearance. Information upon which cases were decided continued to be gathered and retained by the RCMP. In theory, the decisions to grant or withhold clearances were made by senior officials in the government department concerned; but the influence of the RCMP on government officials in matters of this kind should not be underestimated. During the 1970s, reports on the findings of investigations by the RCMP included recommendations as to whether an individual should be granted a security clearance. The practice was eventually discontinued, but it is difficult to imagine departmental bureaucrats frequently bestowing security clearances on people against whom the RCMP had presented serious adverse allegations.

The key operative aspect of CD 35 is its definition of criteria for determining loyalty. As in the CSIS legislation passed twenty-one years later, the political meaning of the security screening process is to be found in the description of persons (or groups, or activities) that constitute threats to the security of Canada. In determining loyalty, CD 35 excludes:

(a) a person who is a member of a Communist or Fascist party or an organization affiliated with a Communist or Fascist party and having a similar nature and purpose;
(b) a person who by his words or his actions shows himself to support a Communist or Fascist party or an organization affiliated with a Communist or Fascist party and having a similar nature and purpose;
(c) a person who, having reasonable grounds to understand its true nature and purpose, is a member of or supports by his words or his actions an organization which has as its real objective the furtherance of Communist or Fascist aims and policies (commonly known as a front group);
(d) a person who is a secret agent of or an informer for a foreign power, or who deliberately assists any such agent or informer;
(e) a person who by his words or his actions shows himself to support any organization which publicly or privately advocates or practices the use of force to alter the form of government.[14]

CD 35 has continued to provide the basis for security screening in the Canadian public service. The McDonald Commission recommended that the criteria for granting security clearances be defined with more precision. The proposed grounds for denial of a security clearance were identical to the definition of threats to the security of Canada that the Commission suggested as the basis for the CSIS legislation itself.[15] That definition was refined in the process of drafting Bill C-157, then re-drafting and finally enacting Bill C-9. But contrary to the McDonald recommendation, a year and a half after Bill C-9 became law, the early-sixties language of CD 35 was still being used as the basis for security screening procedures. Ironically, even CSIS was not using the definition contained in its own statute to screen its employees and prospective recruits; it was applying the provisions of CD 35.

The definitions in CD 35 represent a clear statement of liberal assumptions about threats to national security in the late cold war period. They are straightforward in their explicit naming of Communists (and Fascists) as being the enemies of liberal democracy in Canada. One of the considerable virtues of CD 35, in comparison with other formulations of the genre, is that it does not condemn political ideas as such; it is instead concerned with active participation in or support of political organizations. Paragraph (e), which deals with "subversion," is concerned with the relationship of an individual to an organization that might have the "subversive" quality of advocating or practising the use of force to alter the form of government. Ironically, in this respect, the older CD 35 is less repressive than the CSIS Act: the description of "subversion" in the CSIS legislation could conceivably be interpreted as applying to the act of holding or speaking about certain ideological convictions.[16]

In some obvious respects, the definition of threats in CD 35 is dated. The implied equation of Communist and Fascist parties, as well as the concern with "front groups," bear the stamp of the era in which CD 35 was written. By contemporary standards, the formulation is also simplistic in its assumptions that the "nature and purpose" of Communist or Fascist parties are obvious and unchanging. It might be observed in passing, for example, that social democratic and liberal parties share with Communist parties the *purpose* of achieving full employment, or of achieving world peace. The "aims and policies" of Communist parties are nothing if not constantly changing, for many reasons.

The descriptions of threats to the security of Canada in the CSIS Act are more exact and certainly have a more contemporary ring. They share the concern of CD 35 about espionage and political violence; but they also strike off in new directions. In addition to the tendentious definitions of "subversion," the CSIS Act refers to another presumed threat that has become fashionable during the 1980s bout of cold war fever. Paragraph (b) refers to "foreign influenced activities within or relating to Canada that are detrimental to the interests of Canada and are clandestine or deceptive or involve a threat to any person."

The McDonald Royal Commission had recommended that

"foreign interference" be regarded as a threat to the security of Canada. This was defined as meaning "clandestine or deceptive action taken by or on behalf of a foreign power in Canada to promote the interests of a foreign power."[17] The transformation of McDonald's concern about "foreign interference" to the mandated interest of CSIS in "foreign influence" is not without significance. An echo of the 1950s obsession with "Reds" or their "dupes" or "stooges" or "fellow travellers" in high places emerged in the 1980s in the guise of a preoccupation about Soviet "agents of influence." This anxiety has been articulated mainly by writers known for their comfortable relationships with the more conservative elements in the British and American intelligence communities.

John Barron raised the issue of "agents of influence" in his book *KGB: The Secret Work of Soviet Secret Agents*, a work that is highly recommended by both the CIA and senior CSIS personnel. In discussing agents of influence, Barron claims that "through them the Soviet Union endeavours to develop its own disguised voices in foreign, governmental, political, journalistic, business, labor, artistic, and academic circles. While agents of influence may incidentally transmit intelligence, their overriding mission is to alter opinion and policy in the interests of the Soviet Union."[18]

Barron readily acknowledges that the opinions advocated by "agents of influence" often appear to be indistinguishable from the opinions that might be held by a person who is not working for the KGB. And indeed, the belief that a person is such an agent is usually a matter of faith. Barron concedes that "there is rarely legal proof that his counsel represented anything other than his own honest judgement."[19]

Richard H. Schultz and Roy Godson are among the most enthusiastic "agents of influence" buffs. For them, such agents may be so subtle that they themselves don't even know they are agents. In their book *Dezinformatsia*, Schultz and Godson observe that "there are several different types of influence agents, including *the unwitting but manipulated individual*, the 'trusted contact,' and the controlled covert agent."[20] (Emphasis added.)

To be sure, various governments have long practised the art of infiltrating other countries with "controlled covert agents," either for espionage or for other purposes. But an *unwitting* agent would be a contradiction in terms; one could hardly act on *behalf* of another nation without being aware of it, unless one were in a trance. If the idea of unwitting influence agents seems offbeat, the reaction to Schultz and Godson's work within the intelligence community is equally bizarre. The two authors have been closely involved in the Washington-based Consortium for the Study of Intelligence, a body that for several years has promoted a decidedly conservative view of the proper role for U.S. intelligence agencies. Its publications have consistently urged relaxing the restraints imposed during the post-Watergate period. *Dezinformatsia* was reviewed in the CIA's own internal publication, *Studies in Intelligence*. The reviewer, Avis Boutell, is a CIA analyst with many years of experience. She observed that Schultz and Godson "begin with extraordinarily naive assumptions and resort to specious arguments to prove the obvious."[21] She concluded her review by remarking that "Naive assumptions and erroneous history make good propaganda but bad policy. They serve neither scholarship nor the national interest."[22] Ironically, *Dezinformatsia* has been looked upon favourably by at least some members of CSIS.

Despite the fact that certain key assumptions, particularly those about cold war issues, are almost universally shared, the ideology of the Western intelligence community is by no means monolithic. Inter-organizational competitiveness plays an important role, as do rivalries within agencies. In addition, on the fringes of the intelligence community various academics, journalists, and politicians play roles similar to that played by Schultz and Godson, in that they openly promote the views of one or other faction within the security and intelligence agencies. They too play an ideological role in the cold war system.

The well-known journalist Chapman Pincher, who has for years made no secret of his intimate relationship with senior figures in the British security and intelligence community, represents the visible portion of the larger struggle that has gone on between the right and the left within the community. He has written extensively attempting to prove allegedly treasonous activities on the part of other senior members of the same community,[23] and he is also enthusiastic about the issue of Soviet agents of influence. In *The Secret Offensive* he implies that agents of influence not only operate as Members of Parliament[24] and as trade union leaders,[25] but also include religious leaders who support "African terrorists"[26] and photographers who "angle their pictures to show 'police brutality'."[27] Another menacing aspect of this problem, according to Pincher, is that "cartoonists are assiduously sought as agents of influence with apparent success in all countries of the West."[28]

It is tempting to dismiss the agents of influence mania as droll nonsense, which on one level is exactly what it is. However, it also has serious aspects. The spectre of agents of influence is particularly dangerous because it can provide a powerful argument for erasing the distinction between dissent and subversion. Quite simply, this conspiratorial view of history and politics is profoundly anti-democratic. The logic of the argument is circular: the Soviet Union relentlessly seeks to destroy all non-Communist governments, therefore anyone who criticizes the status quo in a non-Communist country is, consciously or not, advancing the aims of the Kremlin. If this simplistic view of the world were to be taken seriously, it could have a devastating effect on the democratic political process. Moreover, the logic is essentially the same as that of the most notorious witch-hunters of the original cold war period, who used the "Red smear" on anyone who criticized them or refused to co-operate with them. The implication is that the only truly loyal and reliable citizens are those who at all times uncritically support the status quo.

The agents-of-influence argument can also be used in an attempt to justify blanket political surveillance of the population by the security services. The case for this approach has been put succinctly in an article by Roy Godson and Arnold Beichman. They claim that

> There is substantial evidence that terrorists and some of those who will eventually begin to work as agents of influence or spies for foreign powers are drawn to this work through legal political activities. When these individuals consciously decide to engage in illegal acts, they will begin to take precautions to ensure that they are not subject to surveillance. If they have not been identified or subject to any surveillance at an earlier and legal stage of their activities — i.e., if there is a weak or non-existing data base — the work of the CI [Counter Intelligence] operatives will be much more difficult later on.[29]

If the logic of this argument is accepted, then there is no reason for not turning liberal democracies into police states. It is indeed an expression of a dark view of human nature; but it is a public expression of the general position that has long been taken by elements of the right wing of the international intelligence community.

These elements have also suffered over the years from what

might aptly be called "mole fever." This disease is characterized by an obsessive fear that Soviet spies, or "moles," have burrowed deeply into Western governmental structures, particularly the intelligence services, where they remain buried for years or decades, gnawing away at vital organs on behalf of their masters in the Kremlin. Like most phobias, the fear of moles has a basis in reality. Kim Philby, Donald Maclean, Guy Burgess, and Anthony Blunt, for example, were real. They were Soviet agents, and they did harm the interests of the West. The entertaining word "moles" can accurately be applied to them.

Other less spectacular cases of Soviet espionage have, of course, been discovered in Western countries from time to time. These have frequently involved people in relatively humble positions who have had access to secret material and who have been persuaded to divulge it illegally through blackmail, monetary payment, or the satisfaction of some neurotic need. Although much political hay is often made of the detection of such spies, it is in fact a relatively routine matter. Discovering such agents, regardless of which country they are working for, is the proper work of the security services.

But the trauma of the Philby case has left an enduring legacy of fear in these organizations: there must be other Philbys. Many millions have been spent and much learned ink has been expended in speculation as to the identity of the elusive fifth man, sixth man, or twenty-seventh man from the "Cambridge Comintern" of the early 1930s, or as to the identity of their collaborators or spiritual offspring. The latter-day attacks on Herbert Norman and innuendoes against Lester Pearson and Pierre Trudeau arise out of this legacy of fear.

In the world of the mullahs of counter-intelligence, no one is above suspicion: the safeguarding of Western security depends upon a continuing, long-term, painstaking piecing together of the puzzle. No detail is too small, no fragment too trivial in this time-defying effort. Each snippet of information might have significance — if not immediately, then later, when the outline of the big picture becomes more discernible. Today's gossip and tittle-tattle just might be the crucial final piece of the puzzle that will complete the picture next year or fifteen years from now.

This approach has a limited kind of validity. It would apply in a static world, in which the strategic purposes of states never vary, and in which the ideas and purposes of individuals are equally

174

fixed and unchanging. This may be the nature of the world inhabited by spies and counter-spies. But for all its emphasis on piecing together puzzles through time, it is a world out of history. In the real historical world, the only certainty is that everything is in a constant state of change. Thus, for example, one's understanding of the world and what one should do in it at the age of twenty is bound to be drastically altered by the time one reaches forty or sixty. This is true because of the interaction between the way one grows intellectually and the way the world in which one lives evolves.

What was most interesting about the careers of Philby and Maclean was not that they knew each other at Cambridge in 1932 in the Communist left. It was not to be found in any of the minutiae of their lives. Nor was it that they were both working for the British government in Washington in 1946 and were Soviet agents, although these facts are important, to be sure. What is most significant is that in order to be the incredibly successful mole that he was, Kim Philby had to stop being a thinking political person the minute he changed from revolutionary to spy. The life of a revolutionary, or of any serious political activist, is a never-ending series of struggles: struggles to understand the world and the way it changes, struggles to determine the right course of action at a given time, struggles with others, struggles with one's own conscience. The way ahead is never entirely clear or obvious.

A high-level, long-term espionage agent cannot afford the intellectual luxury of such struggles. He must be like the deadest bureaucrat in that for him the way is clear: he must serve his masters. He can be clever and shrewd, devious and innovative; but he cannot allow himself to question his motives or the rightness of the cause he serves.

The twists and turns of the policies of the Soviet Union and of the world Communist movement from the 1930s imposed enormous pressures on the members of every Communist Party. They were forced to accept that Social Democrats were class enemies in 1934 but allies in 1935, that the fight against Fascism was of paramount importance until the Hitler-Stalin Pact of 1939, whereupon peace was of the greatest importance until June 1941. Then, suddenly, no effort was to be spared in the effort to win the war against Hitler. Until 1956 Stalin was a great revolutionary and friend of the world's peoples; after that he was a cruel despot. A great many dedicated Communists in every country left the Party after each of these — and many other — reverses. Those who stayed, for the most part, did so only through struggle. They did so with doubts. They stayed because they were convinced by their comrades that the Party, in spite of its deplorable inconsistency, offered the best hope for humanity. In a relatively small number of cases, those who stayed were Party bureaucrats with a cynical personal interest in maintaining the organization. Philby had to be like the cynical Party bureaucrat, only more so. He could not entertain doubts and he could not take part in political struggle.

John le Carré has eloquently made the point that the world as viewed by the Soviet spy and the world as seen from inside a secret intelligence service are not very dissimilar. It is worth quoting him at length:

> I do not much believe in the political motive of Kim Philby; but I am sure that the British secret service kept it alive as no other environment could have done. The British intelligence world described here is apolitical. Once entered, it provides no further opportunity for spiritual development. The door that clanged behind the new entrant protected him as much from himself as from reality. Philby, once employed, met spies, conundrums, technique; he had said goodbye to controversy. Such political opinions as sustained him were the opinions of his childhood. The clearer air of the outside world would have blown them away in a year.... He was left with a handful of clichés whose application had ceased in 1931. Similarly, the posturing chauvinism of his superiors would long have passed for idiotic in the outside world; in the secret world it passed for real. Thus in the same secret place, under the same secret sun, the anachronisms of his quarry were sheltered from the changing frosts of reality. Citadel and avenger, both unnaturally protected, were fighting out the battles of the thirties.[30]

It is the contradiction between the static, airless world shared by the moles and their hunters, on the one hand, and the real world of political battle on the other, that makes mole fever a dangerous disease. In the frantic excitement of the hunt, it is all too easy to rip apart entire organizations and societies. Those whose suspicion is limitless are ultimately damaged as much as those whom they suspect.

Perhaps the greatest mole hunter of all is James Jesus Angleton, the CIA Chief of Counterintelligence until his retirement in 1974.

Angleton apparently believes that there is a world-wide Communist conspiracy. He has expressed the view that various splits within the Communist world, including the historic divide between the Soviet Union and China, are simply clever ruses designed to fool the gullible West. In counter-intelligence he was a master at collating every scrap of information on a subject, searching for a discrepancy, and then, when one was found, searching for a motive, which might well, in his view, be deliberate deception.

A similar inclination to view the world through a prism of almost universal suspicion also existed for decades in the RCMP Security Service. One of the legacies of the Gouzenko affair was the suspicion it left with the Security Service that, in addition to the Soviet espionage activities revealed by the Kellock-Taschereau Royal Commission in 1946, other Soviet agents inside the Canadian government had gone undetected.

The "Featherbed" file on suspected Communist moles was established in great secrecy in the early 1950s.[31] Herbert Norman's name was only the first on a list that eventually held those of hundreds of persons suspected of having once been Communists and of then having spent years or decades pretending to be loyal Canadians while in fact being Soviet agents all the while. Resources devoted to expanding the Featherbed file were increased during the 1960s. It came to encompass not only those suspected of having been secret members of the Communist Party, but also large numbers of Canadians active in other left-wing political activities. The operative assumption was in effect that left-wing thought in general predisposes an individual to become a Soviet spy. Thus the net had to be cast not only over persons rendered suspect by their past political associations, but also ultimately over those responsible for advocating or enacting "subversive" public policy.[32]

James Angleton, not surprisingly, shared the opinion of the Featherbed operatives that the government of Canada had been penetrated by moles. Consequently, the RCMP Security Service and the CIA Counterintelligence Division co-operated closely in their efforts to discover and keep track of persons regarded as suspected Soviet agents and "subversives" in the political arena and the public service. Ironically, a senior Security Service custodian of the Featherbed file, Leslie James Bennett, himself fell under suspicion and was forced out of the RCMP.

The case against Bennett was based partially on some members of his family in Wales having been involved in left-wing politics

177

JAMES LITTLETON

in the 1930s, and also partly on his having challenged James Angleton on the value of McCarthyism as a way of guarding democracy. When he was being interrogated in Ottawa by his RCMP colleagues in 1972, Bennett was confronted on his opposition to McCarthyism. He had expressed his doubts about it at a Washington party attended by two senior British security and intelligence officers, James Angleton, Angleton's assistant Ray Rocca, and Angleton's favourite Soviet defector, Anatoli Golitsin.

According to Bennett, "it became a very acrimonious discussion with the two men from the CIA really trying to, I suppose from their viewpoint, put me right on my incorrect evaluation of McCarthyism and the value it had to the United States security." When asked if his dislike of McCarthyism had been used against him, Bennett replied, "Yes, it was used as an example of possibly the fact that I may not be as loyal to democracy as I should be."[33] Bennett was forced into early retirement from the RCMP in 1972 and given a small medical pension. From his exile in Perth, Australia, Bennett is able to savour the ironies of his fate. In one conversation, he wryly observed that those still seeking proof of his alleged guilt might find it in the fact that he is employed by a private company called Mole Engineering, Ltd., which specializes in excavation projects.

William Kelly was Director-General of the Security Service during the 1960s and retired as Deputy Commissioner of the RCMP in 1970. In a revealing comment on the prevalence of a kind of McCarthyesque obsessive suspicion in the world of security and intelligence, Kelly observed that

> Bennett would know that once under suspicion [although no evidence was found], he would have no way to prove his innocence, a nearly impossible thing to do.
>
> Even if the original suspicions were unfounded, it would have been equally impossible for him to regain the complete and necessary trust of his RCMP colleagues and those in other security agencies. Such is the nature of the atmosphere in which security work is carried out.[34]

The internal manoeuvrings and purges of most bureaucracies are often of little consequence except to insiders who are directly affected. But this is not so in the case of the security services. Their scrutiny extends far beyond their own members, past the

178

ranks of the federal state, to the farthest reaches of all civil society. James Angleton has come to symbolize the tendency of secret agencies to embody and perpetuate the essentially anti-democratic values inherent in the cold war stance. But Angleton is merely a representative of a type: the kind of intelligence officer who subjectively, because of his knowledge of "the secrets," and objectively, because of organizational imperatives, believes that he knows better than anyone what is best for the people. His mission, ultimately, is to ensure that serious deviations from the essentials of his ideology do not become too frequent or too influential.

This mission is normally accomplished unobtrusively, with subtlety. The widespread acceptance of cold war assumptions, in both East and West, is evidence of the success of this effort. This is not to suggest a simplistic theory that political attitudes in general are created and manipulated by secret services for their own benefit. Far from it. History is not made by conspiracies. History unfolds on its own dynamics. Individuals are shaped by their experiences and make their own decisions. The ways in which people think about what goes on around them, and the limits to what they consider to be thinkable, are influenced by the information they receive.

Because of their own imperatives, secret agencies inevitably attempt, wittingly or not, to place limits on public discourse on certain matters. These limits naturally are most evident in the area of national security, which is to say in the central area of cold war preoccupations. In their eyes, to question the basic assumptions upon which the cold war edifice rests is to move towards disloyalty.

A strikingly clear example of the ideological role of the security services occurred in Britain in the summer of 1985. A respected British newspaper, the *Observer*, revealed an intimate link between the much-esteemed British Broadcasting Corporation and the British Security Service, MI5. For years the BBC has had a resident officer whose job is to run security checks on BBC personnel.[35] The political views of journalists and others are gleaned from the "domestic subversion" desk of MI5, which has a computer containing the names of half a million "subversive" Britons. BBC interviewing boards do not ask subjects about their political opinions, but if MI5 gives a negative report, a person's professional life might be destroyed, without the individual's being aware of the reason. The *Observer* editorialized that:

"security" governs access to state secrets; it is there to detect foreign spies, not to exclude journalists from BBC jobs because they may (or may not, as it turns out) hold views on social and political issues that fall outside a narrowly defined official orthodoxy. In how many other areas of our national life is this intrusion going on? In far too many, one suspects.[36]

The McDonald Royal Commission reported on the extent to which such meddling had been taking place in Canadian life. It discovered extensive and disturbing intrusions. None that were reported were as boldly manipulative as the BBC-MI5 case. Nevertheless, one of the remarkable aspects of the BBC-MI5 case is the fact that it was discovered. The case casts a glaring light on the wider and more subtle danger faced not only by journalists but by other citizens as well. It is that without our being fully aware of it, our perception of the world, our inquiry, and our thinking are limited to an increasingly narrow orthodoxy. Clichés and assumptions are taken for granted. State interference does not have to be direct to be effective.

Canada is a minor player in the world compared with the superpowers. Even a fading imperial Britain has greater global pretensions. It also has more severe domestic social conflict. Consequently, it should not be surprising that British security services tend to play a more openly intrusive role than do their counterparts in Canada.

The history of CSIS is too short for any clear pattern to have been established regarding its relationship to the democratic political process. In considering its performance, however, certain factors are particularly salient. The overwhelming fact is that CSIS is inescapably an integral part of the international intelligence community. For that reason it is necessarily subject to enormous pressures to conform to the standards, practices, and values that comprise the culture of that community.

CSIS inherited a vast number of arrangements that had existed between the RCMP Security Service and similar organizations in other countries. Some of these arrangements are formal, documented, and authorized at the diplomatic level. Others are informal and are based on an "implicit understanding of co-operation." Still others exist, but only as verbal agreements.[37] The total bulk of the documented arrangements is described by Ron Atkey,

Chairman of the Security Intelligence Review Committee, as t
ing up four to five feet of space on a bookshelf.[38] This would a....
up to many thousands of pages.

The McDonald Royal Commission reported that responsible
cabinet ministers were for the most part unaware of the terms of
these international arrangements.[39] It is not a subject about which
either the RCMP or CSIS is inclined to be forthcoming. The McDonald
Commission itself had to do a great deal of research even to determine that a great many arrangements did in fact exist.[40] Five
years later, the Security Intelligence Review Committee reported
that "CSIS did not have the information organized or collated in a
way which would have allowed Committee members to review all
of it," although this was subsequently done at the committee's
request.[41] The McDonald Commission had warned about the dangers of liaison agreements, particularly if they were not subject to
government scrutiny. The Commission also warned that "Another, less tangible, problem related to foreign agreements is the
danger of Canada's security intelligence agency adopting the outlook and opinions of a foreign agency, especially of an agency
which has come to be depended upon heavily."[42]

The transfer of responsibility for security intelligence in Canada from the RCMP to CSIS has been the cause of a good deal of
anxiety in the international intelligence community. Even before
the McDonald Commission had finished its work and made its
recommendations, James Angleton was worried about the prospect
of the RCMP losing the security function. He reasoned that if a
man had to spend five or ten years as a Mountie doing regular
police work in Canada, his background, attitudes, and reliability
could be thoroughly checked. The always-cautious Angleton feared
that a civilian security intelligence service in Canada would be in
much greater danger of penetration by Soviet moles. He also was
concerned that Canadians who had played what in his view had
been a brave part in the battle against Communist subversion
would be victimized in the witch-hunt that he was sure would
ensue.[43] No such retribution ever did take place. Indeed, not one
member of the RCMP was prosecuted and convicted for the wrongdoing that was reported by the McDonald Commission.

The enactment of the CSIS legislation has caused consternation
within the Western intelligence community — Angleton's apprehension of moles is only one aspect. The provisions in the CSIS

Act for "oversight" procedures, that allowed for a continuing inspection of CSIS's activities by the Security Intelligence Review
Committee, have caused additional concern in allied intelligence
organizations. Any external review of security and intelligence
practices is viewed with alarm by the hard-liners in the international intelligence community. In their minds, no one but they
themselves, no outsiders, can be trusted with the secrets. Members
of the Federal Cabinet, CSIS, and the Security Intelligence Review
Committee have all taken considerable pains to reassure the allied
organizations that their secrets and their ways of operating will
not be jeopardized by the new Canadian set-up.[44] The process of
CSIS and the Review Committee attempting to prove their tough-
ness and reliability in these terms is likely to go on for years.

Although it was the creation of the Trudeau government, CSIS
had barely begun to function before Brian Mulroney and his Progressive Conservative government were swept into office. Mulroney's oft-repeated promise to make better relations with the
Americans his first priority must have given considerable satisfaction to the Reagan administration and to the chiefs of its intelligence agencies.

Elmer MacKay was Brian Mulroney's choice as Solicitor-General, the Cabinet Minister who would be in charge of both the
RCMP and CSIS. The appointment was a source of deep satisfaction
for MacKay. Joe Clark had made Allan Lawrence his Solicitor-
General in 1979. MacKay bitterly resented this, even though he
was in the Clark Cabinet as Minister of Regional Economic Expansion. He became one of Mulroney's earliest and most fervent
supporters. Giving up his parliamentary seat of Central Nova so
that Mulroney could occupy it temporarily was only one of a great
many services he provided the future Prime Minister.

Elmer MacKay had been fascinated both by the RCMP and by
problems of national security for many years. As the son of a
prosperous, stern, and conservative lumber operator, he had grown
up with a strong sense of moral obligation. The people of his
native Pictou County have little time for pretension or posturing;
they value strength and reliability. They voted for Brian Mulroney
in 1983 because Elmer MacKay told them they should. He had
earned their respect almost twenty years earlier as a tough lawyer
who delighted in foiling the local Mounties whenever they tried
to harass or entrap a citizen.

Elmer MacKay, fighter for the ordinary citizen, was asked to

182

run for Parliament by Robert Stanfield in 1971. Over the years MacKay's conception of the proper stance for a champion of the people underwent changes. He was a fierce critic of Pierre Trudeau in the House of Commons. He became the friend and defender of the rank-and-file members of the Security Service, directing his fire at Liberal Solicitors-General and the senior officers of the RCMP. He dedicated himself early on to realizing the idea of a civilian security service. In a conversation on his father's Pictou County farm in the summer of 1980, he lamented the bureaucratic mythology that protected the institutional structure of the RCMP. He said, "You have this automatic response that I've run into, no matter if you have them cold, there's always an explanation, there's always an attempt to paint anyone who comments however objectively on the RCMP as somehow subversive, somehow anti-Canadian, somehow despicable. Unless you're in complete support of all they stand for, you're going to be a very, very unpopular man if you say anything that questions their omnipotence and their essential goodness."

I suggested that this might cause one to wonder how valid are the threats to national security that Canadians have been worried about for years. Elmer MacKay considered the idea and replied obliquely: "The part that strikes me as so funny in a macabre sort of way is that there are never any occasions that they're less than perfect, and that's their weakness, because now they are becoming objects of derision. Think back when you were a kid, how many cartoons did you ever see criticizing the RCMP? Now the papers are full of them."[45]

Five years later, as the Conservative Solicitor-General, Elmer MacKay's earlier concerns about the RCMP bureaucracy seemed to have been replaced by a strong determination to make CSIS work. He wanted to apply the perspective he had gained from his rank-and-file friends to the running of the organization. The atmosphere of the new cold war was propitious. MacKay could live in harmony with the allies, the CSIS organization, and even the RCMP high command. Towards the end of his time as Solicitor-General, he was becoming frustrated. There were still too many impediments to the kind of action-oriented organization he wanted. There was still bureaucratic friction between the RCMP and CSIS, despite or perhaps because of the fact that CSIS was populated largely by RCMP Security Service veterans (according to the Security Intelligence Review Committee, "95 per cent of the members of the RCMP Security Service chose to transfer to the new agency"[46]). The ambiguity and compromise that the reality of politics inevitably imposes were making themselves felt for Elmer MacKay.

The CSIS legislation reflects many of the attitudes that were prevalent during the *détente* period in which it had its genesis. An important question is whether the vestiges of that period will be anachronistic in the late 1980s. Ultimately, the letter of any law, including the CSIS legislation, is not as important as the spirit in which it is observed. At present, CSIS is in many respects the RCMP Security Service under a different name.

Whether the political culture that was criticized by the McDonald Royal Commission but inherited by the new service will prove to be a problem to the wider Canadian society is another question. A more serious question is whether the political context, both domestic and international, in which CSIS operates will encourage or discourage a reassertion and entrenchment of the cold war values of suspicion and intolerance of dissent.

In the second half of the 1980s, the prospects are not particularly bright. Cold war attitudes, especially in international relations, have been in the ascendancy in the United States since the late 1970s. The geographical importance of Canada to the achievement of the strategic aims of the Reagan administration is becoming increasingly apparent. The nature of the cold war system, particularly the strong links within the international security and intelligence community, suggests that the pressures on CSIS to conform by adhering to cold war values will be considerable. The extent of that conformity remains to be seen.

Epilogue

B ecause it occupies such a strategically important piece of real estate, Canada is being and will continue to be subjected to considerable pressure to accommodate the American Strategic Defense Initiative and other related schemes that require the utilization of Canadian territory. The quality and extent of political debate in the country will determine the stance that will finally be taken on these issues. In a situation in which the cold war establishment in Washington perceives its vital interests to be at stake, it is to be expected that the international intelligence community will play a key role in ensuring that these interests are protected.

The tendency among conservative elements in the intelligence community to automatically accept cold war assumptions about international relations suggests that those who exceed orthodox limits in this debate may at some point be perceived as representing threats to national security. This perception can apply not only to the traditionally defined left, but also to mainstream politicians and other opinion leaders when they are seen to obstruct vital schemes for the defence of the West. After all, some members of the Reagan administration did little to conceal their loathing for Pierre Trudeau during his peace initiative in his last year as Prime Minister of Canada.

The extreme form of resistance to the politics of peace on the part of members of the cold war establishment is found in a remarkable statement by George K. Young, a former Deputy Director of Britain's secret intelligence service, MI6. Under the heading "When Treason Can Be Right," Young claims that:

> There is still the disturbing prospect of treason in high places. And what of a government willing to pursue *détente* to the point of complete surrender? At that stage the officers of a special operations executive or the Security Service may feel that the only course of action is to grab their Top Secret Files and head — if not to the hills — at least for the United States embassy.[1]

185

Perhaps George Young, like James Angleton, was a bit of an extremist in the international intelligence community. It would be misleading to suggest that his view is representative of that of most of the responsible leaders in the intelligence community. But the willingness of such men to subvert democratic political processes if these lead in directions that they dislike is striking. Their own words reveal that they are not finally concerned to protect democracy from subversion; they almost seem to want to do the opposite.

George K. Young's vision is dark and melodramatic. There are other, less dramatic ways of ensuring that the interests of the western alliance are protected. Again, one recalls the more subtle means that are employed by the CIA to influence the policies of other countries as described by General Vernon Walters — former Deputy Director of the CIA, advisor to a number of U.S. presidents, President Reagan's "Ambassador at Large" and principal world trouble-shooter, and presently U.S. Ambassador to the United Nations — when he remarked that a general method "is to seek to alter in the long term the thinking in the target nation in such a way as to make them perceive that their interest does not lie in hostility to the first nation.... The most successful action of this type takes place without anyone in the target nation being aware of it."[2]

The relationship between democracy and subversion is exceedingly complex. Democracy cannot simply be identified with one set of interests; it is a dynamic process. Ultimately, it cannot subvert itself. That can only be done by those who allow a narrow vision of the world to obscure the fact that democracy is a human project that never ends, and never can end.

Notes

Introduction
1. Vernon A. Walters, "The Uses of Political and Propaganda Covert Action in the 1980s," in Roy Godson, ed., *Intelligence Requirements for the 1980s*, Vol. IV: *Covert Action* (Washington, D.C.: National Strategy Information Center, 1981), p. 115.

Chapter 1 Areas of Influence
1. See Escott Reid, *Time of Fear and Hope: The Making of the North Atlantic Treaty, 1947-1949* (Toronto: McClelland and Stewart, 1977), pp. 20ff.
2. Victor Marchetti and John D. Marks, *The CIA and the Cult of Intelligence* (New York: Dell, 1975), p. 48. See, for example, Cord Meyer, *Facing Reality* (New York: Harper and Row, 1980), especially Chapter 5, "Cold War," for an account by a former CIA officer with direct knowledge of many of the events. Details of CIA activity in post-war Europe were confirmed and elaborated in an interview with Cord Meyer by the author in Washington, D.C., on April 28, 1981.
3. D.F. Flemming, *The Cold War and Its Origins, 1917-1960*, Vol. I (New York: Doubleday, 1961), pp. 174-87.
4. See Daniel Yergin, *Shattered Peace* (Boston: Houghton Mifflin, 1977), pp. 324-26, and Isaac Deutscher, *Stalin: A Political Biography* (Harmondsworth: Penguin, 1966), pp. 504ff.
5. For an elaboration of this argument, see Richard J. Barnet, *The Alliance* (New York: Simon and Schuster, 1983) and Reid, *Time of Fear and Hope*.
6. See Frank J. Donner, *The Age of Surveillance* (New York: Knopf, 1980), pp.86-87.
7. J. Edgar Hoover, *Masters of Deceit* (New York: Henry Holt, 1958), p. 319.
8. See Victor Navasky, *Naming Names* (New York: Viking, 1980).
9. *Time*, July 23, 1951, p. 13.

10. Irving Saypol, CBS Radio Network programme, August 10, 1950 (CBC Radio Archives, "McCarthy Era Tapes," #5008-1).
11. Ibid.
12. Quoted in Richard H. Rovere, *Senator Joe McCarthy* (New York: Harper Colophon, 1973), p. 182.
13. See Reginald Whitaker, "Origins of the Canadian Government's Internal Security System, 1946-1952," *The Canadian Historical Review*, vol. LXV, no. 2 (June 1984), pp. 154ff.
14. "To bar reds from positions in public service," Ottawa *Journal*, March 24, 1947, cited in ibid., p. 160.
15. See *The Report of the Royal Commission to Investigate the Facts Relating to and the Circumstances Surrounding the Communications, by Public Officials and Other Persons in Positions of Trust, of Secret and Confidential Information to Agents of a Foreign Power* (Ottawa: King's Printer, 1946) (generally referred to as the Kellock-Taschereau Commission Report).
16. Robert Bothwell and J.L. Granatstein, *The Gouzenko Transcripts* (Ottawa: Deneau, n.d.), p. 14.
17. See John Sawatsky, *Gouzenko: The Untold Story* (Toronto: Macmillan, 1984), for many previously unpublished candid opinions of Gouzenko, mainly from persons who were in close contact with him.
18. This conclusion is based on interviews in 1981 with six of the persons who were alleged by the Royal Commission to have been involved in the espionage ring.
19. Interview with Raymond Boyer, Montreal, June 22, 1981.
20. Interview with Freda Linton, January 28, 1981.
21. Kim Philby, *My Silent War* (New York: Grove Press, 1968), p. 163.
22. Interview with Don Wall, Portland, Ontario, June 18, 1984; interview with Christopher Dwyer, Rodney, Ontario, November 24, 1984.
23. Cited in Whitaker, "Internal Security Systems," p. 160.

Chapter 2 The Mythology of Treason

1. "Were Commies in control here?" in Toronto *Sun*, April 12, 1981, p. 1.
2. Ibid.
3. Roger W. Bowen, ed., *E.H. Norman: His Life and Scholarship* (Toronto: University of Toronto Press, 1984), p. x.
4. Pat Sloan, ed., *John Cornford: A Memoir* (London: Jonathan Cape, 1938), p. 99.
5. Ibid., p. 110.
6 Interview with Robert Bryce, Ottawa, October 20, 1980.
7. See, for example, William F. Buckley, Jr., and L. Brent Bozell, *McCarthy and His Enemies* (Chicago: Henry Regnery, 1954).

8. Bowen, *E.H. Norman*, p. *x*.
9. Transcript of Senate Internal Security Subcommittee session, August 7, 1951. Published in *U.S. News and World Report*, April 26, 1957, p. 121.
10. Ibid.
11. David Caute, *The Great Fear* (New York: Simon and Schuster, 1978), p. 56.
12. "Former red courier links Montreal man to espionage system," Montreal *Gazette*, June 6, 1949.
13. Transcript of Executive Session of United States Senate Subcommittee to Investigate the Administration of the Internal Security Act and Other Internal Security Laws of the Committee on the Judiciary, Washington, D.C., August 14, 1951, pp. 3-4.
14. Memorandum (100-364-301) from Special Agent in Charge, FBI New York, to Director, FBI, September 28, 1951, p. 4.
15. Ibid., p. 7.
16. Ibid., p. 9.
17. FBI (Hazen Edward Sise, 8/5/49) New York file #100-95076 MLB, pp. 3-4.
18. Roger W. Bowen, "Cold War, McCarthyism, and Murder by Slander: E.H. Norman's Death in Perspective," in Bowen, *E.H. Norman*, p. 63. Discussions with the following persons have also been useful in arriving at the conclusions set out here. Naturally, each subject would not necessarily agree with the conclusions: Robert Bryce, Ottawa, October 17, 1980; George Glazebrook, Toronto, January 10, 1981; Terry Guernsey, Toronto, February 19, 1981, and September 26, 1981; George B. McClellan, Montreal, February 11, 1981.
19. Interview with Robert Bryce, Ottawa, October 20, 1980.
20. Bowen, *E.H. Norman*, p. 63. Note that, with respect to security screening procedures in this period, the McDonald Royal Commission (*Second Report*, Vol. II, p. 781) pointed out that: "In March 1948 a system of security screening was formalized in Cabinet Directive 4, and with it the basic pattern for security clearances was established. The RCMP was instructed to screen all employees and candidates for employment in security sensitive positions. The findings of these security investigations were reported to the individual's department where the decision to grant the security clearance would be made."
21. Interview with Robert Bryce, Ottawa, October 20, 1980.
22. William Rusher, *Special Counsel* (New Rochelle: Arlington House, 1968), p. 199.
23. Interviews with Mrs. Irene Norman, Ottawa, January 14 and January 15, 1981.

Chapter 3 The Self-Perpetuating System

1. For two interpretations of the Cold War as self-perpetuating, see Reg Whitaker, "What Is the Cold War About and Why Is It Still With Us?", *Studies in Political Economy*, Spring 1986; and Thomas Powers, "What Is It About?", *The Atlantic Monthly*, January 1984, p. 54.
2. Harold Innis, *Essays in Canadian Economic History*, M.Q. Innis, ed. (Toronto: University of Toronto Press, 1956), p. 407.
3. "New Zealand warned not to close its ports to U.S. nuclear ships," Toronto *Globe and Mail*, July 17, 1984, p. 9.
4. *New York Times*, February 14, 1985 (reported by Peter Goodspeed in *Toronto Star*, February 15, 1985 — "Canada obliged to take nuclear arms in crisis, U.S. says," p. A1).
5. "Chief of CIA and Senate critic meet on issue of pro-Soviet bias," *New York Times*, December 3, 1985, p. 4.
6. John Prados, *The Soviet Estimate* (New York: Dial Press, 1982), p. 250.
7. The most comprehensive account of the scope and magnitude of this activity is in James Bamford, *The Puzzle Palace* (Boston: Houghton Mifflin, 1982). This estimate arises out of discussions with James Bamford in August 1983.
8. For a more comprehensive discussion of these agreements and of Canada's SIGINT activities, see Chapter 6.
9. Royal Canadian Mounted Police, *Law and Order in Canadian Democracy* (Ottawa: Queen's Printer, 1952), p. *vii*. Cited in Carolyn and Lorne Brown, *An Unauthorized History of the RCMP* (Toronto: James Lorimer & Co., n.d.), p. 95.
10. Ibid., p. 1, also cited in *An Unauthorized History*.
11. John le Carré, "Introduction" to Bruce Page, David Leitch, and Phillip Knightly, *The Philby Conspiracy* (New York: Ballantine, 1981), p. 8.
12. Ibid., p. 9.

Chapter 4 American Confidence

1. See, for example, Colin Gray and Keith Payne, "Victory Is Possible," *Foreign Policy*, Summer 1980; Eugene Rostow, "The Case Against SALT II," *Commentary*, January 1979; Richard Pipes, "Why the Soviet Union Thinks It Could Fight and Win a Nuclear War," *Commentary*, July 1977.
2. John T. Elliff, *The Reform of FBI Intelligence Operations* (Princeton: Princeton University Press, 1979), pp. 4ff.

3. *United States* v. *United States District Court*, 407 U.S. 297, cited in ibid., p. 9.
4. Charles Mohr, "Frustration, resignation and the CIA," *New York Times*, September 30, 1985.
5. Interview with James J. Angleton, Washington, D.C., March 17, 1981.
6. Jay Peterzell, "The Intelligence Transition," *First Principles*, vol. VI, no. 4 (January 1981), p. 3.
7. Ibid. See volumes on various aspects of Intelligence published by the consortium, the third of which is Roy Godson, ed., *Intelligence Requirements for the 1980s*, Vol. III: *Counterintelligence* (Washington, D.C.: National Strategy Information Center, 1980).
8. Peterzell, "Intelligence Transition," p. 1.
9. Ibid.
10. Ibid., p. 2.
11. Ibid.
12. *Intelligence: The Acme of Skill* (Washington, D.C.: CIA, n.d.), p. 28.
13. See United States Senate, *Intelligence Activities and the Rights of Americans*, Book II: *Final Report of the Select Committee to Study Governmental Operations with Respect to Intelligence Activities* (Washington, D.C.: U.S. Government Printing Office, 1976), especially "Recommendations," pp. 296-339. See also "The CIA Becomes Central Again," *The Economist*, April 28, 1984, p. 38.
14. David Ignatius, "Casey raises morale and budget at CIA, but not public image," *Wall Street Journal*, January 11, 1985, p. 1.
15. Philip Taubman, "Aggressive CIA chief," *New York Times*, April 19 1984.
16. Ibid.
17. Judith Miller, "Reagan widens intelligence role, gives CIA domestic spy power," *New York Times*, December 5, 1985, p. 11.
18. Leslie Gelb, "Shift is reported on CIA actions," *New York Times*, June 11, 1984, p. 1.
19. "America's Secret Warriors," *Newsweek*, October 10, 1983, pp. 38ff.
20. Gelb, "CIA actions," p. 4.
21. Ibid.
22. "Reflections on Peace and Security," remarks by the prime minister to the Conference on Strategies for Peace and Security in the Nuclear Age, University of Guelph, Ontario, October 27, 1983, p. 2.
23. Bill Fox, "Reagan avoided specifics with PM," *Toronto Star*, December 17, 1983.
24. Carl Mollins (Canadian Press), "PM reportedly called 'erratic leftist'," Toronto *Globe and Mail*, December 16, 1983; Carl Mollins (Canadian Press), "U.S. aide named in 'pot' slur on PM," *Toronto Star*, December 22, 1983.

25. "'As a species threatened with extinction we must prevent the chance of nuclear war'," *Toronto Star*, November 14 1984, p. A8.
26. Robert Jackson, *World Military Aircraft Since 1945* (New York: Scribner's, 1979), p. 128.
27. David Halloway, *The Soviet Union and the Arms Race* (New Haven: Yale University Press, 1983), p. 89.
28. Quoted in ibid., p. 91.
29. Nicolas Lemann, "Caspar Weinberger in Reagan's Pentagon: The Peacetime War," *The Atlantic Monthly*, October 1984, p. 94.
30. "U.S. defends NATO after Trudeau remarks," Toronto *Globe and Mail*, November 15, 1984.

Chapter 5 Strategic Considerations

1. "'The Relationship of Defence Policy to Foreign Policy,' excerpts from an address by Prime Minister Trudeau to a Dinner of the Alberta Liberal Association, Calgary, April 12, 1969," in *Statements and Speeches*, No. 69/8 (Ottawa: Information Division, Department of External Affairs), p. 4.
2. Senate of Canada, *Proceedings of the Special Committee of the Senate on National Defence*, Issue No. 2, February 22, 1984, p. 9.
3. Quoted in James Eayrs, *In Defence of Canada*, Vol. II: *Appeasement and Rearmament* (Toronto: University of Toronto Press, 1965), p. 183.
4. Ibid.
5. Ibid., p. 184.
6. Trevor Lloyd, "Canada's Strategic North," *International Journal*, vol. II, no. 2 (Spring 1947), p. 144.
7. F.H. Soward, *Canada in World Affairs: From Normandy to Paris, 1944-46* (Toronto: Oxford University Press, 1950), p. 267.
8. Canada, House of Commons, *Debates*, August 3, 1944, p. 5844.
9. Lloyd, "Canada's Strategic North," p. 145.
10. Blair Fraser, "The Watch on the Arctic," *Maclean's*, December 1, 1946, pp. 7-8, 69-71.
11. L.B. Pearson, "Canada Looks Down North," *Foreign Affairs*, July 1946, pp. 643-44.
12. J.W. Pickersgill and D.F. Forster, eds., *The Mackenzie King Record*, Vol. 3: 1945-1946 (Toronto: University of Toronto Press, 1970), p. 362.
13. Ibid., p. 364.

14. Ibid., p. 366.
15. Ibid., p. 367.
16. Ibid.
17. Canada, House of Commons, *Debates*, February 12, 1947, p. 346, cited in Robert A. Spencer, *Canada in World Affairs, 1946-1949* (Toronto: Oxford University Press, 1959), p. 306.
18. James Eayrs, *In Defence of Canada*, Vol. III: *Peacemaking and Deterrence* (Toronto: University of Toronto Press, 1972), p. 355.
19. See Fred Kaplan, *The Wizards of Armageddon* (New York: Simon and Schuster, 1983), pp. 232-48. See also Gregg Herken, *The Winning Weapon* (New York: Knopf, 1980), pp. 198ff.
20. David Alan Rosenberg, "The Origins of Overkill: Nuclear Weapons and American Strategy, 1945-1960," *International Security*, vol. VII, no. 4 (Spring 1983), p. 14.
21. Ibid., p. 23.
22. "NSC 20/4, U.S. Objectives with Respect to the U.S.S.R. to Counter Soviet Threats to U.S. Security, 23 November 1948," cited in Rosenberg, "Origins of Overkill," p. 14.
23. Rosenberg, "Origins of Overkill," p. 16.
24. JCS 1496/3, September 19, 1945, and JCS 1518, September 19, 1945, cited in ibid., p. 17.
25. Rosenberg, "Origins of Overkill," p. 23.
26. Ibid., p. 34.
27. JCS, op. cit.
28. NSC-68, April 14, 1950, pp. 263-64, cited in John Lewis Gaddis, *Strategies of Containment: A Critical Appraisal of Post-War American National Security Policy* (New York: Oxford University Press, 1982), p. 91.
29. NSC-68, cited in Rosenberg, "Origins of Overkill," p. 25.
30. Lawrence Freedman, *The Evolution of Nuclear Strategy* (New York: St. Martin's Press, 1981), p. 126.
31. Memorandum Op-36C/jm, *Briefing given to the representatives of all services at SAC Headquarters*, Offutt Air Force Base, Omaha, March 15, 1954, reproduced in David Alan Rosenberg, "A Smoking, Radiating Ruin at the End of Two Hours," *International Security*, vol. VI, no. 3 (Winter 1981/82), p. 27.
32. Ibid., p. 19.
33. Cited in Rosenberg, "Origins of Overkill," p. 26.
34. Eayrs, *Peacemaking and Deterrence*, p. 356.
35. Gregg Herken, *Counsels of War* (New York: Knopf, 1985), p. 63.
36. Rosenberg, "Origins of Overkill," p. 26.
37. Eayrs, *Peacemaking and Deterrence*, p. 369.
38. Ibid.

39. Lewis Hertzman, John Warnock, and Thomas Hockin, *Alliances and Illusions* (Edmonton: Hurtig, 1969), p. 63.
40. Donald Creighton, *Canada's First Century* (Toronto: Macmillan, 1970), p. 327.
41. Ibid., p. 326.
42. Pierre Elliott Trudeau, "Pearson ou l'abdication de l'esprit," *Cité Libre*, Avril 1963, pp. 9-10.
43. The Honourable Douglas Harkness and Rear Admiral Jeffrey Brock, quoted in "The Space Between", film 3 of television series "Defence of Canada" produced by Canadian Broadcasting Corporation and National Film Board of Canada, February 5, 1986, transcript, p. 12.
44. William Arkin and Richard Fieldhouse, *Nuclear Battlefields* (Cambridge, Mass.: Ballinger, 1985), p. 76.
45. Ibid., pp. 79, 216-19; Jeffrey T. Richelson and Desmond Ball, *The Ties That Bind* (Boston and Sydney: Allen and Unwin, 1985), p. 201.
46. The Honourable Joe Clark, Secretary of State for External Affairs, *Minutes of Proceedings and Evidence of the Standing Committee on External Affairs and National Defence*, Ottawa, Issue no. 51, December 4, 1985, p. 15.
47. General Robert T. Herres, USAF, "Aerospace Defence Command: Keeping Watch on the Skies of North America," *Signal*, Vol. 39, No. 7 (March 1985), pp. 18-21.
48. John Anderson, *Minutes of Proceedings and Evidence of the Standing Committee on External Affairs and National Defence*, Ottawa, Issue no. 52, December 6, 1985, p. 23.
49. *Canada's Territorial Air Defence*, Report of the Special Committee of the Senate on National Defence (Ottawa: Minister of Supply and Services, 1985), p. 10.
50. This account and the LeMay statement are reported in Fred Kaplan, *The Wizards of Armageddon* (New York: Simon and Schuster, 1983), pp. 132-35.

Chapter 6 Canada and the Western Intelligence Community

1. Jeffrey T. Richelson and Desmond Ball, *The Ties That Bind* (Boston and Sydney: Allen and Unwin, 1985), p. 301.
2. Ibid., p. 303.
3. David Wise and Thomas B. Ross, *The Invisible Government* (New York: Bantam, 1965), pp. 116-20. Jonathan Bloch and Patrick Fitzgerald, *British Intelligence and Covert Action* (Dingle, Ireland: Brandon Publishers, 1983), p. 112.
4. Interview with Senator Michael Pitfield, Ottawa, July 20, 1984.

5. Peter St. John, "Canada's Accession to the Allied Intelligence Community, 1940-1945," *Conflict Quarterly*, vol. IV, no. 4 (Fall 1984), p. 5.
6. Ibid., p. 7.
7. Ibid., p. 9. See also David Kahn, "Introduction" to Herbert O. Yardley, *The American Black Chamber* (New York: Ballantine, 1981), p. *xv*.
8. St. John, "Canada's Accession," p. 12.
9. Ibid.
10. Ibid., p. 13.
11. Ibid., p. 14.
12. J.L. Granatstein, *A Man of Influence* (Ottawa: Deneau, 1981), p. 181.
13. James Bamford, *The Puzzle Palace* (Boston: Houghton Mifflin, 1982), p. 309.
14. Jeffrey T. Richelson, *The U.S. Intelligence Community* (Cambridge, Mass.: Ballinger, 1985), p. 198; CBC television programme "The Espionage Establishment" in series "The Fifth Estate," January 9, 1974, interview with Winslow Peck, transcript, p. 9.
15. Bamford, *Puzzle Palace*, p. 315.
16. Duncan Campbell, "The Threat of the Electronic Spies," *New Statesman*, February 2, 1979, p. 142.
17. Interview with Kevin O'Neill, Ottawa, June 21, 1984.
18. House of Commons, *Minutes and Proceedings and Evidence of the Standing Committee on Miscellaneous Estimates*, Issue no. 18, Ottawa, March 24, 1975, p. 20.
19. Interview with Senator Michael Pitfield, Ottawa, June 20, 1984.
20. Bamford, *Puzzle Palace*, p. 77.
21. Winslow Peck, "U.S. Electronic Espionage: A Memoir," *Ramparts*, August 1972, pp. 36-50.
22. Canada, House of Commons, *Debates*, January 10, 1974, p. 9226.
23. Interview with Kevin O'Neill, Ottawa, June 19, 1984.
24. William Johnson, "Trudeau gives few answers, but tells Commons Canada doesn't engage in espionage abroad," Toronto *Globe and Mail*, January 11, 1984, p. 1.
25. Canada, House of Commons, *Debates*, January 11, 1974, p. 9275.
26. Walter R. Agre, Brig. Gen., USAF, Memo to Co-ordinator of Joint Operations re "Proposed U.S.-Canadian Agreement," June 7, 1948 (2-1926).
27. Ibid.
28. See Richelson and Ball, *Ties That Bind*, p. 145.
29. Memorandum for the Chief of Staff, U.S. Army, from Maj. Gen. LeRoy Irwin, GSC, AC of S, G-2, on Canadian participation in forth-

coming Intelligence Conference, June 23, 1950, G-2/IWW-EST/73442, p. 1.

30. Ibid.

31. *IRSIG — 3rd edition Document, Part 1, Official Secrets Act Declaration COMINT Indoctrination: Declaration to be Signed after Briefing for Communications Intelligence,* reproduced in Richelson and Ball, *Ties That Bind,* p. 148.

32. Interview with Kevin O'Neill, Ottawa, June 19, 1984.

33. CBC-TV, "Fifth Estate" transcript, p. 12.

34. Ibid.

35. Desmond J. Ball, "Uneasy hosts, secretive guests," Sydney *National Times,* May 17, 1984.

36. Ibid. See Desmond Ball, *A Suitable Piece of Real Estate* (Sydney, Australia: Hale and Iremonger, 1980).

37. Ball, "Uneasy Hosts."

38. James A. Nathan, "Dateline Australia: American's Foreign Watergate," *Foreign Policy,* no. 49 (Winter 1982-83), p. 171.

39. Richard Hall, *The Secret State: Australia's Spy Industry* (North Melbourne: Cassell, 1978), p. 4.

40. Ibid., p. 84.

41. Interview with James J. Angleton on the Australian Broadcasting Corporation programme "Correspondents Report," June 12, 1977, cited in Ball, *Suitable Piece of Real Estate,* p. 145n, and Nathan, "Dateline Australia," p. 173.

42. Nathan, "Dateline Australia," p. 179.

43. Quoted in Ball, *Suitable Piece of Real Estate,* p. 170.

44. Nathan, "Dateline Australia," p. 176.

45. Chapman Pincher, *Inside Story* (London: Sidgwick and Jackson, 1978), p. 34.

46. Ibid., pp. 38-39.

47. Quoted in Bamford, *Puzzle Palace,* p. 19.

48. Interview with Don Wall, Portland, Ontario, June 18, 1984.

49. Canada, House of Commons, *Debates,* March 16, 1984, p. 2179.

50. Interview with Senator Michael Pitfield, September 10, 1983 (telephone).

51. Ibid.

52. *Proceedings of the Special Committee of the Senate on the Canadian Security Intelligence Service,* Ottawa, September 22, 1983, p. 32.

53. *Delicate Balance: A Security Intelligence Service in a Democratic Society.* Report of the Special Committee of the Senate on the Canadian Security Intelligence Service (Ottawa: Minister of Supply and Services, November 1983), p. 19.

54. Interview with the Honourable Ronald Atkey, PC, Chairman of the

Security Intelligence Review Committee, Toronto, September 25, 1985.

55. *RCMP Operational Manual*, May 23, 1970, LIA, p. 1079.
56. Ibid.
57. *RCMP Operational Manual*, September 25, 1970, LIA, p. 1110.
58. *Commission of Inquiry Concerning Certain Activities of the Royal Canadian Mounted Police* (McDonald Commission), *Second Report, Freedom and Security Under the Law*, vol. I (Ottawa: Canadian Government Publishing Centre, 1981) (hereinafter cited as McDonald Commission Reports), p. 635.
59. Ibid., p. 634.

Chapter 7 Political Violence
1. Quoted in William Johnson, "War on terror: FBI, CIA stand to gain from new mood in U.S.," *Globe and Mail*, July 3, 1985, p. 2.
2. "Terrorism and the Modern World," address by U.S. Secretary of State George P. Shultz, New York, October 25, 1984. Reprinted in the *New York Times*, October 26, 1984.
3. "Terrorism: Reagan on the record," *Wall Street Journal*, July 19, 1985.
4. Ibid.
5. Flora Lewis, "The big bark," *New York Times*, July 12, 1985, p. 23.
6. "Excerpts from the address by Shultz on fighting terror," *New York Times*, December 10, 1984.
7. Bernard Gwertzman, "Global actions to fight terror urged by Shultz," *New York Times*, June 25, 1985.
8. Lewis, "Big bark," p. 23.
9. "CIA study plays down Soviet terrorism tie," Toronto *Globe and Mail*, March 30, 1981.
10. Interview with U.S. Secretary of State Caspar Weinberger, Washington, D.C., March 17, 1981.
11. "CIA study plays down Soviet terrorism tie."
12. Ibid.
13. George P. Shultz, "America and the Struggle for Freedom," address to the Commonwealth Club of California, San Francisco, February 22, 1985; excerpts in *New York Times*, February 23, 1985.
14. Paul Wilkenson, *The New Fascists* (London: Grant McIntyre, 1981), p. 118.
15. Magnus Linklater, Isabel Hilton, and Neil Ascherson, *The Nazi Legacy: Klaus Barbie and the International Fascist Connection* (New

York: Holt, Rinehart and Winston, 1984). See especially pp. 278-308 for an account of the involvement of Stefano della Chiaie and other neo-Fascists in European terrorism, right-wing political activities in Latin America, and collaboration with various military and intelligence services.

16. See Martin A. Lee and Kevin Coogan, "The Agca con," New York *Village Voice*, December 24, 1985, pp. 19-23.

17. John Tagliabue, "Rome prosecutor urges acquittal of three Bulgarians," *New York Times*, February 28, 1986, p. 1.

18. The theory of a "Bulgarian Connection" was advanced, for example, in Claire Sterling, *The Time of the Assassins* (New York: Holt, Rinehart and Winston, 1983), and in Paul Hinze, *The Plot to Kill the Pope* (New York: Scribner's, 1983). These writers have also argued that the American mass media suppressed the evidence of the "Bulgarian Connection" because of "liberal bias" or "Soviet influence."

19. For instance, speaking in Amsterdam in 1872, Marx stated that: "We are aware of the importance that must be accorded to the institutions, customs and traditions of different countries; and we do not deny that there are countries like America, England (and, if I knew your institutions better, I would add Holland) where the workers can achieve their aims by peaceful means." Quoted in David McLellan, *The Thought of Karl Marx* (London: Macmillan, 1971), p. 209.

20. For a lucid discussion of "insurrectionary politics" in Marxist theory, see Ralph Miliband, *Marxism and Politics* (Oxford: Oxford University Press, 1977), pp. 166-75. For a detailed account of the application and the distortion of Marxist theory in the world Communist movement, see Fernando Claudin, *The Communist Movement: From Comintern to Cominform* (Harmondsworth: Penguin, 1975).

21. See, for example, "May 1968" in E.J. Hobsbawm, *Revolutionaries* (New York: New American Library, 1973), pp. 234-44.

22. This process has generated a vast body of literature. See, for example, Miliband, *Marxism and Politics*, and Raymond Williams, *The Year 2000* (New York: Pantheon, 1983); also successive issues of *New Left Review* (London), *Socialist Review* (New York), the annual *Socialist Register* (London), *Studies in Political Economy* (Ottawa), etc.

23. See, for example, Henri Michel, *The Shadow War: European Resistance 1939-1945*, translated by Richard Barry (New York: Harper and Row, 1972).

24. See "Mao's Primer on Guerrilla War," translated by Brigadier General Samuel B. Griffth II, in Lt. Col. T.N. Greene, ed., *The Guerrilla — And How to Fight Him* (New York: Praeger, 1962), pp. 5-21.

25. Department of State Bulletin, May 8, 1961, p. 660, cited in Brian Loveman and Thomas M. Davies, Jr., "Introduction," in Che Guevara, *Guerilla Warfare* (Lincoln: University of Nebraska Press, 1985), p. 26.

26. *International Development and Security Act, House Hearings*, pt. 1, p. 73, as cited in Raymond Estep, *United States Military Aid to Latin America* (Maxwell Air Force Base, Alabama: Documentary Research Division, Aerospace Studies Institute, Air University, 1966), p. 75, cited in Loveman and Davies, "Introduction," p. 26.

27. John S. Pustay, *Counterinsurgency Warfare* (New York: Free Press, 1965), p. 100.

28. Ibid.; Jonathan Bloch and Patrick Fitzgerald, *British Intelligence and Covert Action* (Dingle, Ireland: Brandon Publishers, 1983), p. 73.

29. Pustay, *Counterinsurgency Warfare*, p. 102.

30. Ibid., pp. 101, 102.

31. See Brian Loveman and Thomas M. Davies, Jr., *The Politics of Anti-Politics* (Lincoln: University of Nebraska Press, 1978).

32. See, for example, Richard A. Hunt, "Strategies at War: Pacification and Attrition in Viet Nam," in Richard A. Hunt and Richard H. Schultz, *Lessons from an Unconventional War* (New York: Pergamon, 1982), pp. 23-47.

33. For a comprehensive account of the political dynamics of the Vietnam War, see Gabriel Kolko, *Anatomy of a War: Viet Nam, the United States, and the Modern Historical Experience* (New York: Pantheon, 1985).

34. Ibid.; Richard A. Hunt, "Introduction," p. *xii*.

35. See Fred Halliday, *The Making of the Second Cold War* (London: Verso, 1983), p. 92.

36. Colonel John D. Waghelstein, "Post Viet Nam Counterinsurgency Doctrine," *Military Review*, vol. LXV (May 1985), p. 48.

37. *The Defense Monitor* (Washington, D.C.), vol. XIV, no. 2 (1985), p. 1.

38. Quoted in ibid., p. 2.

39. Waghelstein, "Post Viet Nam Counterinsurgency Doctrine" p. 42.

40. Colonel James B. Motley, "A Perspective on Low-Intensity Conflict," *Military Review*, January 1985, pp. 5-9.

41. Edward N. Luttwak, "Notes on Low-Intensity Warfare," *Parameters: Journal of the U.S. Army War College*, vol. XIII, no. 4 (December 1983), pp. 11-12.

42. Ibid., p. 13.

43. Carlos Marighella, "Minimanual of the Urban Guerrilla," Appendix to Robert Moss, *Urban Guerrilla Warfare* (London: International Institute of Strategic Studies, 1971), p. 40.

44. Warren Hinckle, Preface to "Guerrilla War in the U.S.A.," *Scanlans*, vol. I, no. 8 (January 1971), p. 12.
45. Canada, House of Commons, *Debates*, October 16, 1970, p. 215.
46. Ibid., pp. 223-24.
47. Ibid., p. 213.
48. "Plan to supplant Quebec government caused Ottawa to act," *Toronto Star*, October 26, 1970, p. 1.
49. "Knew about 'the plot that never was' Trudeau says," Toronto *Globe and Mail*, October 31, 1970.
50. Interview with Gordon Robertson, Ottawa, June 17, 1981.
51. Edward Luttwak, *Coup d'Etat* (Harmondsworth: Penguin, 1969), p. 11.
52. Canada, House of Commons, *Debates*, November 2, 1977, p. 564, cited in McDonald Commission, *Second Report*, Vol. I, p. 67.

Chapter 8 The Reform of the Security Service

1. Interview with Senator Michael Pitfield, Ottawa, June 19, 1984.
2. McDonald Commission, *Second Report*, Vol. II, p. 669.
3. Interview with George B. McClellan, Montreal, February 11, 1981; interview with Mark McClung, Ottawa, October 23, 1980.
4. See, for example, Pierre Elliott Trudeau, *The Asbestos Strike*, translated by James Brooke (Toronto: James Lewis and Samuel, 1974). Regarding Trudeau's having been barred from entry to the United States, see Douglas Stuebing, John Marshall, and Gary Oakes, *Trudeau: A Man for Tomorrow* (Toronto: Clarke, Irwin, 1968), p. 26.
5. *Report of the Royal Commission on Security* (the MacKenzie Commission) (Ottawa: Queen's Printer, 1969), p. 1.
6. Ibid., p. 105.
7. Ibid., p. 19.
8. Quoted in McDonald Commission, *Second Report*, Vol. II (Ottawa: Minister of Supply and Services, 1981), p. 671.
9. Canada, House of Commons, *Debates*, June 26, 1969, p. 10637.
10. Interviews with John Starnes, Ottawa, June 17 and August 6, 1981.
11. Interview with James J. Angleton, Washington, D.C., March 17, 1981.
12. Jeff Sallot, *Nobody Said No* (Toronto: James Lorimer, 1979), p. 95.
13. Interviews with Donald McCleery, Montreal, October 28, 1980, and June 8, 1981. In the early 1970s McCleery was a Staff Sergeant in the RCMP Security Service in Montreal and played a key role in several investigations of the FLQ.

14. The 527 pages of the *Third Report* of the McDonald Commission are largely devoted to detailed descriptions of "certain RCMP investigative practices that were not authorized or provided for by law." For additional details on police activities in Quebec during and after the October Crisis, see *Rapport de la Commission d'enquête sur les opérations policières en territoire québécois* (Gouvernement du Québec, 1981) (The Keable Commission Report).

15. McDonald Commission, *Second Report*, Vol. I, pp. 478-84. For a detailed account of the politics of the Ontario Waffle see Robert Hackett, "Pie in the Sky: A History of the Ontario Waffle," *Canadian Dimension*, vol. 25, nos. 1 & 2 (October-November 1980), pp. 2-72.

16. Personal information.

17. Quoted in McDonald Commission, *Second Report*, Vol. I, p. 481.

18. Quoted in ibid., p. 482.

19. Ibid., p. 483.

20. Ibid., p. 73.

21. Ibid., p. 74.

22. Ibid., p. 75.

23. *Official Secrets Act, Revised Statutes of Canada 1970*, Chapter 0-3 (amended 1973-74, Statutes of Canada, Chapter 50, sections 5, 6).

24. Ibid.

25. Interview with the Honourable Warren Allmand, PC, Ottawa, October 23, 1980.

26. This section is based on a series of conversations with Warren Hart in Washington, D.C., on April 26 and 27, 1981.

27. Film interview with Warren Hart by James Littleton and Donald Brittain, Washington, D.C., April 27, 1981.

28. Ibid.

29. The Commissioners warned that: "No police force protecting the peace can be effective unless it has the trust of the people it seeks to protect; no security intelligence agency can be effective without the trust of citizens. Moreover, neither can be effective without the trust of government" (McDonald Commission, *Second Report*, Vol. I, p. 15).

30. Interview with Fred Gibson, Ottawa, September 17, 1981.

31. McDonald Commission, *Second Report*, Vol. I, p. 10.

32. This has been directly confirmed by Sir William Stephenson (private information).

33. See, for example, William Stephenson's hagiographical *Intrepid's Last Case* (New York: Ballantine, 1983).

34. Richard Friedman, "Spymaster Intrepid snubs Trudeau at award ceremony," *Toronto Star*, September 23, 1983, p. A12.

35. Interview with Andrew Caddell (press officer for Solicitor-General Robert Kaplan), Ottawa, June 21, 1984.
36. These impressions are based on discussions with Archie Barr in Ottawa on a number of occasions, including December 3, 1982, and August 17, 1983.
37. Interview with Deputy Solicitor-General Fred Gibson, Ottawa, August 17, 1983.
38. Interview with the Honourable Roy McMurtry, Toronto, July 5, 1983.
39. Interview with Peter Russell, Toronto, July 20, 1983.
40. First Session, Thirty-Second Parliament, Bill C-157, Section 14(1).
41. Ibid., Section 23(1)(a).
42. Ibid., Section 2(a).
43. Robert H. Jackson, "The Federal Prosecutor," *Journal of American Judicature Society*, June 1940, cited in Frank J. Donner, *The Age of Surveillance* (New York: Knopf, 1980), p. *xvi*.
44. Bill C-157, Section 2(d).
45. Interview with Ronald Dworkin, London, England, August 25, 1983 (for radio broadcast).
46. McDonald Commission, *Second Report*, Vol. I, p. 430.
47. Ibid., p. 441.
48. Ibid., p. 442.
49. Ibid., p. 441.
50. Interview with Solicitor-General Robert Kaplan, Ottawa, August 18, 1983.
51. Interview with T.D. Finn, Ottawa, August 17, 1983.
52. Ibid.
53. Senate of Canada, *Proceedings of the Special Committee of the Senate on the Canadian Security Intelligence Service*, Issue no. 2, August 18, 1983, p. 49.
54. *Delicate Balance: A Security Intelligence Service in a Democratic Society*. Report of the Special Committee of the Senate on the Canadian Security Intelligence Service (Ottawa: November 1983), p. 15.
55. Interview with the Honourable Elmer MacKay, PC, September 14, 1983 (telephone).
56. Interview with Senator Michael Pitfield, Ottawa, June 20, 1984.

Chapter 9 Legacy of Fear

1. "Summary Outline of *An Act to Establish the Canadian Security Intelligence Service*," news release from the Solicitor-General of Canada, Ottawa, May 18, 1983.
2. *An Act to Establish the Canadian Security Intelligence Service*,

Section 2, (a), (b), (c), (d). For discussion of these definitions, see Chapter 8.
3. See McDonald Commission, *Second Report*, Vol. I, pp. 415-17, for discussion of uses to be made of security intelligence.
4. McDonald Commission, *Second Report*, Vol. II, p. 930.
5. Ibid., p. 929.
6. Robert Goldstein, *Political Repression in Modern America* (Cambridge, Mass.: Schenkman, 1978), p. 324.
7. Ibid.
8. Athan Theoharis, *Spying on Americans* (Philadelphia: Temple University Press, 1978), p. 196.
9. Ibid., p. 210.
10. McDonald Commission, *Second Report*, Vol. II, p. 782.
11. For a detailed account of this history, see John Sawatsky, *Men in the Shadows: The RCMP Security Service* (Toronto: Doubleday, 1980), pp. 124-37.
12. A major review of security policy towards homosexuals was conducted in this period, on the initiative of R.B. Bryce, Secretary to the Cabinet, and Don Wall, Assistant Secretary for Security Policy.
13. Interview with Don Wall, Ottawa, December 7, 1985.
14. Cabinet Directive No. 35, *Security in the Public Service of Canada*, December 18, 1963, p. 2.
15. McDonald Commission, *Second Report*, Vol. II, p. 797. August 1981.
16. For a more complete discussion of the CSIS Act definition of subversion, see Chapter 8.
17. McDonald Commission, *Second Report*, Vol. II, p. 797, Recommendation no. 119.
18. John Barron, KGB: *The Secret Work of Soviet Secret Agents* (New York: Reader's Digest Press, 1974), p. 35.
19. Ibid., p. 37.
20. Richard H. Schultz and Roy Godson, *Dezinformatsia* (Washington: Pergamon-Brassey's, 1984), p. 133. Emphasis added.
21. Review of Schultz and Godson, *Dezinformatsia*, by Avis Boutell, originally published in *Studies in Intelligence* (Winter 1984); reprinted in *Foreign Intelligence Literary Scene*, Vol. IV, no. 4 (August 1985), p. 5.
22. Ibid.
23. See, for example, *Their Trade Is Treachery* (London: Sidgwick and Jackson, 1981), in which Pincher attempts to show that the former head of MI5, Sir Roger Hollis, was a Soviet spy. This allegation was investigated and rejected by the Thatcher government.
24. Chapman Pincher, *The Secret Offensive* (London: Sidgwick and Jackson, 1985), p. 178.
25. Ibid., p. 173.

26. Ibid., p. 172.
27. Ibid., p. 178.
28. Ibid.
29. Arnold Beichman and Roy Godson, "Legal Constraints and Incentives," in Roy Godson, ed., *Intelligence Requirements for the 1980s*, Vol. III: *Counterintelligence* (Washington, D.C.: National Strategy Center, 1980), p. 287.
30. John le Carré, "Introduction," to Bruce Page, David Leitch, and Phillip Knightly, *The Philby Conspiracy* (New York: Ballantine, 1981), p. 3.
31. John Sawatsky, *For Services Rendered* (Toronto: Doubleday, 1982), p. 254.
32. Ibid., p. 257.
33. Australian Broadcasting Corporation interview with Leslie James Bennett, Perth, Australia, June 1981. This section is also based on telephone interviews with Bennett by the author November 10, 11, 12, and 16, 1982, and on personal correspondence from Bennett.
34. W.H. Kelly, "Bennett biography offers insight into RCMP" (a review of Sawatsky, *For Services Rendered*), Montreal *Gazette*, November 27, 1982, p. 36.
35. David Leigh and Paul Lashman, "Revealed: How MI5 vets BBC staff," *The Observer*, London, August 18, 1985, p. 1.
36. "Saving the BBC's soul," *The Observer*, London, August 25, 1985, p. 8.
37. Security Intelligence Review Committee, *Annual Report, 1984-85* (Ottawa: Department of Supply and Services, 1985), p. 18.
38. Interview with the Honourable Ronald Atkey, PC, Chairman, Security Intelligence Review Committee, Toronto, September 25, 1985.
39. McDonald Commission, *Second Report*, Vol. I, p. 633.
40. Ibid.
41. Security Intelligence Review Committee, *Annual Report, 1984-85*, p. 18.
42. McDonald Commission, *Second Report*, Vol. I, p. 632.
43. Interview with James J. Angleton, Washington, D.C., March 17, 1981.
44. Interview with the Honourable Elmer MacKay, PC, Solicitor-General of Canada, Halifax, Nova Scotia, August 13, 1985. Interview with the Honourable Ronald Atkey, Toronto, September 25 and October 9, 1985.
45. Interview with the Honourable Elmer MacKay, PC, Lorne, Nova Scotia, July 27, 1980.
46. Security Intelligence Review Committee, *Annual Report, 1984-85*, p. 19.

Epilogue
1. G.K. Young, *Subversion and the British Riposte* (Glasgow: Ossian, n.d.), p. 154.
2. Vernon A. Walters, "The Uses of Political and Propaganda Covert Action in the 1980s," in Roy Godson, ed., *Intelligence Requirements for the 1980s*, Vol. IV: *Covert Action*, p. 115.

Bibliography

BOOKS

Ackroyd, Carol, Karen Margolis, Jonathan Rosenhead, and Tim Shallice. *The Technology of Political Control*. Markham, Ontario: Penguin, 1977.

Adams, Ian. *S — Portrait of a Spy*. Toronto: Gage, 1977.

Agee, Phillip. *Inside The Company: CIA Diary*. Markham, Ontario: Penguin, 1975.

—— and L. Wolf, eds. *Dirty Work: The CIA in Western Europe*. New York: Lyle Stuart, 1978.

Alperovitz, Gar. *Atomic Diplomacy: Hiroshima and Potsdam*. Second edition. Harmondsworth: Penguin, 1985.

Anderson, Perry. *Considerations of Western Marxism*. London: NLB, 1976.

Andrew, Christopher. *Secret Service: The Making of the British Intelligence Community*. London: Heinemann, 1985.

Arkin, William, and Richard Fieldhouse. *Nuclear Battlefields*. Cambridge, Mass.: Ballinger, 1985.

Avakumovic, Ivan. *The Communist Party in Canada*. Toronto: McClelland and Stewart, 1975.

Bahro, Rudolph. *The Alternative in Eastern Europe*. London: Verso, 1978.

Ball, Desmond. *A Suitable Piece of Real Estate*. Sydney, Australia: Hale and Iremonger, 1980.

Bamford, James. *The Puzzle Palace*. Boston: Houghton Mifflin, 1982.

Barnet, Richard J. *The Alliance*. New York: Simon and Schuster, 1983.

Barron, John. *KGB: The Secret Work of Soviet Secret Agents*. New York: Reader's Digest Press, 1974.

——. *KGB Today: The Hidden Hand*. New York: Reader's Digest Press, 1983.

Bell, J. Bowyer. *The Secret Army*. Cambridge, Mass.: MIT Press, 1970.

Berlin, Isaiah. *Four Essays on Liberty*. London: Oxford University Press, 1969.

Bloch, Jonathan, and Patrick Fitzgerald. *British Intelligence and Covert Action*. Dingle, Ireland: Brandon Publishers, 1983.

Bothwell, Robert, and J.L. Granatstein. *The Gouzenko Transcripts*. Ottawa: Deneau, n.d.

Bowden, T. *Beyond the Limits of the Law*. Harmondsworth: Penguin, 1978.

Bowen, Roger W., ed. *E.H. Norman: His Life and Scholarship*. Toronto: University of Toronto Press, 1984.

Brown, Carolyn, and Lorne Brown. *An Unauthorized History of the RCMP*. Toronto: James Lorimer & Co., n.d.

Brown, N. *The Future Global Challenge: A Predictive Study of World Security, 1977-1990*. London: Royal United Services Institute for Defence Studies, 1977.

Buckley, William F., Jr., and L. Brent Bozell. *McCarthy and His Enemies*. Chicago: Henry Regnery, 1954.

Bunyan, Tony. *The History and Practice of the Political Police in Britain*. London: Julien Friedman, 1976.

Camilleri, Joseph A. *Australian–American Relations: The Web of Dependence*. Melbourne: Macmillan, 1980.

Campbell, Duncan. *Big Brother is Listening: Phonetappers and the Security State*. London: New Statesman, 1981.

———. *The Unsinkable Aircraft Carrier: American Military Power in Britain*. London: Michael Joseph, 1984.

Cannon, Lou. *Reagan*. New York: Putnam's, 1982.

Caplan, Gerald. *The Dilemma of Canadian Socialism*. Toronto: McClelland and Stewart, 1973.

Carillo, Santiago. *Eurocommunism and the State*. London: Lawrence and Wishart, 1977.

Caute, David. *The Fellow Travellers*. London: Quartet, 1977.

———. *The Great Fear*. New York: Simon and Schuster, 1978.

Chapman, Brian. *Police State*. London: Macmillan, 1970.

———. *The Canadian Police: A Survey*. Manchester: University of Manchester Press, 1977.

Chomsky, Noam. *Towards a New Cold War*. New York: Pantheon, 1982.

———, Jonathan Steele, and John Gittings. *Superpowers in Collision*. Harmondsworth: Penguin, 1982.

Clarkson, Stephen. *Canada and the Reagan Challenge*. Toronto: James Lorimer, 1982.

Claudin, Fernando. *The Communist Movement: From Comintern to Cominform*. Harmondsworth: Penguin, 1975.

Clemens, Diane Shaver. *Yalta*. Oxford: Oxford University Press, 1978.

Cline, Ray S., and Yonah Alexander. *Terrorism: The Soviet Connection*. New York: Crane Russak, 1984.

Cochran, Thomas B., William M. Arkin, and Milton M. Hoenig. *U.S. Nuclear Forces and Capabilities*. Cambridge, Mass.: Ballinger, 1984.

Commager, Henry Steele. *Freedom, Loyalty, Dissent*. New York: Oxford University Press, 1954.

Copeland, Miles. *The Real Spy World*. London: Weidenfeld and Nicolson, 1975.

Crawford, Alan. *Thunder on the Right: The New Right and the Politics of Resentment*. New York: Pantheon, 1980.

Creighton, Donald. *Canada's First Century*. Toronto: Macmillan, 1970.

Cuff, R.D., and J.L. Granatstein. *Ties That Bind*. Toronto: Samuel Stevens Hakkert & Company, 1977.

———. *American Dollars, Canadian Prosperity*. Toronto: Samuel Stevens, 1978.

Dahl, R.A. *Who Governs?* New Haven: Yale University Press, 1961.

Davis, David Brion, ed. *The Fear of Conspiracy: Images of Un- American Subversion from the Revolution to the Present*. Ithaca: Cornell University Press, 1971.

Deutscher, Isaac. *The Great Contest*. London: Oxford University Press, 1960.

———. *Stalin: A Political Biography*. Harmondsworth: Penguin, 1966.

Donner, Frank J. *The Age of Surveillance*. New York: Alfred A. Knopf, 1980.

Doran, Charles F. *Forgotten Partnership: U.S.–Canada Relations Today*. Baltimore: Johns Hopkins, 1984.

Dower, John W., ed. *Origins of the Modern Japanese State: Selected Writings of E.H. Norman*. New York: Pantheon, 1975.

Dworkin, Ronald. *Taking Rights Seriously*. Cambridge, Mass.: Harvard University Press, 1977.

Eayrs, James. *In Defence of Canada*: Vol. I: *From the Great War to the Great Depression*; Vol. II: *Appeasement and Rearmament*; Vol. III: *Peacemaking and Deterrence*; Vol. IV: *Growing Up Allied*; Vol. V: *Indochina: Roots of Complicity*. Toronto: University of Toronto Press, 1964-83.

———. *Canada in World Affairs, 1955 to 1957*. Toronto: Oxford University Press, 1959.

Elliff, John T. *The Reform of FBI Intelligence Operations*. Princeton: Princeton University Press, 1979.

Elliot, Stuart Robert. *Scarlet to Green: A History of Intelligence in the Canadian Army 1903-1963*. Toronto: Canadian Intelligence and Security Association, 1981.

Ferguson, Thomas, and Joel Rogers. *The Hidden Election*. New York: Random House, 1981

Flemming, D.F. *The Cold War and Its Origins, 1917-1960*. 2 vols. New York: Doubleday, 1961.

Freedman, Lawrence. *The Evolution of Nuclear Strategy*. New York: St. Martin's Press, 1981.

French, Richard, and André Béliveau. *The RCMP and the Management of National Security*. Toronto: Institute for Public Policy, 1979.

Freudenberg, Graham. *A Certain Grandeur: Gough Whitlam in Politics*. Melbourne: Macmillan, 1977.

Friedman, Milton. *Capitalism and Freedom*. Chicago: University of Chicago Press, 1962.

211

Gaddis, John Lewis. *The United States and the Origins of the Cold War, 1941-1947*. New York: Columbia University Press, 1972.

———. *Strategies of Containment: A Critical Appraisal of Post-War American National Security Policy*. New York: Oxford University Press, 1982.

Godson, Roy, ed. *Intelligence Requirements for the 1980s*: Vol. I: *Elements of Intelligence*, 1979; Vol. II: *Analysis and Estimates*, 1980; Vol. III: *Counterintelligence*, 1980; Vol. IV: *Covert Action*, 1981; Vol. V: *Clandestine Collection*, 1982. Washington, D.C.: National Strategy Information Center.

Goldsmith, James M. *Counter Culture*. London: Private Publications, 1985.

Goldstein, Robert. *Political Repression in Modern America*. Cambridge, Mass.: Schenkman, 1978.

de Gramont, Sanche. *The Secret War*. New York: Putnam, 1962.

Granatstein, J.L. *A Man of Influence*. Ottawa: Deneau, 1981.

———. *The Ottawa Men: The Civil Service Mandarins, 1935-1957*. Toronto: Oxford University Press, 1982.

Gray, Colin S. *Canadian Defence Priorities: A Question of Relevance*. Toronto: Clarke, Irwin, 1972.

Greene, T.N., ed. *The Guerrilla — And How to Fight Him*. New York: Praeger, 1962.

Gross, Bertram. *Friendly Fascism*. New York: M. Evans, 1980.

Guevara, Che. *Guerilla Warfare*. Lincoln: University of Nebraska Press, 1985.

Hall, Richard. *The Secret State: Australia's Spy Industry*. North Melbourne: Cassell, 1978.

Halliday, Fred. *The Making of the Second Cold War*. London: Verso, 1983.

Halloway, David. *The Soviet Union and the Arms Race*. New Haven: Yale University Press, 1983.

Halperin, Morton, Jerry Berman, Robert Borosage, and Christine Marwick. *The Lawless State: The Crimes of the U.S. Intelligence Agencies*. New York: Penguin, 1976.

Hamilton, P. *Espionage, Terrorism and Subversion in an Industrial Society*. London: Peter A. Heims, 1979.

Harrison, W.E.C. *Canada in World Affairs 1949 to 1950*. Toronto: Oxford University Press, 1959.

Harvison, C.W. *The Horsemen*. Toronto: McClelland and Stewart, 1967.

Heaps, Leo. *Hugh Hambleton, Spy*. Toronto: Methuen, 1983.

Heilbroner, Robert. *Marxism: For and Against*. New York: Norton, 1980.

Hellman, Lillian. *Scoundrel Time*. New York: Little Brown, 1975.

Herken, Gregg. *The Winning Weapon*. New York: Alfred A. Knopf, 1980.

———. *Counsels of War*. New York: Alfred A. Knopf, 1985.

Herman, Edward S. *The Real Terror Network*. Montreal: Black Rose, 1982.

Hersh, Seymour M. *The Price of Power*. New York: Summit, 1983.

Hertzman, Lewis, John Warnock, and Thomas Hockin. *Alliances and Illusions*. Edmonton: Hurtig, 1969.

Hinsley, F.H. *British Intelligence in the Second World War*, Vols. I-III. London: Her Majesty's Stationery Office, 1979-85.

Hinze, Paul. *The Plot to Kill the Pope*. New York: Scribner's, 1983.

Hobsbawm, E.J. *Revolutionaries*. New York: New American Library, 1973.

Hofstadter, Richard. *The Paranoid Style in American Politics and Other Essays*. Chicago: Phoenix, 1979.

Holmes, John W. *The Shaping of Peace: Canada and the Search for World Order, 1943-1957, Vol. I.* Toronto: University of Toronto Press, 1979.

Hoover, J. Edgar. *Masters of Deceit*. New York: Henry Holt, 1958.

Hunt, Richard A., and Richard H. Schultz. *Lessons from an Unconventional War*. New York: Pergamon, 1982.

Hyde, H. Montgomery. *The Atom Bomb Spies*. London: Hamish Hamilton, 1980.

Innis, Harold. *Essays in Canadian Economic History*. M.Q. Innis, ed. Toronto: University of Toronto Press, 1956.

Jackson, Robert. *World Military Aircraft Since 1945*. New York: Scribner's, 1979.

Jacobs, Harold, ed. *Weatherman*. Palo Alto, Calif.: Ramparts Press, 1970.

Kahn, David. *The Codebreakers*. New York: Macmillan, 1967.

Kaldor, Mary. *The Disintegrating West*. Harmondsworth: Pelican, 1979.

Kaplan, Fred. *The Wizards of Armageddon*. New York: Simon and Schuster, 1983.

Kelly, Nora, and William Kelly. *The Royal Canadian Mounted Police: A Century of History*. Edmonton: Hurtig, 1973.

Kent, Sherman. *Strategic Intelligence for American World Policy*. 2nd edition. Hamden, Conn.: Archon Books, 1963.

Kierstead, B.S. *Canada in World Affairs 1951 to 1953*. Toronto: Oxford University Press, 1956.

Kirkpatrick, Lyman S., Jr. *The U.S. Intelligence Community*. New York: Hill and Wang, 1973.

Klare, Michael. *Beyond the Viet Nam Syndrome*. Washington, D.C.: IPS, 1981.

Knelman, F.H. *Reagan, God and the Bomb*. Toronto: McClelland and Stewart, 1985.

Kolko, Gabriel. *The Politics of War: The World and United States Foreign Policy, 1943-45*. New York: Vintage, 1968.

―――. *Anatomy of a War: Viet Nam, the United States, and the Modern Historical Experience*. New York: Pantheon, 1985.

Kolko, Joyce, and Gabriel Kolko. *The Limits of Power*. New York: Harper and Row, 1972.

Kupperman, Robert H., and Darrell M. Trent. *Terrorism: Threat, Reality, Response*. Stanford: Stanford University Press, 1979.

La Feber, Walter. *America, Russia and the Cold War, 1945-1980*. New York: Wiley, 1980.

Laqueur, Walter. *Terrorism*. London: Weidenfeld and Nicholson, 1977.

————. *A World of Secrets: The Uses and Limits of Intelligence*. New York: Basic Books, 1985.

Lasch, Christopher. *The Agony of the American Left*. New York: Vintage, 1969.

Laurie, Peter. *Beneath the City Streets*. London: Granada, 1970.

Leiden, Carl, and Karl M. Schmidt, eds. *The Politics of Violence: Revolution in the Modern World*. Englewood Cliffs: Prentice-Hall, 1968.

Lenin, V.I. "Left-Wing Communism — An Infantile Disorder"; "The State and Revolution"; "What Is to be Done?"; in *Selected Works of V.I. Lenin*. Moscow: Progress Publishers, 1969.

Linklater, Magnus, Isabel Hilton, and Neil Ascherson. *The Nazi Legacy: Klaus Barbie and the International Fascist Connection*. New York: Holt, Rinehart and Winston, 1984.

Lipset, Seymour Martin, and Earl Raab. *The Politics of Unreason*. New York: Harper and Row, 1970.

Loveman, Brian, and Thomas M. Davies, Jr. *The Politics of Anti-Politics*. Lincoln: University of Nebraska Press, 1978.

Luttwak, Edward. *Coup d'Etat*. Harmondsworth: Penguin, 1969.

MacLaren, Roy. *Canadians in Russia, 1918-1919*. Toronto: Macmillan, 1976.

Macpherson, C.B. *The Life and Times of Liberal Democracy*. Oxford: Oxford University Press, 1977.

————. *The Real World of Democracy*. Toronto: CBC Enterprises, 1965.

Mann, Edward, and John Alan Lee. *RCMP vs. The People*. Toronto: General Publishing, 1979.

Marchetti, Victor, and John D. Marks. *The CIA and the Cult of Intelligence*. New York: Dell, 1975.

McCall-Newman, Christina. *Grits: An Intimate Portrait of the Liberal Party*. Toronto: Macmillan, 1982.

McLellan, David. *The Thought of Karl Marx*. London: Macmillan, 1971.

McLin, Jon B. *Canada's Changing Defence Policy, 1957-1963*. Baltimore: Johns Hopkins, 1967.

McRoberts, Kenneth, and Dale Postgate. *Quebec: Social Change and Political Crisis*. Toronto: McClelland and Stewart, 1980.

Meyer, Cord. *Facing Reality*. New York: Harper and Row, 1980.

Michel, Henri. *The Shadow War: European Resistance, 1939-1945*. Tr. Richard Barry. New York: Harper and Row, 1972.

Miles, Michael W. *The Odyssey of the American Right*. New York: Oxford University Press, 1980.

Miliband, Ralph. *Parliamentary Socialism*. London: Allen and Unwin, 1961.

———. *Marxism and Politics*. Oxford: Oxford University Press, 1977.

———. *The State in Capitalist Society*. London: Weidenfeld and Nicholson, 1969.

Morton, Desmond. *A Military History of Canada*. Edmonton: Hurtig, 1985.

Moss, Robert. *Urban Guerrilla Warfare*. London: International Institute of Strategic Studies, 1971.

Navasky, Victor. *Naming Names*. New York: Viking, 1980.

Newman, Peter C. *True North: Not Strong and Free*. Toronto: McClelland and Stewart, 1983.

Oshinsky, David. *A Conspiracy So Immense*. New York: Free Press, 1983.

Page, Bruce, David Leitch, and Phillip Knightly. *The Philby Conspiracy*. New York: Ballantine, 1981.

Pearson, Lester B. *Mike: The Memoirs of Rt. Hon. Lester B. Pearson*. 3 vols. Toronto: University of Toronto Press, 1972.

Pelletier, Gérard. *The October Crisis*. Tr. Joyce Marshall. Toronto: McClelland and Stewart, 1971.

Penner, Norman. *The Canadian Left*. Toronto: Prentice-Hall, 1977.

Perlmutter, Amos. *The Military and Politics in Modern Times*. New Haven: Yale University Press, 1977.

Philby, Kim. *My Silent War*. New York: Grove Press, 1968.

Phillips, Dennis. *Cold War 2 and Australia*. Sydney: George Allen and Unwin, 1983.

Pickersgill, J.W., and D.F. Forster, eds. *The Mackenzie King Record*. 4 vols., 1939-48. Toronto: University of Toronto Press, 1960-70.

Pincher, Chapman. *Inside Story*. London: Sidgwick and Jackson, 1978.

———. *Their Trade Is Treachery*. London: Sidgwick and Jackson, 1981.

———. *Too Secret, Too Long*. London: Sidgwick and Jackson, 1984.

———. *The Secret Offensive*. London: Sidgwick and Jackson, 1985.

Plate, Thomas, and Andrea Darvi. *Secret Police*. New York: Doubleday, 1981.

Popper, Karl. *The Open Society and Its Enemies*. London: Routledge and Kegan Paul, 1962.

Powers, Thomas. *The Man Who Kept the Secrets*. New York: Alfred A. Knopf, 1979.

Prados, John. *The Soviet Estimate*. New York: Dial Press, 1982.

Pringle, Peter, and William Arkin. *S.I.O.P.: The Secret U.S. Plan for Nuclear War*. New York: Norton, 1983.

Prouty, L. Fletcher. *The Secret Team*. New York: Ballantine, 1973.

Pustay, John S. *Counterinsurgency Warfare*. New York: Free Press, 1965.

Radwanski, George. *Trudeau*. Toronto: Macmillan, 1978.

Rapoport, David C. *Assassination and Terrorism*. Toronto: CBC Enterprises, 1971.

Raskin, Marcus G. *The Politics of National Security*. New Brunswick, N.J.: Transaction Books, 1979.

Rawls, John. *A Theory of Justice*. London: Oxford University Press, 1972.

Reid, Escott. *Time of Fear and Hope: The Making of the North Atlantic Treaty, 1947-1949*. Toronto: McClelland and Stewart, 1977.

Renouf, Alan. *The Frightened Country*. Melbourne: Macmillan, 1979.

Richelson, Jeffrey T. *The U.S. Intelligence Community*. Cambridge, Mass.: Ballinger, 1985.

—— and Desmond Ball. *The Ties That Bind*. Boston and Sydney: Allen and Unwin, 1985; Harper Colophon, 1973.

Rovere, Richard H. *Senator Joe McCarthy*. New York: Harcourt Colophon, 1973.

Rusher, William. *Special Counsel*. New Rochelle: Arlington House, 1968.

Sallot, Jeff. *Nobody Said No*. Toronto: James Lorimer, 1979.

Sawatsky, John. *Men in the Shadows: The RCMP Security Service*. Toronto: Doubleday, 1980.

——. *For Services Rendered*. Toronto: Doubleday, 1982.

——. *Gouzenko: The Untold Story*. Toronto: Macmillan, 1984.

Scharr, David. *Clearing the Air*. Boston: Houghton Mifflin, 1977.

Scheer, Robert. *With Enough Shovels: Reagan, Bush and Nuclear War*. New York: Random House, 1982.

Schneir, Walter, and Miriam Schneir. *Invitation to an Inquest*. New York: Pantheon, 1983.

Schultz, Richard H., and Roy Godson. *Dezinformatsia*. Washington, D.C.: Pergamon-Brassey's, 1984.

Schumpeter, J.A. *Capitalism, Socialism, and Democracy*. London: Unwin, 1943.

Simpson, Jeffrey. *Discipline of Power: The Conservative Interlude and the Liberal Restoration*. Toronto: Macmillan, 1980.

Sloan, Pat, ed. *John Cornford: A Memoir*. London: Jonathan Cape, 1938.

Sokolovskiy, V.D. *Soviet Military Strategy*. Third edition. Ed. Harriet Fast Scott. New York: Crane Russak, 1980.

Soward, F.H. *Canada in World Affairs: From Normandy to Paris, 1944-46*. Toronto: Oxford University Press, 1950.

Spencer, Robert A. *Canada in World Affairs, 1946-1949*. Toronto: Oxford University Press, 1959.

Steele, Jonathan. *Soviet Power: The Kremlin's Foreign Policy — Brezhnev to Andropov*. New York: Simon and Schuster, 1983.

Stephenson, William. *A Man Called Intrepid*. New York: Ballantine, 1976.

——. *Intrepid's Last Case*. New York: Ballantine, 1983.

216

Sterling, Claire. *The Time of the Assassins.* New York: Holt, Rinehart and Winston, 1983.

Straight, Michael. *After Long Silence.* New York: Norton, 1983.

Stuebing, Douglas, John Marshall, and Gary Oakes. *Trudeau: A Man for Tomorrow.* Toronto: Clarke, Irwin, 1968.

Talbott, Strobe. *Deadly Gambits.* New York: Alfred A. Knopf, 1984.

Taylor, Charles. *Six Journeys: A Canadian Pattern.* Toronto: Anansi, 1977.

Theoharis, Athan. *Spying on Americans.* Philadelphia: Temple University Press, 1978.

Thompson, Edward. *Beyond the Cold War.* New York: Pantheon, 1982.

———— *et al. Exterminism and Cold War.* London: NLB, 1982.

Trudeau, Pierre Elliott. *The Asbestos Strike.* Tr. James Brooke. Toronto: James Lewis and Samuel, 1974.

Turner, Stansfield. *Secrecy and Democracy: The CIA in Transition.* Boston: Houghton Mifflin, 1985.

Vallières, Pierre. *White Niggers of America.* Tr. Joan Pinkham. Toronto: McClelland and Stewart, 1971.

Volkman, Ernest. *Warriors of the Night.* New York: Morrow, 1985.

Walsh & Munster. *Secrets of State.* Melbourne: Angus and Robertson, 1982.

Wardlaw, Grant. *Political Terrorism: Theory, Tactics and Countermeasures.* Cambridge: Cambridge University Press, 1982.

Warnock, John W. *Partner to Behemoth.* Toronto: New Press, 1970.

Watt, David. *The Law of Electronic Surveillance in Canada.* Toronto: Carswell, 1979.

Weisbord, Merrily. *The Strangest Dream: Canadian Communists, the Spy Trials, and the Cold War.* Toronto: Lester & Orpen Dennys, 1983.

West, Nigel. MI6: *British Secret Intelligence Service Operations 1909-45.* London: Weidenfeld and Nicolson, 1983.

Whitaker, Reg. *The Government Party.* Toronto: University of Toronto Press, 1978.

Wilkenson, Paul. *Terrorism and the Liberal State.* London: Macmillan, 1977.

————. *The New Fascists.* London: Grant McIntyre, 1981.

Williams, Raymond. *Culture and Society 1780-1950.* Harmondsworth: Penguin, 1961.

————. *The Year 2000.* New York: Pantheon, 1983.

Winterbotham, F.W. *The Ultra Secret.* New York: Dell, 1974.

Wise, David, and Thomas B. Ross. *The Invisible Government.* New York: Bantam, 1965.

Wright, S. *Repression and Repressive Violence.* Amsterdam: Swets and Zeitlinger, 1977.

Yardley, Herbert O. *The American Black Chamber.* New York: Ballantine, 1981.

Yergin, Daniel. *Shattered Peace*. Boston: Houghton Mifflin, 1977.

Young, G.K. *Subversion and the British Riposte*. Glasgow: Ossian, n.d.

GOVERNMENT PUBLICATIONS

Canada. House of Commons. *Debates*, various issues.

————. Senate. *Territorial Air Defence*. Report of the Special Committee of the Senate on National Defence. Ottawa: Minister of Supply and Services, 1985.

Commission of Inquiry Concerning Certain Activities of the Royal Canadian Mounted Police, *Reports*. Ottawa: Minister of Supply and Services, 1981. (The McDonald Commission.)

Delicate Balance: A Security Intelligence Service in a Democratic Society. Report of the Special Committee of the Senate on the Canadian Security Intelligence Service. Ottawa: Minister of Supply and Services, 1983.

Intelligence Activities and the Rights of Americans. Washington, D.C.: U.S. Government Printing Office, 1976.

Intelligence and Security. Canberra: The Commonwealth Government Printer, 1978.

Law and Order in Canadian Democracy. Ottawa: Queen's Printer, 1952.

Minutes of Proceedings and Evidence of the Standing Committee on External Affairs and National Defence. Ottawa: various issues.

Minutes of the Standing Committee on Miscellaneous Estimates. Ottawa: March 24, 1975.

Proceedings of the Special Committee of the Senate on National Defence.

Proceedings of the Special Committee of the Senate on the Canadian Security Intelligence Service. Ottawa: various issues.

Rapport de la Commission d'enquête sur les opérations policières en territoire québécois. Gouvernement du Québec, 1981. (The Keable Commission Report.)

Report of the Royal Commission on Security. Ottawa: Queen's Printer, 1969. (The MacKenzie Commission.)

Report of the Royal Commission to Investigate the Facts Relating to and the Circumstances Surrounding the Communications, by Public Officials and Other Persons in Positions of Trust, of Secret and Confidential Information to Agents of a Foreign Power. Ottawa: King's Printer, 1946. (The Kellock-Taschereau Commission.)

Report to the President by the Commission on CIA Activities Within the United States. Washington: U.S. Government Printing Office, 1975. (The Rockefeller Commission Report.)

Security Intelligence Review Committee. *Annual Report, 1984-85*. Ottawa: Minister of Supply and Services, 1985.

Security in the Public Service of Canada. Directive No. 35. Ottawa: December 18, 1963.

Senate Select Committee to Study Governmental Operations With Respect to Intelligence Activities. *Reports*. Washington, D.C.: U.S. Government Printing Office, 1976. (The Church Committee Reports.)

Transcript of Executive Session, United States Senate Subcommittee to Investigate the Administration of the Internal Security Act and Other Internal Security Laws of the Committee on the Judiciary. Washington, D.C.: August 14, 1951.

INTERVIEWS

Allmand, the Honourable Warren. Ottawa, October 23, 1980; April 24, 1981.

Anderson, John. Ottawa, April 6, 1982.

Angleton, James Jesus. Washington, D.C., March 17, April 26, 30, 1981.

Atkey, the Honourable Ronald, PC. Toronto, September 25 and October 9, 1985.

Bagalki, Gus. Ottawa, July 27, 1981.

Baldwin, Gerald, MP. Ottawa, January 14, 1981.

Ball, Desmond. Washington, D.C., August 29, 30, 31, 1983.

Bamford, James. Boston, August 23, 1983.

Barr, Archie. Ottawa, December 3, 1982; August 17, 1983.

Barron, John. Toronto, August 12, 1983.

Bayfield, Cecil. Vancouver, December 23, 1980 (phone); January 6, 1981.

Bennett, Leslie James. Perth, Australia, November 10, 11, 12, 16, 1982 (phone).

Boyer, Raymond. Montreal, June 22, 1981.

Bryce, Robert B. Ottawa, October 17, 20, 22, 1980.

Caddell, Andrew. Ottawa, June 21, 1984.

Carr, Sam. Toronto, January 12, 1981.

Cobb, Donald. Ottawa, September 9, 10, 17, 1981.

Dombrain, Nicholas. Ottawa, January 14 and 16, 1981.

Douglas, the Honourable T.C. Toronto, October 31, 1980.

Dworkin, Ronald. London, August 24 and 25, 1983.

Dwyer, Christopher. Rodney, Ont., November 24, 1984.

Endicott, James. Toronto, October 30, 1980.

Finn, T.D. Ottawa, August 17, 1983.

Gibson, Fred. Ottawa, September 17, 1981; August 17, 1983.

Glazebrook, George. Toronto, January 10, 1981.

Godin, Gerald. Montreal, September 30, 1981.

Guernsey, Terry. Toronto, September 29, November 20, 1980; February 19, September 26, 1981.

Halperin, Morton. Washington, D.C., November 5, 1980.

Hamilton, the Honourable Alvin. Ottawa, October 22, 1980.

Hart, Warren. Washington, D.C., April 26, 1981.

Holmes, John W. Toronto, October 19, 1980.

Hughes, Royden. Ottawa, October 20, 1980.

Kamoff, George. Ottawa, August 6, 1981.

Kaplan, the Honourable Robert. Ottawa, April 21, 1981; Toronto, August 15, 1983; Ottawa, August 18, 1983.

Kennan, George. Princeton, N.J., February 16, 1981 (phone).

Lawrence, the Honourable Allan. Ottawa, June 23, 1981.

Lewis, David. Ottawa, November 25, 1980.

Lindsay, Dr. George. Ottawa, April 6, 1982.

Linton, Freda. January 28, 1981.

Lisgar, Joel (Staff Director, Senate Committee on Security and Terrorism). Washington, D.C., March 18, 1981.

MacKay, Elmer. Lorne, N.S., July 27-28, 1980; Ottawa, January 15, 1981; Halifax, August 13, 1985.

MacPherson, C.B. Toronto, November 11, 1980.

Maury, John. Washington, D.C., April 29, 1981.

Mazerall, Edward. Winnipeg, December 23, 1980 (phone).

McCleery, Donald. Montreal, October 28, 1980; June 8 and 22, 1981.

McClellan, George B. Montreal, February 11, 1981.

McClung, Mark. Toronto, September 25, October 23, 1980.

McCordick, John. Toronto, November 27, 1980.

McIlraith, the Honourable George. Ottawa, April 22, 1981.

McMurtry, the Honourable Roy. Toronto, July 5, 1983.

Meyer, Cord. Washington, D.C., April 28, 1981.

Norman, Irene. Ottawa, January 14 and 15, September 17, 1981.

O'Neill, Kevin. Ottawa, June 19 and 21, 1984.

Pearson, Geoffrey. Ottawa, January 14, 1981.

Penner, the Honourable Roland. Toronto, June 27, 1983.

Pitfield, Senator Michael. Ottawa, July 25, 26, 27, 1983; September 10, 1983 (phone); June 19 and 20, 1984.

Reid, Escott. Toronto, February 19, 1981.

Ritchie, Charles. Ottawa, October 22, 1980; June 19, 1984.

Robertson, Gordon. Ottawa, February 6, June 17, 1981.

Robertson, Mrs. Norman. Toronto, July 14, 1981.

Russell, Peter. Toronto, October 7, 1981; June 14, 1984.

Ryerson, Stanley B. Montreal, January 27, 1981.

Salzberg, J.B. Toronto, January 5, 1981.

Sedgwick, Joseph. Toronto, January 21, 1981.

Sherwood, Percy. Ottawa, April 21, 1981; August 17, 1983.

Shoemaker, Michael J. Ottawa, April 21, 1981.

Smith, Arnold. Ottawa, January 13, 1981.

Starnes, John. Ottawa, November 13, 1980; June 17, August 6, 1981.

Toohey, Brian. Melbourne, Australia, August 11, 1983.

Wall, Don. Portland, Ont., various occasions.

Weinberger, Caspar. Washington, D.C., March 17, 1981.

Index